PETER F. DRUCKER, Editor

Graduate School of Business Administration
New York University

Preparing
Tomorrow's Business Leaders
Today

A symposium on the occasion
of the fiftieth anniversary of the
Graduate School of Business Administration
New York University

Prentice-Hall, Inc., Englewood Cliffs, New Jersey

Library of Congress Catalog Card Number: 69–15233

Printed in the United States of America

Current printing (last digit):
10 9 8 7 6 5 4 3 2 1

Prentice-Hall International, Inc., *London*
Prentice-Hall of Australia, Pty. Ltd., *Sydney*
Prentice-Hall of Canada, Ltd., *Toronto*
Prentice-Hall of India Private Ltd., *New Delhi*
Prentice-Hall of Japan, Inc., *Tokyo*

Contributors

H. M. Boettinger   is assistant Comptroller—Management Sciences of the American Telephone & Telegraph Company. Educated at Johns Hopkins and New York Universities, Mr. Boettinger is the author of "Big Gap in Economic Theory" (*Harvard Business Review*, July–August 1967) and of a forthcoming book on the presentation of ideas.

H. F. R. Catherwood   has been Director-General of the National Economic Development Council of Great Britain since May 1966. He was managing director of The British Aluminum Company Limited before joining the Department of Economic Affairs in October 1964 as Chief Industrial Adviser. Among his books are *The Christian in Industrial Society* and *Britain with the Brakes Off*.

Clifford D. Clark   assumed the position of Dean at the School of Business of the University of Kansas with the academic year 1968–1969. From 1957 to 1968 he had been associated with the Graduate School of Business Administration of New York University as Associate Professor, Professor and Vice Dean. An economist, Dean Clark is the author of numerous articles on technological change and tax policy. His books include *Workmen's Compensation in New York State* and, with others, *The Theory and Measurement of Rent*.

iii

John T. Connor assumed in 1967 the Presidency of Allied Chemical Company after having served for two years in President Johnson's Cabinet as Secretary of Commerce. Earlier he had for ten years been President of Merck & Co., Inc. A lawyer by training (Harvard Law School 1939), he went into industry in 1947 after five years in government service as an administrator, counsel for scientific research activities, and an intelligence officer in the Marine Corps.

G. A. Costanzo is Executive Vice President of the First National City Bank of New York in charge of the bank's international business. Prior to joining City Bank in 1961 he was for six years Deputy Director of the Western Hemisphere Department of the International Monetary Fund. A native of Birmingham, Alabama, with a doctorate from the University of Virginia, Dr. Costanzo began his career as a teacher of economics at the University of Maryland in 1941 and as an economist in the U.S. Department of Commerce in 1942.

John Diebold is President and Chairman of the Board of The Diebold Group, Inc., management consultants, and Chairman of its parent company, John Diebold Incorporated, a management and investment company. He is active in public as well as business life and has held several presidential appointments. He is the author of numerous books and articles, among them *Automation—the Advent of the Automatic Factory* (1952) and a collection of his speeches and articles, *Beyond Automation* (1964).

Peter F. Drucker is Professor of Management at the Graduate School of Business Administration of New York University. He served for a number of years as Chairman of the Management Area. Among his books are *The Practice of Management* (1954); *Managing for Results* (1964); and *The Effective Executive* (1967).

Christian Gasser is known in his native Switzerland both as academician and as industrialist. He served as Professor of Industrial Management at the Graduate School of Business Administration of St. Gallen from 1947 to 1953. He then joined one of Europe's largest foundries, Georg Fischer A. G. in Schaffhausen as Vice President in charge of Finance, Accounting and Personnel. In 1960 he bought control of Mikron Machine Works Ltd. which manufactures and exports precision machine tools, and instruments. He also founded Mikron Holding Ltd. and added a Swiss and a British company to the Group. He is now Chairman of the Board of the Mikron companies. Among his publications are *Der Schweizer Kapitalmarkt; Mensch und Betrieb*; and *Der Mensch im Modernen Industriebetrieb*.

Gerald J. Glasser is Professor of Business Statistics at the School of Commerce and the Graduate School of Business Administration, New York University. He is co-author of the book, *Statistics for Business Decisions*, and has published numerous articles on statistical theory and its applications in professional journals in this country and abroad.

iv

He also serves as a consultant in statistics with a number of business firms and governmental agencies.

Howard C. Harder has been President of Corn Products Company since 1965. A native of Texas, he attended the University of Texas, and joined the company as an accountant in 1937. Mr. Harder's special interest has long been the role of the corporation in modern society— and in particular the role of the multi-national corporation.

David B. Hertz is currently a Director of McKinsey & Company, Inc., management consultants, and joined them in 1962. He was Associate Professor of Industrial Engineering at Columbia University from 1949 through 1953 and since 1954 he has been a Lecturer in Operations Research at that university. During 1964 he served as President of The Institute of Management Sciences (TIMS). Dr. Hertz is a Founding Member, Council Member (1964–67) and Editor for Publications (1959–present) of the Operations Research Society of America. He is the author of *The Theory and Practice of Industrial Research* (McGraw-Hill), *Elegance in O. R., Marketing As a Social Discipline, Risk Analysis in Capital Investment, Investment Policies That Pay Off* and other books and articles.

Howard W. Johnson has been President of the Massachusetts Institute of Technology since 1966. He was Dean of the Alfred P. Sloan School of Management at M.I.T. from 1959 to 1966. He first came to M.I.T. in 1955 as associate professor and Director of the Sloan Fellowship Program at the School. Mr. Johnson is a member of the President's Advisory Committee on Labor-Management Policy and the National Manpower Advisory Committee. He is chairman of the board of directors of the Federal Reserve Bank of Boston, and a member of the board of Federated Department Stores, the John Hancock Mutual Life Insurance Company, and the Putnam Funds.

Michael J. Kami has been interested in planning since his days with the IBM Corporation from 1952 to 1964, where he was successively Director of Product Planning, Director of Advance Planning, and Corporate Director of Long-Range Planning. From 1964 to 1967 he was Vice President of Corporate Planning for the Xerox Corporation. He is now President of Corporate Planning Associates in Lighthouse Point, Florida. He is the author of many articles on planning, and frequently lectures on the subject of advanced management in major universities.

Ernst Keller has been Managing Director of ADELA the multi-national equity-investment company for Latin America since the company was first founded in 1964. Earlier he had been for seven years Senior Partner of Ernst Keller Associates, S.A., consulting engineers, and from 1960–1964 also President of PERUINVEST, a multi-national private development finance company in Lima, Peru. Mr. Keller who is Swiss by birth and a graduate of the Eidgenoessische Technische Hochschule in Zuerich first came to Latin America in 1953 as Industrial Engineer

v

and later became General Industrial Manager for W. R. Grace & Co. in Peru.

Herman E. Krooss is Professor of Economic History at the Graduate School of Business Administration of New York University. He served for a number of years as Chairman of the Economic Area. Among his books are *American Economic Development, Financial History of the United States*, and *The American Economy* (with E. A. J. Johnson).

Franklin A. Lindsay has been President and Chief Executive Officer of ITEK Corporation since 1962. Earlier he was a member of the management consulting firm of McKinsey & Co. After wartime service Mr. Lindsay worked till 1953 for the U.S. Government, primarily on international problems. He has remained active in international affairs as a member of a number of Presidential Task Forces and of various study groups. He is a Director of the First National Bank of Boston and the author of *New Techniques of Management Decision Making* (1958).

Akio Morita is a founder and Executive Vice President of SONY Corporation, and also Chairman of SONY Corporation of America. His best-selling book *Gakureki Muyoron (Career Problems of Japanese Management)*, which appeared in 1966, has been widely read and discussed in Japanese business circles.

Rudolph A. Peterson has headed the Bank of America as President and Chief Executive Officer since 1963. He is a graduate of the University of California and in 1968 was named Alumnus of the Year and was the recipient of an honorary Doctor of Laws degree from his alma mater. Mr. Peterson has special interest in the international monetary system as well as the country's domestic monetary and fiscal system and the institutional forms under which the systems function.

John J. Powers Jr. has been chief executive officer of Chas. Pfizer & Co., Inc. since 1965; until 1968 as President, and since then as President and Chairman of the Board. A lawyer by training, Mr. Powers first joined Pfizer in 1941. From 1953 until his assumption of the Presidency of the parent company in 1965, Mr. Powers was chief executive officer of Pfizer International and thus a leading participant in the creation of the multi-national corporation which his chapter discusses.

Reinaldo Scarpetta, a native of Bogotá and a graduate of Georgia Tech, worked with W. R. Grace & Company in Colombia as an industrial engineer and Assistant to the President. In 1959 he joined IMP, a Colombian steel products fabricating company as manufacturing manager. In 1964 he became Dean of Social and Economic Sciences at the Universidad del Valle where he founded the Graduate School of Business and the University Foundation, serving as the Foundation's first president. Dean Scarpetta is a director of twelve institutions and corporations, was National Vice President of INCOLDA, the Colombian Management

Association, and has represented Colombia at several international congresses. His main interest lies in multi-national business.

Michael Schiff is Professor of Accounting and Chairman of the Accounting Area at the Graduate School of Business Administration of New York University. He is the author of *Practical Distribution Cost Analysis* (co-author), *Cases and Problems in Distribution Cost Accounting and Analysis, Cost Accounting* (co-author), *State Business Taxes, Financial Handbook* (contributing editor), *Accountant's Handbook* (contributing editor), *Cost Handbook* (contributing editor), *Financial Management of the Marketing Function,* and *Control of Maintenance Costs.*

Joseph H. Taggart has been Dean of the Graduate School of Business Administration of New York University since 1959, having been Associate Dean for three years before that. He is also Executive Dean of the University's Schools of Business. He serves on several company Boards of Directors and as a Governor of the American Stock Exchange. From 1945 to 1952 Dean Taggart served the United States Government in various capacities at home and abroad. From 1947 to 1956 he was a member of the faculty at Rutgers University, first as Professor of Finance and then as Professor of Economics. He is the author of *The Federal Reserve Bank of Boston* (1938) and of articles in economic journals and of papers on business education.

Dale E. Zand is Professor of Management and Chairman of the Management Area at the Graduate School of Business Administration of New York University. An engineer by training, Dr. Zand specializes both in quantitative methods such as Operations Research and in behavioral approaches, e.g. sensitivity training. He is the author of *Managing the Board of Directors, The Impact of an Organization Development Program on Perceptions,* and several studies of organizational change and small-group behavior.

Preface

Fifty years ago, toward the end of World War I, New York University first offered graduate instruction in business. It was, of course, not the first institution of higher learning to do so. In 1918 the Amos Tuck School at Dartmouth was almost twenty years old, and the Harvard Business School was approaching its tenth anniversary. Yet New York University, in its first venture into graduate education, however, did establish a "first." It was first to establish a graduate business curriculum leading to an advanced degree for educated men already well established in their business careers—primarily at that time young executives in banking and finance. The educational venture of 1918, out of which the present Graduate School of Business Administration of New York University grew, was perhaps the first example of what we would now call "advanced management" education or "continuing" education for business executives. Significantly, this new institution was not established on a college campus or contiguous to it as its older sister institutions had been. It opened its doors in the heart of New York's financial district, surrounded by Wall Street banks, brokerage houses, and headquarters office buildings. By its choice of location, the new educational ven-

ix

ture of New York University, fifty years ago, announced that it considered itself as much a part of the business community as of the educational community.

Today's GBA (to use the familiar abbreviation by which the Graduate School of Business Administration of New York University has become known) has grown far beyond its modest beginnings. It now has a student body of 3,765 and a faculty of 80. It still offers a graduate business education leading to the master's degree to qualified young men and women in mid-career. But, where fifty years ago the first students worked largely for Wall Street's financial institutions, the GBA student body now represents the broadest spectrum of American and international business: the big banks as well as the big, multinational corporations; retailers large and small, as well as science-based companies working on the frontier of technology; manufacturing businesses, but also business services such as public accounting, the big law firms, and management consultants. Non-profit institutions—schools, hospitals, federal, state, and local government agencies, and the military—are also well represented in the GBA student body.

There is also a substantial "day program" which prepares carefully selected younger men for the master's degree and for a career in business. A large Ph.D. program develops future scholars and teachers of business. And GBA has a larger number of foreign students—especially from the emerging countries—than any other graduate business school in the United States. Although graduate instruction began fifty years ago in a few rooms in a small red sandstone building (designed in Victorian Gothic and originally used by neighboring Trinity Church), GBA now has its own modern ten-story building erected less than ten years ago which will soon be joined by an even newer building next door.

Yet, in one essential, GBA has not changed in its fifty years. It still considers itself as much a part of the nation's business community as it is a part of the educational community. To be true to the vision of its founders, GBA must serve both communities with equal excellence.

This tradition underlies the design of this volume. Planned to mark the fiftieth anniversary of GBA, it proceeds from the realization that the men and women who will head our major business enterprises by the year 2000 are now students in our graduate business schools. What are the challenges they will have to be ready for? Where will their opportunities lie? What are the trends ahead in business, economy, and society? These are the questions discussed in this volume by perceptive business educators.

x

In the twenty years since the end of World War II, business has been a major stabilizing influence throughout the free world. It has become one of few truly international organs in a strife-torn world, a true agent of peace, progress, and worldwide cooperation. At the same time, business has become ever more demanding and ever more challenging. Tomorrow's business leaders will build upon a strong foundation inherited from their predecessors. But they will have to be capable of tackling new tasks and of wielding new tools if they are going to be true to this heritage. To contribute understanding and inspiration to this important task is the purpose of this volume.

*   *   *

The book begins with a summing up of the major structural changes in business and in business schools since GBA started fifty years ago. It then looks at the changing environment in which business operates—in politics, in the local community, in respect to money and finance, technology information, and so on. Next, it discusses major new developments within business enterprise, from the rise of systematic entrepreneurship and of the knowledge organization to new concepts and tools available to the business leader. The survey of the social and economic business scene is then completed with a number of essays on business abroad, on the multi-national corporation, and on the multi-national executive.

Finally, the book turns to systematic business education. It presents a number of views on what the business school could be and should be to provide professional leadership in the business community, and to serve society as an organ of knowledge and responsibility.

The result is something much more important, I believe, than another list of courses, subjects, or curricula. The twenty-three distinguished contributors to this volume, each of them a leader in his field, open up new vistas, confront us with new challenges, and call for even greater dedication and seriousness on the part of business educators. They also make clear that it is not just the business school that has to develop new ways to prepare tomorrow's business leaders. Indeed business itself, the contributors point out, is a major educational institution, and, as such, it has to address itself to the task of preparing tomorrow's business leaders today. One conclusion derived from the discussion in this volume is that the business *school* and business *enterprise* have to work together if tomorrow's business leader is to be prepared adequately for the great challenges and demands ahead.

There is, this volume makes abundantly clear, no royal road to business education. Every business school in the world will have to work out its own program, its own ways, and its own solutions. And so will every major business. The task calls for experimentation, for diversity, indeed, for dynamic pluralism.

This book will therefore, I predict, serve us at GBA for years to come as a guide to our own continuing self-examination. It will challenge again and again our "conventional wisdom." I am confident also that our friends and neighbors, the other collegiate business schools of the free world, will find this volume relevant and valuable to them in thinking through their own direction and course of action. Above all, however, I hope that business leaders here and abroad will be stimulated by these essays and will find them of help in thinking through what they and their companies could and should do today to prepare their own young people for the opportunities and responsibilities that await them.

* * *

Like any human institution, GBA has its memories, some happy, some sad, some bittersweet. It has had its heroes. It has been blessed, in good measure, with great teachers and great scholars. We, of today's GBA faculty as well as thousands of alumni, fondly and proudly remember these men whose vision and efforts built GBA. They were strong men because they looked forward rather than back. It is in their spirit that we at the faculty of GBA decided to celebrate our fiftieth anniversary by looking ahead. It is in their spirit that I, as Dean of the Graduate Business School at New York University, on this fiftieth anniversary of the School, rededicate GBA, its faculty, and its students to the preparation of tomorrow's business leadership today.

In conclusion, I wish to express my sincere appreciation to the Nichols Foundation for a generous grant which made possible the Symposium and this volume commemorating the fiftieth anniversary of the Graduate School of Business Administration.

JOSEPH H. TAGGART

Contents

xiii

HERMAN E. KROOSS
AND
PETER F. DRUCKER

How We Got Here: Fifty Years of Structural Change in the Business System and the Business School, 1918-1968

1

As "everybody" knows, the American economy has undergone a "revolutionary change" in the last fifty years. But what everybody knows is often misleading. Most of us believe that we have undergone a "revolution" in production, productivity, and wealth, that is, in the quantitative aspects of the economy. But this is wrong. Quantitatively, the change that has occurred since 1917 has not been much different from the change that took place in any previous half century of American economic history.

The familiar statistics are, of course, important; but they tell only a part of the story of the transformation of the American economy since graduate business education was first offered by New York University in the heart of downtown New York fifty years ago. The qualitative, the institutional, the structural changes rather than the quantitative ones in income and production are the truly significant ones for business policy, for the tasks of management, and for educating and developing today's and tomorrow's business leaders.

1

The truly "revolutionary" aspects of these past fifty years are the changes in the structure of the work force, in its education, and in job content; in business structure and in the job and role of the businessman. This brief review of the last fifty years of American economic history shall, therefore, take for granted the facts and figures the reader would expect to find in the standard dissertations of the economic analyst, confining itself to those developments that give *meaning* to the figures.

I

Fifty years ago at the end of World War I, the United States had become the world's foremost industrial power. Yet it was still predominantly rural, with a little over half its population living in rural areas and small towns, and three in ten living on farms. Seven in ten Americans were involved in the production of physical goods as factory hands or farmers.

Today, by contrast, fewer than one in three Americans lives in the country, and not one in ten lives on a farm. Most Americans live in an urban sprawl, which the Census calls a "Standard Metropolitan Statistical Area." This is a congeries of urbia, suburbia, and exurbia running thirty-five miles or more out from a central city. It is a community altogether different from the large city of fifty years ago which was still relatively compact and had an average radius of ten to fifteen miles.

In these fifty years the population has doubled—from 100 million in 1917 to 200 million now. At the same time, the labor force has also doubled, for the proportion of the adult population that is at work has remained singularly stable all through American history at about 57 per cent. A little less than half of the working population are in the white collar group, and another sixth, approximately, are classified as service workers. Together these two categories account for almost two-thirds of the labor force—twice the proportion that prevailed in the earlier part of the century.

While the labor force has grown, working hours have fallen appreciably. In 1917 the average work week was about fifty hours; today it is about forty. Total hours worked have therefore risen a good deal less than population. Indeed, in farming they have declined drastically, while in manufacturing they are only 50 per cent higher than in 1917. Yet manufactured products have multiplied four times, and total product five times, which means that productivity or output per man hour has risen at a much faster rate than ever before. This remarkable achievement has been primarily the result of better work management, which in turn has in no small degree been the result of a higher level of education. In 1917, half the adult population had attended school for less than eight years, and only seven out of every hundred could boast of having been to college. In 1967, half the population has been through high school, and almost half of those between eighteen and twenty-one are attending college.

American society has become an educated society, and the American economy has become a service economy. It is the only example in history of an economy in which the strategy for raising productivity has shifted from brawn to brain. This explains not only America's unprecedented labor force and job structure, but also the unprecedented challenges offered to management—the challenge to manage educated people doing work that has always been considered "professional"; to manage innovation; and to manage highly complex social organizations.

II

The American economy has become mature, not in the sense that the term was used during the depression of the 1930's to describe a tired, old, and moribund economy, but in the sense of an economy that has outgrown its adolescence. At the risk of some oversimplification, one can squeeze the explanation for the country's economic maturity into a simple formula; what we have achieved is a product of technological change, which prominently includes the skills of management.

Over the lifetime of the American economy, technology has evolved in step with the evolution of the whole economy. In the beginning, technological development was geared to meet the needs of an adolescent economy; the objective was to develop and acquire machines and machine tools, and the process was highly extensive. In the middle period, the emphasis shifted more to the needs of a growing economy; the objective was to develop more effective power—steam, later electricity, and still later, the internal combustion engine. That essentially was still the kind of technological development that characterized the economy in 1917. In more recent years, however, the objective has been to meet the needs and answer the questions posed by a well-advanced economy. Research, development, and managerial efficiency have become the dominant themes in the science and art of technology. At the same time, the process of technological change has speeded up, both in terms of those who create technological change and in terms of the length of time between the birth of an idea and its commercial success. Schools of science have been so fruitful that 90 per cent of all the scientists who have ever lived are alive today. The time between "invention" and full utilization has narrowed from fifteen years to four.

Still another sign that our economy has reached a state of maturity from the adolescence that still characterized it in 1917, is the transformation that has occurred in the composition of manufactures. Fifty years ago, the five leading industries accounted for the overwhelming portion—about two-thirds—of all the value added by manufacturing. Today production is more widely dispersed. Instead of producing two-thirds, the five largest industries produce only half of all value added. And these five leaders are not the same as the five leaders in 1917. Then the leaders were metals, food processing, textiles, paper and printing, and lumber. The manufacture of metals is still the largest industry, but it is now followed by automobiles, food, non-electric machinery, and paper and printing.

There have been other fundamental changes in the mix of manufacturing. Perishable goods are not nearly as conspicuous as they used to be. Their leadership role has been taken over by consumer durables. All of this shifting about in manufactured output has had wide repercussions on income and consumption and on the market structure and the nature of competition.

Let us consider briefly what has happened to income and what has happened to the ways in which consumers manage their incomes, that is, their saving and spending habits. Despite popular belief to the contrary, today's consumer saves no less and no more in proportion to his disposable income than his grandfather did. But his income is much higher. It is estimated that fifty years ago, only half the population were in the "comfortable" or "well-to-do" class. The others lived at the poverty or bare subsistence level. Today about four-fifths can be classified as living above bare subsistence.

Since income has risen so substantially and the percentage saved has remained about the same, the total amount of dollars spent on consumption has also multiplied. But much more important than the number of dollars spent is the change in spending behavior.

Students of spending patterns divide total consumption into three categories. There are expenditures for sensitive, somewhat sensitive, and insensitive items. These are roughly the same as the elastic, unit elastic, and inelastic categories used by economists. Sensitive items include those whose consumption increases or decreases at a faster rate than disposable income. For example, spending for sensitive goods like furs, jewelry, boats, and caviar can be expected to rise by about 8 to 10 per cent when the national income is increasing at a rate of 5 per cent. At the same time, spending on less exotic items, such as staple foods, shirts, and housewares, might increase by 2 or 3 per cent. In 1917, perhaps $15 out of every $100 of consumer spending was in the sensitive class; today, the figure is closer to $25 out of every $100.

To say what has just been said in another way, the average consumer's discretionary income is much higher than it used to be. What is important about this rise in discretionary income is that it has created an entirely different market structure to challenge the businessman's marketing ability. It requires a different type of market strategy and a different type of competition to persuade the consumer to spend his dollars when a third of what he earns is discretionary income, than when only a quarter was in that category.

III

Changes have also taken place in the institutional framework to make this era different from others. For one thing, labor unions are much more prominent than they were in those far-off days before two world wars, the great depression, Walter Reuther, and the Wagner Act. Before World War I, only one in ten non-agricultural workers belonged to a labor union compared to three in ten today.

Then, too, the Federal Government, and state and local governments as well, are much more involved in economic life than they were even in the so-called Progressive Era of the early twentieth century. In those days when some authorities were already viewing with alarm the trend toward more government intervention in the economy, Washington was in no sense the center of the nation's finance or of its economy. The total federal debt was just over two and one-half billion dollars. Federal expenditures were approximately $20 per capita, and state and local governments were spending about $25 per capita. But since then, affluence, population growth, urbanization, maturity, and the expanded wants of a democratic society have greatly inflated government activity. The Federal Government alone spends more than the combined spending of the country's fifty largest business firms. Its expenditures per capita amount to $725, and those of the state and local governments amount to $450. The federal debt is well over $300 billion, one hundred and twenty times as much as in 1917.

A third set of institutions, the so-called financial intermediaries, that is, the banks, insurance companies, investment companies, and so forth, have attained a degree of maturity and sophistication that fifty years ago seemed at least a century in the future. At that time the Federal Reserve System was just beginning. The total deposits of all the commercial banks were not very much larger than the deposits of the single largest bank in America in 1968. Indeed, the total claims against all financial institutions were only a little more than twice the total deposits of today's biggest bank. There were in the whole country only a dozen banks capable of lending a million dollars or more to any one customer. Banks were highly specialized, for "department store" banking was still nothing more than an idea in the head of an imaginative innovator.

The security markets in 1917 were also in their adolescence, and the publicly-owned company was still something of a rarity. Just thirty years earlier (in 1888), the shares of only one major manufacturer—the Pullman Company—had been listed on the New York Stock Exchange. It was less than twenty years since the first large corporation—United States Steel—had issued a comprehensive annual report to its stockholders.

By 1967, the assets of the financial intermediaries were approaching one trillion dollars. A third of this trillion was controlled by commercial banks, another fifth by insurance companies, and an eighth by savings and loan associations. The term "people's capitalism" had come into wide use, for it was estimated that one in every five adults owned stock in a publicly-owned corporation. Hectic was too mild a word to describe activity on the stock exchange. Seventeen of the twenty most active days in the history of the New York Stock Exchange occurred in 1966 and 1967. The exchange regularly handled more shares in one hour than the highest number ever traded in an entire day prior to 1917.

The expansion of financial intermediaries was in part a natural result of the growth of national income. But it was also the result of some subtle and ordinarily unrecognized changes in the habits of saving and financing. Year by year, savers did less and less direct investment of their saving and relied more and more on the middlemen in the money and capital markets, that is, the financial intermediaries. At the same time, consumers, while maintaining approximately the same level of saving, did less voluntary saving and more forced saving in the form of pension contributions; they also did more contractual saving through insurance policies, mortgage payments, and so forth. Once it could be said man was responsible for his own sins; now it appeared that he was not even responsible for most of his own saving.

IV

From what has already been said, it is apparent that the process known as economic change is a circular one in which cause and effect are intermeshed. In this reciprocal action, economic institutions and the factors of production play both an active and a passive role. They influence and at the same time they are influenced by what is happening in the external economy. This is especially true of business enterprise, for if the economy is to grow, business enterprise must be more agile than any of the other factors in its ability to adjust to economic change in the external environment.

What exactly therefore has the economic transformation of the last fifty years meant to the manager, to the entrepreneurial spirit, and to the business way of life? How have the so-called population explosion, the coming of affluence, the rise of megalopolis, the ubiquitous white collar, the welfare state, security capitalism, the pluralistic society, and the other much-advertised signs of economic change influenced the businessman?

To begin with, it can be said that what has taken place in economic life has not altered the businessman's basic function. It is still his job to combine the other factors of production. It is still his task to handle production, finance, and marketing. To be sure, his function has been clouded by a great deal of vague discussion of an indefinable category called "social responsibility." Admittedly, economic change has made his life more complicated, and increased complexity requires a greater degree of sophistication. Nevertheless, the businessman's chief responsibility continues to be to manipulate the seven Ms of management: men, methods, money, machines, materials, management, and marketing. Let us take each of these in turn and see how it has been influenced by what has taken place in the external economy.

During the past generation and a half, one of the most fascinating conversation pieces has been the "growth of big business." As population grew and income advanced, the size of the average industrial firm also grew. But while it grew in absolute terms, it did not grow relatively. That is to say, big business is no larger in proportion to the total size of the economy than it was a generation or two ago. To be sure, in the debate over the question whether big business is more powerful than it used to be, there is evidence on both sides. But the consensus among those who know about these things is that concentration of corporate control is lower and the relative size of big business is smaller today than it was fifty years ago. Certainly in proportion to population the number of small businesses is larger today than it was in 1900.

But in absolute terms, big business is very big indeed. It has hordes of owners, armies of employees, and higher revenues than many nations. General Motors Corporation, the tallest industrial giant, employs more people than the total population of the city of Boston; its income is larger than the combined revenue of all the Middle Atlantic and New England states; its payroll is more than double the total personal income of Ireland. Another colossus, the Bell System, has enough stockholders to fill 3,000 Yankee Stadiums with enough left over to occupy most of Madison Square Garden. The 500 largest industrial companies represent an insignificant fraction of the total business population, but they nevertheless employ an eighth of all workers and earn a fifth of all profits. It is no exaggeration to say that the country's 200 largest corporations strongly influence directly or indirectly half to three-quarters of American business life. Big business in the form of supermarkets, department stores, and discount chains has even come to dominate retailing, and through a device called corporate farming, it is well on its way to taking over the last bastion of small business—farming.

Much of the growth of big business has been internal. But much of it has also been the result of mergers and consolidation. In the years since 1917, there have been two waves of mergers, one in the 1920's and the other since the end of World War II. The tidal wave of the 1920's involved large corporations, but not the largest. The offspring of these marriages between lesser giants was a conglomerate in the old meaning of the word, that is, a mixture of horizontal and vertical integration involving firms in the same industry. The current merger movement is similar to the one of the 1920's in that it does not involve consolidations of giants. But what is produced is something different from horizontal or vertical integration. Today's mergers are conglomerates in the current meaning of the term: combinations of firms in entirely different kinds of business. Examples are a cigarette manufacturer and a producer of maple syrup, an electronics company and a processor of frozen foods, a steel fabricator and an underwear weaver.

Growth and diversification have brought with them some sweeping changes in the business management of the large-scale enterprise. One of these has been the separation of ownership from control accompanied by the rise of professional management. Fifty years ago, business decisions were still being commonly made by the stereotype tycoon who owned the firm he controlled and managed. But as the business firm grew, to emerge eventually as a corporate colossus, it had to develop a brain and nervous system to match its physical growth. And as the complications of business—its marketing problems, its labor relations, and its government relations—became ever more intricate, it became increasingly difficult for one man to cope with them. Inevitably the direction of big business had to shift from the owner-manager to the career executive. To put it bluntly, the modern corporation became a collective enterprise under the direction of professional managers.

Two other factors, in addition to growth and the increased complexity of managerial problems, contributed to the ascendancy of the professional manager: the influence of bankers and the ownership of business by masses of stockholders. Investment bankers, of course, played a strategic role in the construction of the large corporation earlier in the century. They promoted many of the mergers that created the giants and floated their securities. Contrary to popular notion, the bankers could not, however, take an active part in directing their offspring. Their interests were too diverse and too widespread to allow them to manage companies. They had veto power, of course. But they had to give wide latitude to managers who were, to be sure, beholden to the bankers for their original selection. The classic example of this interrelation between so-called "finance capitalism" and "managerial capitalism" was the Morgan-Gary direction of United States Steel. Elbert Gary was picked by J. P. Morgan to head the company, but he had wide latitude in directing its affairs.

For their part, the shareholders in the giant firms were quite willing to go along with the trend toward professional management. As their numbers multiplied, most stockholders found themselves unable, because of sheer numbers, and unwilling, because of unfamiliarity, to take part in making business decisions. They therefore turned their powers over to the hired managers.

The combination of finance and managerial capitalism was increasingly discernible in the late nineteenth and early twentieth centuries. In 1917 it was still a novelty, but an entrenched novelty. Since then, however, the influence of finance capitalism has dwindled significantly. Professional management has become a thoroughly accepted part of business life with a status all its own. The professional manager is no longer subservient to finance capitalism. He is at the least the senior partner in the relationship. It is he, as a rule, who selects the banker rather than the other way around. Meanwhile, too, the financial part of the business establishment has changed. Internal financing in the form of retained earnings and depreciation allowances has become immensely important, and external financing now incorporates the aid and assistance of new types of financial intermediaries. One of the open questions for the next fifty years is whether the rise of these new fiduciaries—pension funds and mutual trusts—to the status of legal ownership and control of industry will re-establish a new and very different "control of industry by capital."

There is an almost irresistible temptation to exaggerate the extent of the shift from owner to hired manager and the implications that can be drawn therefrom. In its broad outlines the hypothesis is very plausible. It is likely that professional managers constituted less than 5 per cent of the entrepreneurial population in the late nineteenth century compared with 50 per cent today. In a sample of fifty leading entrepreneurial figures in 1917, there were twenty-three owners and eighteen managers. In 1947 the ratio was eleven to twenty-nine and today it is four to forty-two. But in its details and implications the hypothesis is a caricature in black and white, while life goes on in its usual grays. Fifty years ago, career managers were not that rare; and today, the professional executive *sans* shares is not that common, especially in non-financial business. There is a middle group consisting of executives who have a large personal stake in their individual firms even though that stake represents only a small fraction of the firm's total assets.

Thus, we have *three* not two classes of managers: the owner-manager, who is admittedly rapidly disappearing in the large corporation; the propertyless hired manager, who is also rapidly disappearing from industry and trade; and the thriving professional executive with many eggs in the company basket. The difference between this troika and the stereotype tandem is immensely important, especially when one asks the question what motivates the businessman.

Whether completely true or not, the shift from owner-manager to hired manager is generally believed to have had earth-shaking effects on the whole business environment, effects that were even more revolutionary since the hired manager was often thought to be nothing more than a well-paid office boy.

The professional executive is deemed to be more sophisticated and less gauche than the rugged individualist of the past. As many business historians interpret the passing of the old order and the rise of the new, the professional manager is a "cognitive, sophisticated entrepreneur"* who "is supposed to see the long-term and the social impact of his business." According to Thomas Cochran, "the professional manager's conditioning made him a different type from the aggressive and often socially irresponsible small competitor who had built capitalism."

This may be salutary or it may be pernicious depending on the reader's value system. In any event, both the right and the left, those who are pro-business and those who are cool or hostile to business, have sharply attacked the emergence of the professional manager and the growth of big business that made it possible or inevitable.

Conservatives, following in the footsteps of the late Joseph A. Schumpeter, regard the trend toward business collectivism as a threat to capitalism. In their view, the separation of ownership from control has made individual wealth overly liquid, giving it an unsubstantial, an unreal quality. At the same time, since an individual's self-interest is no longer intimately related to the business he manages, the psychological values of ownership have been atrophied.

Another school of critics, which paradoxically includes both liberals and conservatives, is upset with the trend toward collectivism for somewhat different reasons. These critics look back with deep and often hypocritical nostalgia to a past when business was being "run"

*The phrase belongs to Arthur H. Cole.

by genuine entrepreneurs. As the bill of particulars describes it, these older empire builders had an easily understood objective: to maximize profits. And since they owned the businesses they directed, they had a legitimate claim to power. According to these same critics, today's executive has no claim to legitimacy, for in no sense does he represent the owners. He himself has very little equity in his company, and he has no particular feeling of responsibility to the stockholder-owners. Since he has no ownership interest, he no longer has the objective of maximizing profits. If he has any objective at all, it is to have the corporation grow and expand and increase its size, which is already too large for anyone's good.

Some parts of these sweeping indictments are probably valid, some are debatable, and some are probably false. But most of the criticism of modern management is based on an idyllic view of a perfect past and a myopic view of an imperfect present. To some extent, the odious contrast between yesterday's and today's management is an aspect of the American's preoccupation with personalities. Yesterday's heroic entrepreneur was a gay dog, a devil-may-care swashbuckling individualist competing vigorously and maximizing his gains at every opportunity. Today's executive is an anonymous character, an unglamorous "anti-hero" with no desire to compete or to maximize profits.

But this is not quite the way the executives in the company dining room see it. They have more hostages to fortune, more responsibilities to more blocs than the nineteenth-century businessman ever anticipated. That neanderthal entrepreneur made his decisions in a world in which government and labor unions were minor irritants. Later, in the early twentieth century, both institutions were growing, but the businessman of 1917 could still regard them with amused condescension, much as a tolerant parent regards a neighbor's teenage son. The stockholder, too, was treated patronizingly as companies floated non-voting common, common stock *A*, and common stock *B*, issued reports that were ingenious devices containing little intelligence and less information. The World War I manager had to cater to only three groups: his board of directors, with whom he had in any case an *entente cordiale*; his competitors, who often believed in live and let live; and his customers, who had little choice whether to buy or not to buy. The prevalent attitude was summed up by the most successful entrepreneur of the day, Henry Ford. Ford believed that stockholders were people who "bet their money on other people's brains." Competitors did not bother him particularly, and the consumer "could have any color car as long as it was black."

The contemporary executive cannot behave in this way. He may be relatively free from the owner's control, but other groups, comparatively insignificant fifty years ago, exert all sorts of constraints on his behavior. He must pay close attention to competitors and rival products in the market place, labor unions when hiring and firing and in personnel relations, government agencies in pricing, expansion plans, management, and financing. Nor can he ignore public opinion. And he must always be wary of the other members of the inter-corporate hierarchy.

The second point in the indictment—the decline and fall of profit maximization—is much ado about very little. There is no point to discussions of motivation or of the nuances in the behavior of the vast mass of businessmen, for the fact of the matter is that no one knows very much about the motivational pecking order. But one does know that maximizing profits has never been anything more than an idealized and unattainable fiction in a theoretical model.

Business today, as it did fifty years ago, must make a profit merely to survive. Profit, therefore, must be a primary motive, and contrary to what many people believe, it may very well be that today's businessman is more interested in profit than his grandfather was—simply because he is more aware of change, innovation, and risk. It was common among businessmen in the 1920's to deride profits. But it is not the practice today. Businessmen do not in their speeches, writings, or other expressed opinions scorn profit or the profit motive. Amid all the discussions of "social responsibility," great care is taken to put social responsibility within the framework of the profit motive, for contrary to the stereotype, today's managers do have a substantial stake in ownership through stock options, bonuses, and so forth. They may not be exerting their all to maximize profits, but they are interested, very much interested, in profit. "There seems to me," said Alfred P. Sloan, "still to be no question about that. It is, as I see it, the strategic aim of a business to earn a return on capital, and if in any particular case the return in the long run is not satisfactory, the deficiency should be corrected or the activity abandoned for a more favorable one." What has changed is that profitability, like everything else in management, has become more complex. But it has not become less central for all of that—nor should it.

V

Just because of size if for no other reason, big business, it is said, must be static and bureaucratic. The massive corporations, we are told by Professor Galbraith for one, have embedded themselves in the economy and represent the last refuge of standpattism. Year after year, the same "monopolists" rule the roost. There is little turnover, for the giants hold an unassailable position.

Appealing as this thesis may be, it is just not true. Economic change, new products, consumer preferences, and management failures make for considerable mobility among the very large corporations. Of the fifty largest industrial corporations in 1917, thirty-five are still alive. But only nineteen are still in the first fifty positions. Nine are among the second fifty. Seven have sunk below the hundred largest. Fifteen have disappeared, seven by mergers, and eight by failure.

The fifty largest companies in 1917 included nine oil refiners, six steel mills, four copper mines, and three companies each in automobile assembly, meat packing, chemicals, and food. Among the fifty largest of 1967 are thirteen oil refiners, eight chemical companies, four electronics manufacturers, four steel plants, and three in automobiles and in electrical equipment. This is hardly a static picture.

Accusations of bureaucracy in big business fill many pages of the business literature written by both businessmen and academicians. The attorney for a large manufacturing company explained to a court that "the management of X company is responsible for the savings and investment of thousands of shareholders... and for the security of thousands of employees.... The management of a company so situated is likely to be cautious and conservative, and to take the courses involving the least risk." According to an eminent business historian, "the directors of a company ask of their employees devotion to duty, loyalty, and cooperation in a hierarchy rather than rational hedonism in a market." These are by no means new charges. A business commentator said in the late 1920's: "We are raising a lot of thoroughly drilled 'yes Ma'ams' in big corporations, who have no minds of their own; no opinions.... After a man has served twenty or thirty years in one of these monstrous corporations he is not liable to have much of a mind of his own."

The successful executive has not been oblivious to these criticisms.

He has been well aware that bureaucracy must exist in big business, in big government, in big education, indeed, in any big institution. Musing about the problems of General Motors, Alfred P. Sloan commented: "In practically all of our activities, we seem to suffer from the inertia resulting from our great size." When someone told Lammot du Pont that the hired manager was likely to spend the company's money without exercising due caution, du Pont replied, "That's not the point. The danger is that he'll spend it with *too much* caution." But although they recognize the ever-present threat from bureaucracy, able executives also know that large-scale enterprise can be conducted only within the framework of orderly administration. What has to be done is to accept the difficulty and then work out some method to prevent or soften its impact.

One method by which far-sighted executives attempted to contain the threat of bureaucratic stagnation was to reorganize the managerial structure. Centralization, of course, characterized the so-called "one-man" company of the nineteenth century. As the firm grew bigger, committees and departments were created, but these encouraged rather than discouraged the tendency toward bureaucracy. In the twentieth century, especially after the early 1920's, the trend was more toward decentralization and eventually to what Alfred P. Sloan called "decentralized operations with coordinated control, a happy medium between the extremes of pure centralization and pure decentralization."

One explanation for the new trend toward decentralization, an explanation best articulated by Alfred D. Chandler, is that changes in structure are necessitated by changes in strategy. The aggressive entrepreneur is under a constant compulsion to employ his resources in the best possible way. Under the pressures of expanding markets, with better means of transportation and communication, and other alterations in the economic environment, the businessman takes on new functions and moves into new lines. Each move requires a new design for administration. In Chandler's analysis, business was originally organized in single product, single function firms. Then as markets expanded and urban centers flourished, and as improved transportation made it easier to get to the market, business firms took on new functions and became single product, multi-function. In the 1920's, still a third transition occurred. The strategy of the most advanced entrepreneurs moved in the direction of diversification. Firms became multi-product as well as multi-function, and some firms became just as well entrenched in international as in domestic markets. Decentralization replaced centralization in management, and it was hoped that the process would also manage to prevent corporate arthritis.

Changes in management demanded changes in methods. Innovation moved significantly from the factory to the office, from the production line to the desk and the designing board. In proportion to the total labor force, the once great army of production workers dwindled continuously while the ranks of the non-production workers, the office and service workers, swelled with equal consistency.

Whole new concepts came to the fore, and new tools were invented to deal with the eruption of innovation in the office. Research and development became functions, and eventually self-contained businesses, in themselves. Data processing, computers, and model building replaced machine tools and blast furnaces as the center of attention in the task of raising productivity.

The "office revolution" has had other ramifications. For one thing, administrative expenses have risen much faster than operating expenses. As a per cent of total production costs, they account today for perhaps twice as much as they did fifty years ago. Then too, the office has been responsible for reorganizing the economic structure of the nation's largest cities. Once the center of industrial activity, the large cities now concentrate on office work. New York City is the outstanding example. Its industry declines steadily year after year, but, as the hub of megalopolis, it also steadily attracts more and more head offices of the country's largest corporations.

The multiplication of office workers is one chapter in the story of what economic change has done to the human resources employed in business. Another chapter, much more widely read and publicized, deals with the attitude of businessmen toward labor unions. In 1917 employers did not view unions with any particular alarm. To be sure, unions were growing, but they were still small and not powerful enough to be more than a slight nuisance. They were treated patronizingly all through the 1920's. Then, in the 1930's, they took a number of gigantic steps forward, and under the new threat business became bitter and hostile. Anti-unionism was, however, a losing game, and in time businessmen came to recognize this. Their attitude then changed to one of resignation.

The decline in the number of production workers that has been part of economic change has temporarily or permanently stabilized labor union membership, for it is not easy to organize office workers. Yet unions are still too powerful to be disregarded or treated lightly.

Employers, therefore, tolerate them in very much the same way as human beings have adjusted themselves to the annoyances of an aching back.

But employers have also brought new tools, new theories, and new concepts to the task of managing men. Fifty years ago, personnel relations was a topic hidden away in some dreamer's book. Scientific management was inching its way into a few large corporations. The Hawthorne experiment was still ten years in the future. Today, personnel management and human relations are more a part of business than *Business Week* and the *Wall Street Journal*.

Economic change has also altered the management of money. Today's business firms have an inventory policy for money very much as they have an inventory policy for goods. General Motors was one of the earliest corporations to set up a systematic cash inventory policy. In 1922, according to Sloan, General Motors "began calculating a month ahead what our cash would be each day of the month.... Against this projected curve we compared each day the corporation's actual cash balances.... By reducing our cash balances in banks, this system enabled us to invest the excess cash, principally in short-term government securities."

Money, men, machines, and methods—economic change has caused management to alter its approach to each. But what about marketing, probably the most important function of all, simply because management's primary job is to find a customer and to persuade him to buy. For the businessman, the circumstances surrounding this job and the strategy and tactics best suited for accomplishing the objective are much different today from what they were in 1917. Yet nothing the businessman does has given rise to so much criticism as his marketing strategy and policy. Critics, having rung the changes on responsibility, legitimacy, efficiency, and bureaucracy, add some additional notes by charging that big business is monopolistic. It is an octopus that thrives by eating up the smaller fish. It is a price fixer and a practitioner of meaningless product differentiation.

According to the critics, things were better two generations ago. To be sure, they were different from what they are today, but this did not make them better than they are today. Then, competition was still mainly a matter of price. By and large the market was still a virgin market and goods were price-elastic. Henry Ford understood his market very well when he stuck with one model and one color. He knew instinctively that his customers wanted an automobile and wanted it at a price they thought they could afford. He therefore emphasized price, not color, nor design, nor aesthetics—only price. A decade later in 1929, things were already somewhat different. The manufacturing mix and the market structure had undergone profound changes. A replacement market had to a large extent displaced the virgin market. And today, the metamorphosis has progressed much further. Discretionary income has multiplied. Yesterday's luxuries are today's necessities. The job of the marketing department is not so much to persuade the buyer to buy something he doesn't have, but to persuade him to replace what he has with something that seems much better. Needs have been largely filled, and buying for wants has achieved an importance it did not have in yesterday's generation. Price elasticity has given place to income elasticity. Entrepreneurs like Henry Ford would be lost in the new market structure. Ford achieved phenomenal success by emphasizing price in a market in which only one person in ten owned an automobile. He committed a major error by continuing to emphasize price in a market in which one in five owned an automobile. The new era requires an entirely different kind of competition to persuade the customer to buy. Price does not move him as much as it did once. He does not have to buy; what will persuade him is product differentiation, service, style, and automation.

Many professional economists, sociologists, and moralists with a happy facility for ignoring changing times and changing mores, insist that in today's economy there is no competition. Their view is the same as the estimable one held by Adam Smith that competition is higgling over price in a market place of many sellers. Anything else is monopolistic competition, or imperfect competition. But to the businessman, competition is a situation in which two or more sellers are trying to maximize income. Every businessman rightly thinks that he is just as competitive when he dangles an extra geegaw in front of a reluctant buyer as he is when he agrees to drop a dollar off the price. And his reasoning hardly seems wrong in a market in which more goods are sold because of product differentiation than because of price.

VI

None of the changes that have been discussed in the general economy or in business occurred suddenly. To the contrary, economic progress has been an awkward movement consisting of three steps forward and one step back. It can be said with some exaggeration that the last fifty years have been a cycle of rich man, poor man, beggar man, thief, beggar man, poor man, rich man. Although it is rapidly fading away into mellow memory, there are still among the living those who remember the economic catastrophe of the 1930's and the boom that preceded it. Those whose memories are even sharper recall that there were also two mild recessions and a severe although short-lived downturn during the generally prosperous 1920's. But the pattern of that decade has not been repeated in the period since World War II. There has been no downturn similar to the two severe depressions of the 1920's. There have been recessions—four, in fact, in the last twenty years—but altogether they covered only forty-two months. There has, moreover, not been a recession in the last seven years, the longest period of sustained growth in economic history.

We have been so prosperous that there is now a wide-spread conviction that economic depressions are a thing of the past. The most optimistic go so far as to assert that recessions, that is mild down-turns in major economic indicators, are also a thing of the past. But these are the few. The majority believe that recessions will recur, but one and all have relegated to the artifacts of history the earth-shaking economic convulsions that were once considered as inevitable as death and taxes.

There are three essential reasons for the optimism that springs eternal in the crystal ball of the economic forecaster. First of all, he is conscious of how much more he knows about economics than his predecessor fifty years earlier. He assumes that this increased knowledge will enable him to avoid the pitfalls and booby traps that lead to economic disaster. Granted that we know more, and perhaps much more, the assumption that such increased knowledge is power may be nothing more than economic hubris. There is much more substance to the belief that it is the change in the philosophy and practice of fiscal and monetary affairs that has dealt a major blow to the traditional boom and bust business cycle. But it is well to remember that similar beliefs prevailed in all former eras of prosperity. It is still much too early to proclaim that we have at long last solved the riddle of economic depression. Still, the economy has in the last twenty years performed far better than at any other time in our history.

Nothing could please business more than a state of permanent prosperity. Past depressions and severe recessions not only dried up

profits; they also pushed the reputation of the business community
to a dangerously low level. Consider how the businessman's prestige
has been tossed on the waves of economic activity in the last fifty
years. During the prosperity of the 1920's, the businessman achieved
the pinnacle of public fame and fortune. His was the voice of authority
on every subject. Adviser to governments and keeper of the American
value system, he was very much in the position of the academic
intellectual of today. Then came the depression and the businessman's
prestige dwindled to nothing. Ridiculed and derided and dazed by
what was happening to him and his system, he was a pitiful character.
With recovery and unprecedented prosperity since World War II, the
business system has again become respectable and the businessman
acceptable. But neither has regained the heights reached in the 1920's.
Neither is regarded with the veneration that was then bestowed, but
on the other hand, neither are they regarded with the bitter hostility
that was heaped upon both in the 1930's. The prevalent attitude
today is one of indifference, which, of course, may be more deadly
than outright hatred.

What of the businessman's philosophy, his opinions, and his
economic beliefs? Different times and different people have disrupted
his long-cherished beliefs. As has been said, his attitude toward labor
unions is one of reluctant resignation, and he operates under a different
definition of competition. Prosperity and continuous governmental
intervention have persuaded him to accept a new view of the importance of fiscal policy. He is no longer so adamantly opposed to
government debt; he is no longer so committed to a balanced budget.
On the tariff, he is less protectionist than he was in 1917. But it
would be a major error to infer that all businessmen regard government deficits with equanimity, or that many businessmen are free
traders. His opinions, in short, have changed as much since 1917
as the society, economy, and technology in which he lives and works.

VII

But what about the American business school in this half-century
of change? The greatest change has been in its social function—for
society, for the business system, and for the individual.

Even though business schools in America go back almost a century,
their influence fifty years ago, was minimal—both on business and on

education. Since then, however, they have become our educational bellwether, and also the largest segment of higher education—undergraduate, graduate and continuing education.

It was around World War I that the business school in America first expanded rapidly, with a second wave of expansion in the decade after World War II. Most of the existing undergraduate schools of business opened their doors in the World War I decade or soon thereafter, just as most of the existing graduate schools of business were started after World War II. In both eras the business school was the forerunner and "leading indicator" of a general educational change in American society.

It is only reasonable to assume that the tremendous expansion in the last decade of "advanced management education," i.e., business training for educated men in mid-career, again leads a general educational trend.

Altogether the business school has been a major agent for social mobility in these fifty years. Even today in the working-class cities— Detroit or Milwaukee, for example—it is the business school, above all, through which the children of the blue-collar worker are rising into professional work.

At the same time the business schools—and here especially the graduate and advanced management programs—have increasingly become recruiting grounds for business leadership. Increasingly, they attract men of high potential to business careers and prepare highly motivated and successful technicians for the responsibilities and demands of general management.

Viewed as *professional* schools, business education has thus changed greatly; it has become much more central to the business system as well as to our society. But viewed as professional *schools* the changes have been diffuse. Courses and subject matter have changed and are changing again. Indeed, nothing else in higher education has undergone such a thorough metamorphosis. But the concepts and direction of business education have changed little—far less than business and the business system. Where we had "bookkeeping" fifty years ago, we now have "accounting" and may have "management information" tomorrow. But the concept of business education as a bundle of skills is still the rule, no matter how much we talk about "models" and "processes," no matter how much we use "cases" or "business games."

Altogether the business schools in America have tended to react rather than to act. They have codified rather than initiated. The new concepts, ideas, and tools of business have originated largely outside the business school and practically without benefit of academicians. Modern organization was developed by practitioners—the coal company president Henry Fayol in France, for example, and Hamilton Barksdale at DuPont and Alfred Sloan at General Motors.

There are other paradoxes in business education. In marked contrast to fifty or even twenty years ago, the professor today is highly prized as a consultant, primarily, of course, by business, but increasingly by governments, hospitals, school systems, and, above all, by international groups. Indeed, American business education has become one of our most popular exports, with a balance of trade completely and one-sidedly in our favor. Yet few business school professors are ever considered for high or even low places in Washington. Similarly, neither the most thoughtful spokesmen for, nor the most intelligent critics of business are to be found in our business schools. Unlike the faculties of other professional schools, such as law or medicine, the business school professor is disassociating himself from the business community, the very population to which he is supposed to be offering his services.

The picture is, in other words, one of "dynamic disequilibrium," to use a popular euphemism for what fifty years ago would have been called confusion. The changes have been so great that the business school of today differs from its predecessor of fifty years ago as much as today's business and business system differ from those of 1918. Yet the changes concern manners rather than substance, techniques rather than goals, tactics rather than strategy, views rather than philosophy.

Indeed, it can be said that all the fundamental changes in the American business school date back at least forty years, to the mid-twenties. The first of these—after the Wharton School had opened its doors in 1881 as the first collegiate school of business in America—was the establishment of the graduate school of business at Harvard in 1908. Then, in 1918, New York University pioneered in offering advanced, continuing education leading to graduate degrees for business managers and professionals in mid-career. Finally, in the mid-twenties, Harvard again pioneered by shifting the center of instruction in business from functional "technique" to management as a unifying process. And these three acts of our predecessors still largely mold the business school of today.

But as a professional school the American business school must be appropriate to the needs of the business community. Is it appropriate, however, to the needs of today—the needs shaped by the changes in structure, institutions, and expectations of the last fifty years? Or is it still, whatever its technical sophistication, education for the business system of forty and fifty years ago, when today's commonplaces in business education were bold and risky innovations?

And is it altogether enough to be appropriate to what has happened in the past? After all, the top managers of American business in the year 2000 are the graduate business students of today. What does the business school have to be today to be appropriate to the needs of these leaders of tomorrow?

*   *   *

This volume on the preparation of tomorrow's business leaders begins purposely with a survey of the changes in the environment rather than with a history of university education for business. It is not only that the Graduate School of Business Administration at New York University has always been proud to consider itself a part of the business community. It is not only that as students of business we know that the customer creates value and that the producer only creates costs—and business is our customer. Above all we are only too painfully aware of the fact that business—its vision, its demands, its standards—has been ahead of the business school. This may well be something we have to change tomorrow—but today it is still a fact.

To define what preparation for business leadership should and might be, this volume therefore next looks at the needs, the demands, and the opportunities of business and businessmen.

THE CHANGING
ENVIRONMENT

I

EDITOR'S INTRODUCTION

The first task of the business leader is to turn change in the environment—in society, economy, and technology —into economic and entrepreneurial opportunity. He must convert socio-economic need into effective market demand. The first question to which a discussion of tomorrow's business leaders has to address itself is, therefore, what changes are already discernible in the environment of business enterprise. This is the topic of the five chapters of Part One. They range from discussions of government and local community, to the "information revolution," to changes in the character and scope of technology. What is perhaps most startling about the chapters is that each of them assumes a genuine discontinuity in the environment; each asserts that what is ahead for the business leader is not so much greater demands as new demands.

JOHN T. CONNOR

The Political Environment
for Business

2
In my short life—just over fifty years so far—I have witnessed tremendous changes in the business attitude toward government and in the governmental attitude toward business. These environmental changes can be shown by the drastically different forms of advice given at various points in the last forty or fifty years. My father, a small businessman in Syracuse in upstate New York—then still a relatively small city—advised me over and over again as I was growing up: "Stay out of politics. It's a dirty game." When I was at the Harvard Law School, Felix Frankfurter, probably the most successful recruiter of young men for the New Deal, preached: "Don't go to a Wall Street law firm to help defend the capitalists. Go where the action is—to Washington—and help create a new society." Today, I find myself telling young men and women: "By all means include some years of public service in your career, even though its main thrust may be in business or education. You'll be a better businessman or educator if you do, and the governmental process will be better off because of your participation, even for just a few years. Think of 'politics' as public administration in the executive branch of government as well as in the legislative branch. Politics is an integral part of life itself—no longer off by itself having only peripheral effects on our lives."

27

Government is here to stay—to grow and prosper. During the Eisenhower Administration there was a pause in the expansion of governmental power and services at the federal level. But during that period the state and local governments were working double-time to expand the educational, health, welfare and other local services neglected during the war years and needed in increased amounts by an expanding population. But things changed with the inauguration of President John F. Kennedy and, for better or worse, probably never will be the same again. President Kennedy's resounding plea, "ask not what your country can do for you but what you can do for your country," fell on the responsive ears of countless young people who, living in a troubled world, were eager to do what they could to improve the lot of their fellow men all over the world. The resulting "march on Washington" by able people, mostly young and mostly from the universities, had not been matched since the early New Deal days. The ferment caused by their new ideas and programs will undoubtedly have a lasting effect on the country, particularly in the field of government relations with business and labor. The yeast responsible for that ferment disappeared in large part by the end of President Lyndon B. Johnson's third year in office. But by then, so much of the "Great Society" program originating with the Kennedy Administration had been enacted into law that it is quite safe to say there is no turning back now.

The point of no return has been left far behind. Future administrations will busy themselves with filling the gaps and expanding the frontiers of the newer federal fields in civil rights, education, health, welfare, urban development of backward areas, transportation, transportation safety, consumer protection, international business and finance and trade and investment, communications, and countless other fields. Inevitably, more and more of business will find itself under Federal Government regulation and control, and our daily lives will be increasingly affected.

But, quite astoundingly, important policy-making officials of the Kennedy and early Johnson years—now in private life or legislative posts—are stating publicly that these bright new programs and others, now urgently needed to solve the problems of the urban centers and their people, should be turned over to private industry for administration and not left in the hands of the so-called bureaucrats. Equally amazing, more and more corporate leaders and their corporations are volunteering for duty in this new socio-economic area, and are offering their services to work in fields heretofore regarded as the sole province of government acting directly through its employees.

The relationship between business and government is broad and varied. Clearly, the government means different things to different businessmen, and business means different things to different agencies of government. To one business firm, government is primarily a customer. To another, government is principally a regulatory agency. To a third, government is mainly a source—of information and services, of research and development support, or perhaps of subsidy. And to a fourth company, government means little more than the bad news of higher taxes or the good news of an eased tax burden. Government activities, extending from the sale of postage stamps to the moon program, cannot be generalized about easily from any possible direction on the political or economic compass.

Looking at the world around us as it actually exists, it is nothing short of incredible that anyone should consider business and government as adversaries on any broad front. A record of joint achievements, a catalog of dual efforts, and a dossier of mutual concerns comment most forcefully on this score.

On the other hand, I do not believe that a truly meaningful purpose is served by expressions of puffy sentiment stating that business and government will, hand-in-hand, lead the nation to lasting happiness. Although there may often be an identity of long-term goals, government and business do not commonly share an identity of approach. Nor should this be expected in a system that takes its greatest strength from pluralism.

I am not suggesting that merit badges be awarded for dissent any more than blue ribbons are warranted for automatic assent. But our system is tailored specifically to reflect breadth of approach and diversity of interest—that is the purpose of Executive Department and Congressional hearings, of advisory councils and groups playing such a major role in Washington and in our whole government structure and political process.

In essence, our pluralism applies the checks and balances and breadth of input on a national scale, that the Constitution provided for inside the government. The business community, various as it is within itself, can and does make a notable contribution as part of this national process of pluralist decision-making, particularly in activities related to economic growth and development. The list of areas in which business and government are working in partnership is literally endless.

Yet, of course, business's primary role is not contained in any of these individual relationships, nor indeed by all of them together. Economic success remains business's most important product—providing the goods and services, the new products, the wages, profits and revenues—in short, by functioning as the nation's economic and industrial engine. In the final analysis, all else in the practical world depends on this vast and powerful source of motive power. For, if the government expresses the hopes and the aims of our people, it is business primarily that organizes their energies and talents and resources to serve national purposes at home and abroad. It is business initiative and business risk that are the spark and the spark plug of economic growth.

The first and foremost sphere of contact between government and business is the national economy. The government's role is plainly to support an economic environment in which business and other segments of the economy can function with the maximum of freedom and effectiveness. These have obviously been prime ingredients in the results being achieved during these economically soaring Sixties.

II

Looking to the future, the main point I wish to make is this: In addition to functional economic relationships, from fiscal and monetary policies, to subsidies, to regulation, there are jobs to be done in this country today and particularly, tomorrow, that challenge both business and government to new forms of joint or parallel effort. And what we see today, I believe, clearly indicates the potential shape of a tomorrow characterized, first, by what for the moment I will call public problem-solving; and second, by dramatic utilization of technology in a number of areas that will invite comparison with the technological revolution of recent decades in the military and space areas.

In many instances, but by no means all, these two streams will come together—as in transportation and housing, where a massive application of advanced techniques and technologies can be the answer to the public need.

But in other cases, it will be organizational and management ability, motivated by social awareness, that can come more clearly into play—although technology can also be an important tool here. I am thinking, for example, of such matters as education and training, employment, and recreation; and perhaps we should also include the host of items often associated in general terms with aspirations for "quality" as well as "quantity" in our civilization.

The types of mutual business and government activity that we have been discussing, fall within the two general areas of technology and public problem-solving. A third area is special business expertise or domination, where the counsel of business or its particular efforts—as in the balance of payments program—can be the keystone of a national approach, put in place through the responsibly exercised capabilities and talents of the business community.

By public problem-solving, I am referring to all the tasks that cry out for our efforts amid the growing complexities of a vast continental nation in which the population increases by some two and a half million persons each year, and is expected to rise in the next twenty years by a total equal to the current population of all states west of the Mississippi—and year by year, moves onto a smaller and smaller percentage of our land area.

You will note that I did not say "public sector problems." The public requirements that face our nation may well defy the straitjacket implicit in this term.

In solving these public problems, business may indeed stake out a new role for itself in America or, more accurately, extend its traditional role in response to the needs of the times. This evolving role is not only the crux of business's relationship with government. Far more important, it may be central to our national success in meeting the needs of the last decades of the twentieth century.

For example, slums and substandard housing clearly present a festering problem in our urban society, despite the vast urban redevelopment programs that have been undertaken in many parts of the country in recent years by both government and industry. The entry of some of America's major business organizations into this area of housing rehabilitation, in a manner both ambitious and experimental, may well and truly be a landmark development.

Not only can this mean progress and promise in meeting an urgent public need efficaciously without undue cost in time, resources, or disruption of families and neighborhoods, but, whatever the merits or demerits of various techniques being introduced or considered, it also can serve once again to focus attention on the simple truth that there *are* new answers to these kinds of problems.

There is a potential need, a waiting market if you will, for the "production of public services," just as there were for other products that brought success to American business while enhancing the lives of all of us. The public in general—and government at every level—is not only willing, but eager for industry to bring its full guns to bear on these problems, as it does on problems of production and distribution and other more traditional functions having to do with more traditional kinds of products.

And indeed there can and should be a sound profit in the provision of such products and services—the profit that business earns for provision of the other goods or services society seeks. The new factor today is that business, through these innovations, can meaningfully broaden the normal horizons of yesteryear.

The essential fact is that bridges to the future are waiting to be built across the broad flow of contemporary problems. They *will* be built because they represent the next step for America, and our nation and our people simply will not stand still. The questions that we in this generation must determine, however, relate to design of these bridges, who will build them, and how they will be built.

As the years pass, will it fall to government to develop a greater and greater in-house capability for the nation to move ahead? Or will the times dictate that business and industry more and more become the instrument for accomplishing social and economic responsibilities of the government, through contracts such as we now witness in job development and other activities? Can the business community, by turning its unique genius to an increasing extent on public and social problems, respond as effectively through private competitive enterprise to the problems of a new age as it has done in meeting the challenges of earlier times? And is it possible that competitive enterprise, oriented to new types of needs, will assume a greater and greater role in areas that current opinion might look upon as purely functions of government? Certainly, business activities in this sphere of producing public services do not need to stop at the water's edge.

The economic impact of the United States trade, investment, and business activities abroad is immense. Overseas investment, particularly in underdeveloped nations, has always provided spectacular evidence that profit is the instrument of progress.

So far, I have been focusing primarily on business functioning as business both at home and abroad, albeit with an expanded orientation to meet the wants of our times. Obviously, very closely related to such public problem-solving is business's large and growing vital exercise of institutional citizenship—contributing enormously to education, to charities, and to the arts, and participating in all manner of good works on the community, national, and international levels. This, also, is a burgeoning business role that must, and I am certain will, continue to expand with the years.

The distinction traditionally drawn between corporate citizenship and corporate business is, in fact, no longer well delineated. I believe this is as it should be. The enlightened pragmatists who lead American business have tended to stamp "irrelevant" across the entire matter. Are company training programs for school dropouts good business or good citizenship? Does a large corporation's massive study of the effects of automation on society most significantly serve the company planners or the community at large? Is sponsorship of an art show sound advertising or does it fall under the heading of "culture"? American business leadership would surely answer, "both," in each case—if it bothered to ask itself the questions. For there is a demonstrable conviction in the business community that good citizenship is certainly good business, and good business clearly meets the specifications of good citizenship.

III

With such an expanded and exciting role for business and businessmen in prospect, the real question becomes: what kind of businessmen will be needed to manage these activities—in business corporations, under government contracts, and within the Federal Government itself—and where will they come from? Competent management is the vital and absolutely indispensable ingredient of progress—in business, in labor unions, in the universities, and in government.

For these reasons, able young people should indeed be encouraged to go into government service. There will be plenty of jobs available to them in Washington, in state capitals, in county seats and in city halls—interesting and challenging jobs. Some of the best students will choose a government career right from the start. Many will stay in it for several reasons: salaries are good and risks, at least some types of risks, are fewer than on the outside. The work can be highly satisfying.

After four or five years, many of them may also want to branch out, moving into the professions, into teaching, or into business. The experience they will have picked up in Washington or in the state capital or on the local level will be invaluable, especially as government relationships with the private sector broaden and intermesh more and more, as they surely will.

Some of the young people will reverse that procedure. They will take a job on campus first, or go into research, or to one of the foundations. As a professor or instructor of economics, of political science, of law or social science, of mathematics or of any of the physical sciences, they will then find it relatively easy to switch over to government service. Some people do it regularly—they go from classroom and lecture hall to bureau or agency staff. Then they go back again, usually at a higher level, carrying more influence with each swing. Their qualifications will improve with increased experience, wider exposure, and a developing judgment based on first-hand knowledge and personal contact.

Still, a good many frustrations also await the young man or woman right out of school or out of academic work who goes to work for a government. The need for good, imaginative, bold management may be greatest in government service. But it is—so far—little recognized.

Delegation of authority as it is known in business is altogether little used in the Federal Government. Also surprising from the point of view of a businessman coming into government service, is the fact that very little emphasis is placed upon the task of managing existing programs. The entire emphasis is upon devising new programs, getting them approved by the Bureau of the Budget, the President, and then by the Congress, so that political advantages can accrue to the President and the other members of his administration, who become responsible for new trends, new policies, and new programs. In such an environment, not much credit is given for competent management of existing programs, or even small expansion or small contraction of existing programs—no matter how skilfully it may be accomplished.

For these reasons, I venture to predict—and I know that I am totally out of step—that the young, and especially the idealists among them, will find more and more that a career in business is the most effective way to render true public service.

Surely, to make this apparent to our young people is a major challenge to American business. And as American business becomes the vehicle for answering our public problems in a business-like manner—on an economically rational basis and for an earned and adequate profit—a business career should indeed increasingly live up to the motto New York University has chosen for itself: "A private institution in the public service."

But the most exciting prospect I see ahead is that of increasing numbers of business people considering at least a few years of government service as a part of their own business careers. Indeed, it is a highly desirable, if not necessary, experience for the development of managers in this age of a growing symbiosis of government and business in the same crowded social span, because both fields are concerned very much with the same problems and challenges.

This is the only way in which a large corporation can overcome its inability to understand government and the way government works. And in our society this ignorance, unfortunately almost universal, is a fatal flaw. It is the only way in which we can overcome the equally universal ignorance of business—its structure, its folkways, its needs— by government. And that too is a mortal danger—to government, even more than to business and the economy.

This is not going to be easy. The problems may well be larger than difficulties with money and pension benefits and interrupted career ladders. All this, intelligent business policies can cope with. The biggest problem may be the traditional view that government servants, especially in high positions, are fair game. Business managers are used to much higher demands for performance than public service usually exacts. But they are not used to being constantly under suspicion, as politicians are. Theirs is a world of deeds; the politicians' world is one of personalities. And just as politicians—especially men trained in Congress, as were Presidents Kennedy and Johnson—find it hard to get used to the objective demands of executive performance, business executives find it hard to get used to the highly subjective world of politics in which personal loyalty—of necessity, perhaps—means so much, and in which "who is right" always overbalances "what is right."

But the American businessman will have to learn to adapt to the world of politics. He will have to learn to make business and its capacity to perform serve the solution of our public policy problems. He will have to learn to make government and its needs for effective executives become a career opportunity for the rising business manager. Only in this way can we hope to solve the public problems of our country. But only in this way can we also hope to maintain and strengthen our free economy and our business system.

R. A. PETERSON

The New Era in Finance

3

During the second half of the decade of the 1960's, a major transition is underway in finance in the United States and in the world. The post-World War II era is ending and a new era is beginning. The institutional structures which have served well the financial needs of a growing United States economy and a burgeoning international flow of goods and capital are coming under increasing stress in a changing financial environment.

Certainly, the financial industry in the United States and in the world has been characterized by innovation and dynamic change in the period since World War II. The pace of innovation will likely accelerate in the years ahead. However, there are reasons to believe that during the years ahead, financial institutions and financial relationships will undergo structural changes more basic than mere innovational shifts.

The current strains on financial institutions and international financial relations have been intensified by the continued deficits in the United States and British balances of international payments and the large budget deficit in the United States. However, these factors should not be allowed to obscure the more fundamental changes which are occurring over the entire spectrum of financial relations.

Currently there are a number of questions in finance which must be answered during the next few years. The manner in which these questions are resolved will directly influence the basic structure and function of our financial institutions for years to come. In large measure, the answers to these questions will provide the parameters for the new era in finance.

These questions include:

1. How soon and to what degree will improved technology effect a basic change in the domestic payments mechanism of the United States and, to a lesser degree, the payments mechanism in other developed countries?

2. How can federal counter-cyclical monetary and credit policies be implemented effectively without imposing inequitable burdens on certain sectors of the economy?

3. What changes will be required in the current financial institutional structure and government regulatory bodies to insure effective competition and provide adequate financing for a growing economy?

4. What will be the role of gold and the United States dollar in a viable international payments system?

5. How can government and business cooperate effectively to solve the social and economic problems of the central cities of the United States?

While this list is by no means exhaustive, it points up some major areas of serious concern for financial executives in 1968, and for some time to come. There is little doubt that as these questions are resolved, new and perhaps more complex ones will arise. The best preparation for such challenges can only begin with an understanding of the contemporary financial scene.

The New Financial Environment

There is an impressive body of evidence to suggest that the new financial environment in the United States will be characterized by higher interest rates and a relative shortage of available credit compared with average conditions since World War II. In fact, during the greater part of the past four decades, internal economic forces have tended to hold down domestic interest rates and generate excess liquidity and a corresponding surplus of loanable funds.

Throughout the 1930's, the severe economic depression acted to sharply depress credit demands. Following the wave of bank failures in the early 1930's, surviving banks and other financial institutions tended to build up surplus liquid assets. Commercial banks built up substantial excess reserves in the Federal Reserve Banks which earned no return at all. The availability of these excess reserves, combined with the absence of a strong loan demand, tended to maintain abnormally low interest rates.

The United States Government financed World War II at low interest rates in an atmosphere of strong patriotism and sacrifice, relying on direct wage, price, and credit controls to restrain inflationary pressures. A large part of the added federal debt was absorbed by the commercial banking system. The Federal Reserve Banks maintained the price of government securities, and thus the low interest rates, by their willingness to purchase government issues in unlimited quantities at par.

At the close of 1947, more than two years after the end of hostilities, insured commercial banks in the United States held United States Treasury securities equal to 180 per cent of their total loan portfolio. Total loans of these banks were equal to less than 27 per cent of total deposits.

The general excess liquidity in the economy was also reflected in the balance sheets of nonfinancial corporations. At the end of 1947, such corporations had cash and United States security holdings equal to almost 64 per cent of their current liabilities.

Since that time, however, a growing United States economy has generated private credit demands in excess of the growth of financial savings. A large part of these demands were met by a reduction in bank and corporate liquidity. From 1947 to 1966, total loans at all insured commercial banks increased at an average annual rate of almost 10 per cent. During this same period, total deposits grew at a rate of less than 5 per cent per year. As a result, the ratio of bank loans to total deposits increased to well over 60 per cent.

Corporate liquidity also recorded a substantial decline. Corporations increased their holdings of cash and United States Government issues at a rate of less than 3 per cent per year, while current liabilities were increasing at an average annual rate of almost 8 per cent. As a result, the ratio of cash and United States Government securities to current liabilities for all United States nonfinancial corporations fell from 64 per cent to about 24 per cent.

While the reduction in bank and corporate liquidity provided a substantial source of funds for expansion in the private sector of the economy, further reductions in the years ahead do not appear likely. The bulk of the securities currently held by commercial banks are either pledged as collateral for public deposits or required as minimum secondary reserves. Thus, if deposits grow at the same rate in the future as in the post-war period, the rate of commercial bank loan growth will be reduced by half. This slower growth in bank credit will come in a period when business firms will be forced to rely more on credit as they will no longer have the option of liquidity reduction.

Of course there have been transient periods of "tightness" in the financial markets during the past two decades; however, the general environment has been one of credit ease and relatively low interest rates. Available evidence would indicate that an inflection point has been reached in the trend toward reduced liquidity. Liquidity ratios are not likely to trend higher in the years ahead but should remain relatively stable or decline at a significantly lower rate. Assuming a strong and growing economy, a relative shortage of credit funds for expanding public and private needs seems likely to prevail. Indeed, looking across the world, there are unmistakable signs of heavy—perhaps insatiable—demands for funds, especially in the developing countries.

The Domestic Payments System

During the post-war period, business firms and individuals have tended to reduce cash balances to the absolute minimum level consistent with transaction needs and the opportunity costs of alternative uses. There have been many developments and refinements in transactions procedures which have facilitated the reduction of balances. These include lock-box services for collection of funds, improved wire transfer of funds, and greatly improved facilities for communications and transportation. As short-term interest rates have trended higher, the penalties for holding idle funds have also increased, giving further incentive to reduction of balances.

During the post-World War II period, the *total money supply* in the United States, defined as currency in circulation and adjusted demand deposits in commercial banks, increased at an average annual rate of less than one half the rate of increase in the total output of goods and services. Of course, there have been short periods during which the growth of the money supply outpaced the growth in the economy as monetary policy shifted toward ease to encourage expansion of the economy.

Many students of the United States monetary system believe that we are now on the threshold of a major transition in the domestic payments system. The popular phrase used to denote the new system is the "cashless-checkless society." In such a system, a computerized transfer of funds would be accomplished immediately at the time of purchase or sale. The place of sale would be in contact with the relevant banks' computers by means of telephone or other facilities. While equipment is currently available which makes such a payments system technically feasible, there are still numerous economic and legal problems which will take a good deal of time to be resolved. Most important, such a system must also gain customer acceptability, which is far from spontaneous among many groups in our society.

It appears certain, however, that a more versatile and diversified payments system will evolve with automated exchange increasingly supplementing the use of cash and checks. Many of the initial phases are already in operation, such as direct transfer of payrolls and certain periodic payments, including mortgage payments and utility bills. The rapid growth of bank credit cards is also a move in this same direction. The end result of these developments could be more realistically called a "less-check and less-cash society."

The net result of this transition will be a more efficient utilization of the money supply. Thus the money stock and its major component —demand deposits—will continue to grow more slowly than output and expenditures in the economy.

In other developed countries, there will be a continued acceleration in the development of the payments mechanism. In fact, the nationwide system of bank branches in most other developed countries will allow a more rapid transition in the payments system than would be possible in the United States under similar economic conditions where nationwide branch banking is prohibited.

The new era in finance will be one in which demand deposits in commercial banks maintained for transaction purposes will decline in relative importance as a source of loanable funds to business in the United States and in other developed countries.

Federal Monetary and Credit Policy

In an environment of relatively high interest rates and a general shortage of available credit, the efficient and equitable market allocations of available funds and the efficiency of federal monetary and credit policy become increasingly important.

The Federal Government is committed to the pursuit of policies which encourage economic growth with maximum employment and relatively stable prices. It is quite apparent, however, that high employment itself, once achieved, raises many new disturbing cost-price problems which need solutions if the economy is to avoid further serious disruptions. For example, recent experience would seem to indicate that during periods of rising prices, any significant moves toward fiscal restraint in the form of tax increases or reduced federal expenditures are extremely difficult to achieve. Recent experience has also shown that significant moves toward monetary and credit restraint, using the present tools of monetary and credit policy, result in a disproportionate restraint on some sectors of the economy, especially the residential construction industry.

If, in fact, the financial environment of the future is characterized by relatively high interest rates and a fairly chronic credit shortage, the continued use of monetary and credit policy as a major tool of counter-cyclical policy will likely result in increased dislocations in the economy and, ultimately, may contribute to instability. This will be true even in an environment in which the tools of fiscal policy are used in a far more effective manner than has been the case in the very recent past.

At present, federal monetary and credit policy is exercised almost solely by controlling the reserves of the member commercial banks of the Federal Reserve System. The Federal Reserve Board can, within specified limits, set the percentage of deposits of various types which must be maintained in reserves. Additional reserves are provided to member commercial banks either through Federal Reserve purchases of securities in the open market, or through loans to member banks by the regional Federal Reserve Bank.

By controlling the rate of increase in member bank reserves, the Federal Reserve System can control the growth in their deposits and, ultimately, in their loans and investments. In addition to the general control of reserves, the Federal Reserve also regulates the maximum rates member banks can pay on various types of time and savings deposits. In recent years, the Federal Reserve has also used moral suasion to discourage certain types of bank loans.

As befits an area as complex as money and finance, there are a number of competing theories to explain the relationship between financial variables and the general level of economic activity. Many economists argue that changes in economic activity result largely or solely from changes in the money stock. This group contends that the velocity of circulation or rate of turnover of the money stock is relatively stable. Thus, an increase in the money supply at a stable rate consistent with the increase in productive potential in the economy would result in maximum economic growth at stable prices.

If this approach is accepted, then a careful definition of the components of the money supply becomes a paramount concern. The most widely accepted definition of the money stock in the United States includes currency in circulation and adjusted demand deposits in commercial banks. Acceptance of a quantity theory of money and the above definition raises serious questions concerning reserve requirements for time and savings deposits and maximum rate ceilings on such deposits as tools of counter-cyclical monetary policy.

Many proponents of some form of a quantity theory of money also include savings and time deposits of individuals and even large certificates of deposit of corporations and state and local governments in their definition of the money supply. However, recent and current experience should prove conclusively that bank time and savings deposits are more comparable to, and competitive with, other short-term marketable liquid assets and time deposits in nonbank financial intermediaries than to demand deposits and currency.

An alternate monetary theory links the growth in economic activity to the cost and availability of credit. Proponents of this theory argue that investment opportunities offering some prospective rate of return are always available. When such return is greater than the current cost of funds, the investment will be undertaken and economic activity increased. Acceptance of this theory in some form implies that counter-cyclical monetary policy should act to vary the total supply and thus the cost of credit to achieve the most desirable national economic growth and price stability goals.

Of course, the presentation of these two types of monetary theories is oversimplified and there seem to be as many variations as there are theorists. In addition, the influence of institutional structures and market rigidities must be considered in any approach to the formulation of federal economic policy. A major question, for example, which must be answered by the quantity theorists concerns the impact of technologically induced changes in the payments mechanism.

If the goal of federal counter-cyclical monetary policy is to control the growth of credit and the level of interest rates, a restructuring of the present tools of monetary policy is in order. Under the conditions of excess liquidity and monetary ease which prevailed during most of the post-war period, commercial banks were able to contribute actively to the growth of the economy. However, under conditions where credit is in chronic short supply and monetary restraint is more or less constant, this situation cannot be expected to persist.

When commercial bank credit is restrained, business borrowers scramble to line up alternative sources of funds. The large corporations turn to the sale of commercial paper and long-term bonds in the open market.

Continued efforts to control the total growth in credit by controlling commercial bank deposits will almost certainly result in a reduction in the commercial bank share of the total credit market. Leaving aside any question of the equity of such a development, the effectiveness of monetary controls would be impaired. With restraint being applied to a steadily declining proportion of the total credit market, the degree of restraint would have to be progressively more severe to have the same effect on the total market.

The extension of monetary controls to all segments of the credit market under the present institutional structure would be difficult. However, extension to a major share of the market is now essential if counter-cyclical policy is to be effective. Also, the question of equity of policy restraints on commercial banks versus nonbank financial institutions cannot be avoided indefinitely.

There are also the problems of effective and equitable allocation of the supply of credit in a period of chronic shortage. It has been demonstrated that under the present institutional structure, the residential construction industry is disproportionately affected by monetary restraint. Does this imply that in the future, a smaller share of our resources will be allocated to the provision of housing? What changes, if any, will be required in the institutional structure of the financial industry of the United States to allow this industry to compete effectively for an equitable share of available credit?

Underlying all these matters is the crucial issue of whether national economic policy will remain largely linked to general measures of restraint and expansion, or whether there will be a gradual drift into more direct controls with all their administrative and management deterrents. Unfortunately, the present indications are not very reassuring.

The answers to these perplexing questions and many others must be provided within the next few years. It is becoming increasingly clear that a re-examination of the role and the tools of federal monetary and credit policy is in order. We must redefine the goals of government regulation of the financial markets, and develop the type of institutional structure which will allow those goals to be achieved in an efficient and equitable manner in the type of financial environment which lies ahead.

International Finance

International developments will exert increasing influence upon all aspects of finance in the United States in the years ahead. The future role of the United States in the world economy and in the international financial system will be of increasing importance to the financial management of American firms.

The post-World War II period has been characterized by a strong growth in international trade and increasing inter-country flows of capital. This has been accomplished in part by a general relaxation of tariff and non-tariff barriers to trade and fund flows. A large part of the gains in international trade and capital flows can also be attributed to the development of the international payments mechanism.

However, serious questions are now being raised concerning the present gold-dollar exchange standard as a viable basis for the international payments system. There are two distinct, but closely related, problems evident in the present system. These may be characterized as the problem of the United States' balance of payments deficit and the problem of providing a growing reserve base for international finance.

Under the gold-dollar exchange standard, the United States Treasury has stood willing to buy gold from, or sell gold to, foreign official institutions at a fixed price of $35 per ounce. In these circumstances, foreign governments have been willing to accumulate United States dollars as a part of their international monetary reserves. When the United States runs a deficit in its balance of international payments, the deficit is financed either by an accumulation of dollar holdings abroad, or by an outflow of gold.

In the early post-war period, the United States held a major share of the world's monetary gold. During the early reconstruction period immediately following the war, the demand for American goods was so great that gold continued to flow to this country. The United States' gold stock reached a peak of over $24.5 billion in 1949. In the period since 1949, the United States gold stock has persistently declined, while dollar holdings of foreign official institutions have increased.

The persistent payments deficit and the declining stock of United States gold have given rise to serious concern among foreign observers as to the continued willingness and ability of the United States Treasury to make gold available to foreign governments and central banks in unlimited quantities at the $35 per ounce price. These concerns will not easily diminish, and they will become more valid should the United States continue to run a substantial balance of payments deficit.

The various government programs which have been developed to reduce the balance of payments deficit of the United States have been directed mainly toward the reduction of private investment overseas. Although these programs have been labeled as "temporary," they seem to be achieving the character of permanence and have been made progressively more restrictive. Over the long-run, these programs will tend to weaken rather than strengthen the United States balance of payments position. A long-range solution to the balance of payments problem must recognize the necessity to set meaningful priorities for government spending abroad, and to control inflation at home to insure that United States exports remain competitive.

The various programs aimed at reducing the United States' payments deficit may prove successful if we can control domestic inflation, generate a trade surplus, and achieve an early end to the conflict in Southeast Asia which would eliminate a drain of foreign exchange. Should the present program of "restraints" prove insufficient, other measures will have to be taken, such as further reductions in government spending overseas and more restrictive domestic monetary and fiscal policies to control inflation at home. Or, the United States could impose new tariff and nontariff barriers to imports. However, a move in this general direction would likely be countered by restrictions in other countries, with the net result of lower levels of trade and no real reduction in the United States payments deficit.

Should the United States prove unable or unwilling to control its payments deficit, some basic changes ultimately will be forthcoming in the international payments system. These changes could take any of a number of forms and there is considerable speculation about an increase in the dollar price of gold. Aside from the real problem of equity for those countries which have maintained a major portion of their monetary reserves in the form of United States dollars, there are grave doubts concerning the lasting benefit to the United States of an increase in the gold price. An increase in the gold price, would at best only buy time, and would not solve the United States' balance of payments or international reserve problems. It would also disrupt confidence and planning for some time to come.

There is little doubt that if past trends continue, the Treasury will ultimately be forced to stop selling gold. Such an action would result in some form of floating exchange rates. In the short-run it would also bring uncertain, if not chaotic, conditions to the international financial markets. While some economists argue that a system of floating exchange rates would result in a more orderly and efficient international financial system and avoid domestic corrective economic adjustments, the preponderant opinion of government and business leaders is that such a system would be disruptive to actual international trade and capital flows, and ultimately prove unsettling to the domestic economy as well.

Closely linked is the major problem confronting the international financial system's growing shortage of international reserves. With dollar accumulations no longer available to supplement monetary reserves, and with gold production going largely or entirely into private hoards, what will form the monetary base for a growing level of international trade? As is currently the case with most domestic monetary systems, it would appear necessary to develop a managed form of international reserve creation. A first step in this direction has been the development of the Special Drawing Rights in the International Monetary Fund.

While no one can confidently predict how these basic problems will be solved, it is clear that new solutions cannot be long deferred. The actual solutions can have far-reaching effects on interest rates as well as on economic institutions of the United States and the world.

With the continued expansion of the international operations of American firms and the growing influence of international factors on domestic economic policies, developments in the international financial system will be of increasing importance to American business.

It will be imperative that future financial executives have a good knowledge of the functioning of the international financial system and become aware of current and prospective developments in the system.

In the years ahead, it is imperative that a stable and orderly functioning international monetary system be maintained. Such a system, combined with continued progress toward the reduction of barriers to international trade and capital flows, offers the best means for achieving the economic growth and development of all countries.

Government-Business Relations

The next few years will see new directions in government-business relations in the United States which will have noticeable financial overtones. In recent years, the American people have become painfully aware of deep-seated social and economic problems rending the fabric of our society. To some Americans, unemployment, inadequate housing, poor education, and lack of motivation have become a way of life rather than a temporary condition.

The causes of these problems include racial discrimination, rapid rural to urban migration, and technological advances which eliminated large numbers of unskilled jobs. One result has been creation of racial ghettos in most of our large cities—blighted communities characterized by high unemployment, slum housing conditions, high crime rates, rapidly growing welfare rates, and a pervading sense of despair. And recently, many of our cities have experienced violent and destructive riots.

These complex and painful problems must and will be solved. It is apparent that neither the government nor the private sector, acting alone, can provide the solutions. The government does not command the skills nor the resources to provide adequate housing and purposeful job training. The private sector is not able to assume the non-economic risks associated with these basic problems.

Some new way must be found for meaningful and effective cooperation between government and business, especially in the rebuilding of our central cities and the provision of job training for the potentially employable unemployed. Business must be willing to assume normal business risks in these areas with the expectation of a normal profit. Government must be willing to assume the non-economic risks and the added training costs, and condone normal profits for the private participants. Currently, some of the best minds in both government and business are devoted to the development of the basic ground rules under which this type of cooperation can succeed. Problem solving in the nation's urban areas must become an integral part of the profit-making dynamism of the economy, and not relegated to a mere non-profit appendage.

In this business-government cooperation, financial institutions must play a major role, especially in the areas of housing and improved public facilities. Enormous amounts of funds will be required to finance the building efforts contemplated, and financial institutions must find a way to provide these funds. They must, and can, creatively reconcile the demands of their stockholders, but it will not be easy to do.

The Financial Executive in the New Era

The next few years will be a testing period for the basic structure of finance in both the United States and the world. It appears likely that pressures already evident will alter the role and the tools of monetary and credit policy in the United States, and significantly change the financial institutional structures as well. A general environment of relatively high interest rates and a chronic shortage of credit in many areas will likely prevail. The problems of achieving a high employment economy will blend with a new set of problems caused by high employment itself.

Basic changes in the international financial system also appear inevitable if the monetary base is to be expanded to provide the basis for a growing level of world trade and capital flows.

In the period ahead, finance will become an ever more critical variable in every form of economic activity. The availability and the cost of funds, more than ever, will be key elements in every major project undertaken by business or government.

In this type of environment, the role of the financial executive will assume ever increasing importance. The financial executive of the future will need to understand the international financial system as well as the domestic system. All business executives in the United States, and especially financial executives, must become as familiar with balance of payments as they are with corporate balance sheets and income statements. In a period of basic structural change, an understanding of the past, or even current, institutional structure will not be sufficient. The financial executive must understand the subtle range of interactions between international developments and domestic policy actions.

In addition, a new dimension has been added to finance in the United States. That dimension is the new look in relations between business and government. For the first time in history, governments at all levels—national, state and local—have acknowledged that they cannot cope unilaterally with such contemporary domestic problems as air and water pollution, housing, urban development, mass transit, and many others. There are also the many problems of the developing nations which government action has not been able to solve. As a result, government is seeking the help and advice of private business, and appears to want a real partnership with the private sector. The profit incentive must be strengthened, not weakened, in this process, or little will be accomplished. Certainly, an important key to the success of this new government-business partnership is imaginative yet realistic finance.

The period ahead will be an exciting and demanding one for the financial industry. The leaders in the industry must be ready to adapt to, and initiate, the changes necessary for domestic and international economic growth. In addition, the financial leaders must aid in the development of a meaningful partnership with government for the solution of many of the social and environmental problems of our society.

The new era in finance will be characterized by a chronic shortage of funds and growing demands from all sectors. There will be growing stress on many institutional forms, and basic changes in many areas will be required. In this environment, the successful business executive must not only be aware of the complex institutional structures which exist, but must also be aware of the fundamental financial forces pressing for change.

H. M. BOETTINGER

The Impact of Technology

4 In the last two hundred years, civilization has been gripped at different times by two kinds of revolutions —the one noisy and violent, the other silent and gradual.

We have no difficulty identifying revolutions of the first type. Typically, they have been marked by the fall of governments, the start of uprisings, the winning of battles, the signing of manifestos. These have been the political revolutions.

By contrast, the revolutions of the second type have often gone unnoticed until well after their birth. Yet, they have had more impact on our lives than all the political revolutions put together. In fact, they often laid the ground for political, social, and economic upheaval. Such has been the impact of technology—the quiet revolution.

Technology, as that Canadian seer Marshall McLuhan keeps trying to tell us, has done more than merely lighten our physical burdens. It has gone so far as to alter the whole focus of society by literally changing the way we perceive the world. And no sector of society has been more deeply involved in these technological revolutions, and none has been transformed so radically as a result of it, as American business.

Today, we are on the verge of still another quiet revolution, one which must be understood by the managers of business if they are to deal successfully with the great challenges of tomorrow's demanding environment. As a wry comment on man's technological myopia, McLuhan once remarked that the fish was probably the last animal to discover the presence of water. It would be ironic if, years from now, another student of technology observes that business executives were the last people to understand the impact of technology.

What is this quiet revolution I refer to? In order to answer that, let's quickly look at what has been happening to business in the last three hundred years.

Prior to the late eighteenth century, business was virtually synonymous with commerce—the buying and selling of goods. Entrepreneurs in this age devoted themselves to bringing goods and produce into contact with eager markets. As merchants, these men were far more interested in discovering faster, more economical modes of transportation, and in exploring new trade routes, than in improving the productive processes of that time. Significantly, the invention that interested them most was not technological in nature, but financial—the limited liability company. As a result, the productive techniques used in producing food, clothing, and shelter hardly differed from those used in earlier times. They would have been entirely comprehensible to someone born in the Middle Ages.

Then came an age in which technology began to make its mark. England hooked its newly-invented steam engine to a burgeoning market place and the result was the Industrial Revolution. Still, the technology of the day was crude by present standards. Science, as we think of it today, was not yet the handmaiden of industry. Inventions were mostly the brainchildren of inspired mechanics, and technical innovation amounted to little more than a series of successful attempts at harnessing a variety of isolated inventions to the productive process.

This was the age when single inventions fathered whole new industries, or, as in textile-making and shipbuilding, changed old ones so drastically that only their names remained the same. Of course, other things emerged from this turbulent age to haunt us today. Increased strife among the national powers, an exploding world population, wave upon wave of great migrations flooding the cities, a tremendous stockpile of incredibly destructive weaponry—these are the flotsam and jetsam in the wake of the Industrial Revolution.

In following years, business began to consolidate. Once again, the emphasis shifted to financial invention as holding companies, trusts and cartels came into vogue. Business growth during these years resulted mainly from horizontal expansion rather than from great technological advancements. Thus, railroads laid more trackage, steel mills produced more steel, textile mills turned out more cloth, shipbuilders built more ships. In effect, business was still growing cellularly around isolated inventions, just as it had in the previous era. (Some industrial firms born in this stage of the business revolution still bear the name of the invention or the inventor that nourished them in infancy.) Nevertheless, this was the period when technical innovation began having real meaning to the average person. This had great impact on the way a person perceived the world. It was not merely that nations were producing more. It was that the hopes of people were being lifted up in a great tide of progress. In brief, social expectations were rising. A man could look around and see things getting better. He could have faith in his children's future. Men have always dreamed such dreams, but not until this era did they expect to see them fulfilled here on earth. As a result, people began to view technological advancement as one of the vital determinants of social progress. Society's great expectations could only come from greater and greater productivity.

Americans today, believe strongly that technological progress is vital to the nation's economic health. How this progress takes place, though, is something few people really understand. Actually, when it comes to comprehending the modern innovative process, many people still think in terms of the nineteenth century, when innovation sprang from independent inventions. Our folklore fosters this fiction and there is nothing especially harmful in it—*providing the managers of industrial firms do not believe the myth, too.* To see why, let us continue our hurried look at business history by turning now to the first quarter of this century, when another quiet revolution was unfolding in business.

Again, no single event, no celebrations, marked this breakthrough. To find it would have required looking into the minds of men, for that was where the revolution was brewing. What these men had done was *invent the method of invention* by wedding science to technology.

We who have had the scientific method drummed into our heads take this achievement for granted. Innovation, to us, necessarily involves a series of unquestioned steps: you begin with a scientific discovery, then you design and test a laboratory model, and finally, you manufacture the product at a cost attractive to the market and profitable for the business. We are so accustomed to this method that we do not really know how young it is.

What we forget is that fifty years ago science worked in reverse of today's accepted sequence. Scientists became interested in something *after*, not *before*, it was invented. Thus thermodynamics became a rich scientific field when scientists began studying the properties of the steam engine; electromagnetic theory evolved from the study of magnets, coils, and batteries; solid state physics developed from improvements in metallurgy and the production of insulating materials; and pharmacology grew out of an assortment of home remedies.

In contrast to present-day methodology, the innovative process of yesteryear went as follows: the inventor conceived, designed and constructed an apparatus built to do something practical—a telegraph to communicate with, an electric light to see by. If the gadget worked reasonably well, the inventor was satisfied. The fact that he probably could not explain the basic phenomenon underlying the operation of his invention did not disturb him. Edison, for example, did not concern himself with the science of optics when he fiddled with the incandescent lamp. Not until inventors had gone as far as they could in improving their inventions, did they turn to scientists for help. Then, the scientists would explain why the apparatus had worked in the first place and how it could be modified to work even better or in entirely new areas. Out of this tutorial arrangement the industrial laboratory evolved. The revolutionary thing about this development was that industry leaped forward by learning to fall back on the fundamentals of scientific inquiry.

Of course, there were managers who did not like it when industry opened the door to science, for with science came a host of strange characters. Men who had never lifted a crowbar now presumed to advise those who had spent their lifetimes driving the great engines of American industry. "This goddam chemistry," an old-time steel executive once sputtered, "is ruining the steel business." Those who resisted the swing to research as "just another fad" soon found their markets disappearing.

Business finally embraced the new method of invention during the years after World War II, when security analysts began giving black marks to firms with inadequate R & D programs. The impact of research and development in recent years has been tremendous on industry and society. But two side effects from R & D have been disturbing to businessmen.

First, take something as basic as *control*—a fundamental element of the practice of management. Sound management, it goes without saying, is predicated on the ability to plan, organize, and control the operations of a business. But control, at least as the fathers of scientific management visualized it, is something that is practically impossible to exercise over a top-flight research laboratory. How do you control creativity? In fact, tightly-controlled research, aimed exclusively at improving old products or producing new ones, is sometimes a sure-fire formula for sterility.

Second, R & D has speeded the innovative process, but it has also accelerated the rate of obsolescence as well. Coordinating the functional operations of a business has never been an especially easy task, even during stable periods. How much more difficult then, to coordinate the internal workings of an enterprise whose technology is being transformed drastically and rapidly. Too firm a hand on the control lever by top management, too much of a desire for stability, and the result could be stiffer competition not only from traditional competitors, but from entirely different industries as well. Forty years ago, for example, the textile industry suddenly found itself in competition with chemical and petroleum producers, a development that caught the industry by surprise. And wouldn't a locomotive engineer on one of those crack passenger trains back at the turn of the century have laughed if someone had told him that a rickety, kite-like vehicle with a gasoline engine up front (that couldn't even keep the craft aloft two minutes the first time out) would one day put even the most streamlined cross-country railroad cars on the track to desolation.

Thus R & D has spawned a seeming dilemma for industry. Innovation, like a fox, is being pursued by the hounds of obsolescence, and innovation must race on or be devoured. If we pause to reflect on this, however, there is nothing unique about industry's plight, for parallel situations exist everywhere we turn. All nature is subject to the inexorable cycle of growth and decay. The growth curve, from rapid growth in infancy to rapid decay in senility, is the most universal equation of nature.

And yet, if this is true, how can a firm or an industry endure? Those who sensed that R & D would hasten obsolescence, struck on the only logical answer: to heap one technological advancement's life cycle on to another, and another, so that the growth of the new takes over before the old is decaying.

Yet, to know whether a given technology has reached the stage of maturity or decline requires adroit management—and I doubt whether even the best at the game could explain how they do it. Knowing when to phase out a product and to introduce another is high art in management, for it taxes the judgment and involves great risk.

Innovation on this scale also poses an additional problem. While the improvements to come will sustain an enterprise in the future, they are a drag on the present. Yet we must weigh the *futurity of present decisions*. Few things have greater bearing on how well an organization will respond to tomorrow's demands than what is decided today about tomorrow's technology. Technical innovation may not be the entire show, but those who leave it out of their future plans are like stage actors who would perform *Hamlet* without the Prince of Denmark.

How can a business plan ahead for the simultaneous, yet asynchronous, development of new technology? The textbook answer is to "subject these impacts to a completely rational process and organize for it." But this presents two vexing philosophical problems.

First, before you can anticipate change you must adopt a new frame of reference attuned to the future, to the unexpected. A company that does not possess such a frame of reference is no different from the classic clerical department that can handle routine matters with quick dispatch, but which falls apart the moment it has to perform a new task. Giving such organizations unexpected problems to solve is like asking a skilled comptometer operator to do simple addition— *but using Roman numerals*. Most organizations have little difficulty handling the expected. It is the unexpected that throws them.

This raises the second problem. To anticipate change sometimes requires that we train our telescopes not only far ahead into unknown reaches, where immediate rewards are sparse, but also in entirely new directions where it is questionable whether any rewards exist at all. Hard-nosed management often takes a dim view of this kind of research, with the result that only the well-trod, well-defined areas are explored. Companies that adopt this approach to research do not leap into the future—they stumble into it.

One of the things operations research is teaching us today is that we cannot expect to cope with the type of problems produced by today's increasingly varied environment unless our solutions are equally as varied. This is why yesterday's single-product, single-technology mode of management is outdated. At a time when technology is changing more rapidly than ever, we cannot afford to view a kaleidoscopic world through monoscopic lenses. The old single-invention frame of reference is too dangerous an over-simplification for management today.

This brings us to the current stage of business history, in which changing technology is forcing business to employ various new strategies.

One way in which modern industry is countering variety with variety is seen in the rise of the "conglomerates"—large, multifaceted companies active in a variety of unrelated markets. Here we have a throwback to the periods when business resorted to financial invention, rather than technological advancement, to counter the repercussions of technical innovation. Here, we might also say, financial glue is used to tie widely different firms into a single mass of logistic curves at various stages of economic evolution. One of the firms on the logistic curve might be in a stage of incubation, another in a stage of development, and still another in the stage of maturity. Entities in decline, in a stage of decay, are discarded as quickly as possible. By selecting from the entire industrial landscape only those pieces which fit his plan, the promoter aggregates the fate of each firm and, to his credit, minimizes the total risk to *his* overall organization.

But conglomerates, in my judgment, are stop-gap, interim solutions at best. They do not address themselves directly to the quintessential problem: the development of new technology to offset the effects of rapid obsolescence.

A more fruitful strategy is to be found in a relatively new managerial tool known as systems engineering. This strange, often baffling, discipline is used today by the designers who plan the more technically complex man-machine systems which are but parts of even more complex totalities called "systems." The elaborate systems that can transmit a telephone call across the nation or send a rocket to the moon involve the interaction of myriad components, both human and technical. They would have been impossible to build if the system designers had merely calculated how one component behaves in relation to neighboring parts of the system. The problem is that each component is tied to each and every other part of the system. Therefore, these components take on wholly new dimensions by responding in a limitless number of ways to different parts of the network. In short, systems engineering discovered that the whole of the system is greater than the sum of the parts—something the Gestalt psychologist learned long ago about human perception.

Thus, a systems designer asks two fundamental questions in deciding whether a new system is functioning effectively: How well is it responding to the problems it was designed to handle (in which the whole is *equal* to the sum of the parts)?, and, how well is it responding to the real world (in which the whole is infinitely *greater than* the sum of the parts)? These are precisely the questions an organization must ask recurrently if it does not want to be caught in a crossfire of changing technology—from inside and outside the business. How well, the organization must ask, is our own technology performing? And, how well is it performing in relation to what is coming over the hill, or now on the drawingboard?

Notice the similarity of the problems faced by a system designer and the manager of a firm subject to interior and exterior technological advance. The discipline of system design criteria increases rapidly with complexity, and has its roots in *chains of probability* of correct response by each component of apparatus. The discipline of character required to say "yes" or "no" to other men in an environment fueled by rapid technological change also escalates with complexity—yet that is the modern management challenge.

Technology, everybody knows, is accelerating. But the most important fact may be a change in its role in the economy, rather than in its speed. It is becoming a "system" when historically it consisted of separate strands with little interconnections between them. The metallurgist, traditionally, was little affected by whatever went on in optics, let alone in microbiology. Today, scientific disciplines may still be treated as discrete. But technologies are rapidly becoming inter-acting; they rapidly meld with another to form new configurations, rapidly shifting like the individual pieces of colored glass in the kaleidoscope, to form new visions and patterns.

One conclusion from these thoughts is to question the way we prepare young people for business today—and for life altogether.

We prepare for the known, the expedient, the routine. But the unknown of new technologies, new industries, new markets, new products, is increasingly going to be their true test and their effective reality. Yet, to my knowledge, technology as change and challenge is not yet part of the way of life our schools—including, above all, the business schools—inculcate. It is not even a "course," let alone the core of the work in economics and management it deserves to be. And, as long as technology is seen as something *outside* the going business, as something to be done by the "longhairs" in a separate R & D department which produces results in a form which they fit into the going business, enabling it to perpetuate the known profitable routine, young men coming into management will have been trained in the wrong approaches and will have acquired the wrong responses.

But organizational implications also follow. Indeed the "innovative organizations" we need may be quite different from the "managerial organizations" of today. The next "quiet revolution" in business may have its roots in attempts which apply techniques developed to design technology to the *design of the organizations* themselves, which develop, use, and constantly adapt to that technology.

Such attempts would directly take account of the technological dimension of management, which has heretofore, with few exceptions, been neglected. They would look on technology as *central* to the modern management process, and not as something to be resisted, absorbed, or countered in order to restore an elusive equilibrium. Changes in supervisory arrangements and work assignments, designed to develop individual motivation to adapt, will be an essential step in this process.

This revolution, and all the secondary effects it entails, would take its place as a natural evolutionary step. First, we had the isolated single inventions of the nineteenth century. Then, the invention of the *method* of invention which has characterized the first half of our century. We are now on the threshold of methods to employ the method of invention throughout an organization, in ways which make the organization adapt itself to unforeseen events and forces. Such organizations will be self-teachers in the highest sense of that term. Comparatively rigid structures were admirably adapted to a simpler, more leisurely technology. They delivered more than one had a right to expect, if only because we devised ingenious and imaginative means to get around organizational maxims. We did this through the informal organization which puts blood and flesh on the inadequate skeleton of formal, charted relations. But even the best of these informal organizations still encounter great difficulty in dealing with rapid technical change.

Successful solutions to this prime management problem will look on technology not as a disease or epidemic which one must weather from time to time, but as the very air necessary to keep healthy metabolism going.

History is littered with examples of decline or disaster when innovations were met by strategies of rigid response. That has not been *our* way in the past. The greater impacts of technology in our age demand an increase in flexibility, and will stimulate the search for forms, attitudes, and arrangements which nurture it.

The first step on the road to solution must be to recognize and admit that a problem exists. Myths are dangerous when they *hide* problems; and misapplication of earlier experience can grow from retention of belief in the myth of the isolated invention. Veblen stated that immutable conduct, coupled to progressively changing conditions, results in a logical muddle. We are not quite there, but the rapidly changing conditions surrounding managers, which have their origin in technological change, first call for changes in managerial outlook. Only when this is done, can one expect changes in managerial conduct geared to an increasing technological dimension.

The task is awesome. Managers will have to achieve an imaginative grasp of their entire society. At the same time, they must weld together the increasingly sectored knowledge of specialists to produce interactive and supportive systems. If it can be done at all, it will have to be done by men of imagination and experience, both prescient and practical, who know where they are, see where they want to go, and have ideas on how to get there.

Karl Marx predicated his prophecy of capitalism's decline and breakdown on the inability of the business system to adjust to the more frequent and increasingly violent swings of crises caused by technological change. In the one hundred years since the first publication of his book, *Das Kapital*, the greatest factor in frustrating his prophecy has been the flexibility shown by business management in directing technological progress to constructive ends for the benefit of society. Many of the leaders responsible for this outcome would take it as a great compliment if told that they had built organizations "which ran like clockwork." While we are in their debt for the heritage they gave us, future organizations modeled on clockwork will exemplify the kind of rigidity Marx expected and counted on. The technological imperative asks instead that managers today—and tomorrow—develop *organic*, adaptive organizations, capable of transforming the disorderly impacts of technology into impulse energy for healthy growth. This growth should be primarily operative for each *employee*.

Alfred North Whitehead once said: "The tragedy of the world is that those who are imaginative have but slight experience, and those who are experienced have feeble imaginations. Fools act on imagination without knowledge; pedants act on knowledge without imagination."

If we are to continue to prevent the fulfillment of Marx's prophecy, we cannot afford managers who are either fools or pedants. Their response to technological opportunity will show such tendencies up faster than any other sector of the management task.

JOHN DIEBOLD

The Information Revolution

5 We may make significant changes in our process of doing business by using machines, but it is the change in the very nature of what we do, brought about by the social change induced through these machines, that is the real meaning of science and technology to business.

In speaking of so wide a panorama of change, it is necessary to concentrate on certain areas. I am going to discuss, primarily, the application of the new technology of information processing. I will also discuss the new management methods which will stem from the use of this new technology, and how this particular technology affects enterprise and policy decisions in business. Finally, I will look at the problems produced by this technology as it relates to public policy. Four basic themes will flow throughout everything I say. They are:

1. The technological developments in information processing with which we are dealing today are most fundamental. Their scale and proportion can only be surmised.
2. These new technologies are changing what we do, as well as how we do it. They are changing the nature of our business, as well as the methods by which we do business.
3. These technological developments are entirely too important to leave to the technicians. They must be the concern of senior management.

61

4. The human problems arising from these technological changes are by all odds the most important problems with which we must deal, whether we look at this entire development in terms of an individual, or in terms of an enterprise, or in terms of our society.

To begin with, I would like to make a few observations on the new technology itself, and the directions in which it is moving.

To put my subject in perspective, I have chosen a quotation from a learned gentleman and a great American:

It is an extraordinary era in which we live. It is altogether new. The world has seen nothing like it before. I will not pretend, no one can pretend, to discern the end; but everybody knows that the age is remarkable for scientific research into the heavens, the earth, what is beneath the earth; and perhaps more remarkable still is the application of this scientific research to the pursuits of life. The ancients saw nothing like it. The moderns have seen nothing like it until the present generation.... The progress of the age has almost outstripped human belief.

These words were spoken by Daniel Webster in November, 1847 upon opening a new stretch of railroad track in Lebanon, New Hampshire.

More of a parallel exists between that era and our own times than we normally have reason to consider. In that earlier era, science first began to be applied on a wide scale, and out of that process came an entirely new society—an industrial society. Out of it, too, came problems—many of which still plague us. Great opportunities accompanied that era of change. Out of it all came the world in which we live today.

When we look back at that great technological upheaval, the real meaning of those then-wondrous machines to us today is the human and the social changes that accompanied their industrial use.

Information Technology

There are, today, just over 45,000 computers installed in this country and nearly 15,000 installed in Western Europe. There is a backlog of computer orders in this country of about 22,500 and about 6,000 in Europe. The computer industry is an entirely new industry which did not exist very many years ago, but the output in dollars of the industry in 1965 was already $2.6 billion. By 1970, this will have grown to $7.3 billion. A few years ago, investment in computers and related equipment as a percentage of new plant investment was very hard to find on any curve. In 1965, it had already reached 8 per cent of investment in new plant and equipment and, by the turn of the decade, it will exceed 10 per cent. The fact that the sheer hardware comes to 10 per cent of our plant investment begins to make clear, I think, that information technology as an industry has arrived.

Second, and of great importance, is the fact that this is an industry that is rapidly changing. Up to 1945, when the first electronic computer was built, man's calculating speed for several thousand years had been the speed of the abacus. Overnight, it increased five times. From 1945 to 1951, it increased a hundred times again and, from then until now, it has increased a thousand times again.

Our measure of the speed of calculations today is the nanosecond —a billionth of a second. A nanosecond has the same relationship to a second that a second has to thirty years. This is a scale of speed that is very hard to comprehend. But even this speed is not fast enough for some problems. The distance that the electron has to move from one part of a circuit to another part is a very real problem to the people designing this equipment. One of the major reasons for producing smaller and smaller components is to get the pieces closer together so that the electrons will not have to go so far, since they travel at the relatively slow speed of somewhat less than 186,000 miles a second!

These changes in technology produce extraordinary changes in business economics. Between 1963 and 1972—a single decade— there will be a decrease of 85 per cent in the cost of handling a typical business data processing job. During this period, the cost of storage by magnetic tape will go down by 97 per cent, the cost of image storage by 96 per cent, and communication line costs—because of increased speeds of transmission—will decrease by 50 per cent. These changes in economics mean that tomorrow we will be able to bring about very different results with information technology than we can even imagine today.

As a result of the far-reaching changes in the technology, we can no longer think or talk usefully of just a computer. We must talk in the broader terminology of information technology or information systems.

Nowhere is this change brought home more graphically than by the simple cost distribution within a computer system itself. A few years ago, the computer, or central processor, was 75 per cent to 80 per cent of the value of a business computer system. The so-called peripheral equipment—the input-output equipment, outside storage, and communications—was 20 per cent to 25 per cent. By 1972, this relationship will be completely reversed and, as a matter of fact, this reversal has already occurred in some systems. The computer will be 20 per cent to 25 per cent of the value of the system. The peripheral equipment—a term no longer appropriate—is where the real value will lie.

The glassed-in, wood-panelled computer center, reproduced in four colors, will no longer be in the annual report of companies determined to show how modern they are. For we are today dealing with systems that, to an increasing extent, all of you will be using daily—ones which will appear as units in each desk.... a small television screen, a keyboard and a built-in copying device.

These components will be integrated into one device, and, when you ask a question, you will see the answer on the screen. If you want a copy of the answer, you can make it immediately. The actual form of the unit will vary with the needs of the individual using it and the nature of his business. The heart of the system will be a switching center, just as it is in the case of the telephone system. Computers, storage elements of many varieties, and many other devices used as a part of this system will be accessible as you need them, connected through the switching center to the terminal unit at your fingertips.

Such systems are already becoming operational, and more and more companies are placing orders. In the next decade, the typical, new computer installation is going to be of this kind.

Another radical technological change stemming from this new computer system is the relationship between the man and the machine. It is no longer a case of having to carry data down to a computer center, going through a laborious and time-consuming process of getting it into the machine, and then waiting for the results. Each technological development that is taking place is moving us toward an easier and more productive relationship between man and the machine. A dynamic, one might almost say alive, relationship will exist. A dialogue between man and machine is becoming possible.

There are already systems in use in which a light pencil is employed by the operator to draw on a TV screen. For example, when employed in engineering, you can make a sketch and simultaneously see it converted into an engineering drawing. The drawing can be rotated in perspective. When you get what you want, you can then convert to a tape which is used to drive a machine tool that cuts the designed part out of metal. Such systems are already operational.

It is rapidly becoming easier to communicate with the information system. We are going to see much of this happen between now and the mid-seventies. Technology not only makes this possible, but economically feasible. The typical business system in the mid-seventies is going to be of the kind I have described—multi-station input-output, communications-oriented, and with a considerably easier man-machine relationship. This is an important development, and it means a very different use of these systems from that which we make of our systems today. The economics will be very different; the use we make of the information systems will be vastly different.

Changes in the Way We Manage

We first started to apply computers to business operations in 1954. We went through a very difficult experimentation period and were faced with the most puzzling kinds of problems. That was an era that I used to characterize by quoting Damon Runyon. When one of his characters, Harry The Horse, went to the track, he used to say, "I hope I break even today. I need the money." For a long time, this was typical of the thinking of all too many managers trying to put computers to work for the first time. However, we have largely emerged from that period. Today we are using computers in business for everything conceivable—and for much that was not, just a few years ago.

I think we are now coming to the point when senior management is beginning to address itself to the question of what to do with this technology. As this happens, remarkable achievements occur. One of the most important things to come out of this experience is that senior management is beginning to realize that the application of this technology is too important to leave to the technicians. Managers realize now that dramatic things can be accomplished if people who know the objectives of a business take the responsibility of putting these new capabilities to work. An example of what can be accomplished is provided by the International Minerals and Chemicals Corporation, which is applying this technology in a most creative way. It uses it in marketing by building models of customers' farms and solving their problems. By doing this, it is helping to strengthen its own distribution systems and is using computer technology creatively as a marketing weapon.

The key to the future use of this technology, and to the determination of how we are to manage it, is the question of what to do in the area of software. We have the problem of forging a new methodology in this area. We are ten years behind in developing methods for analyzing the information requirements of a business and understanding and determining the best ways to design management information systems. But, we are making a beginning. This is the biggest problem and needs major attention. There is also the problem of determining how much time and money should be allocated for research in this area.

To a certain extent, the very mass of information we can process obscures the real problems of distilling intelligence from it. This condition was well stated in the following passage:

> The modern age has a false sense of superiority, because of the great mass of data at its disposal. But the valid criterion of distinction is rather the extent to which man knows how to form and master the material at his command.

This was written by Johann Wolfgang von Goethe in 1810. It is pertinent to us today—as are so many of his writings.

As progress is being made in the technological field, new questions and problems arise. So very many questions in this area come to mind that there seems no end to them.

There are union negotiation questions. Where and when do you make a stand? For example, you find a number of owners of newspapers throughout the country making a stand—in some cases willing to sacrifice the very existence of their enterprise—on the question of putting in a computer to prepare punched paper tape used to drive linecasting machines. Just over the horizon, that entire process will be bypassed. Is it worth basing an enterprise on a technology which is in transition, and on a process that is disappearing? Soon, type will not have to be set. There will be direct preparation of material for the press. Images will be converted directly from the computer to the printing plates. This is but one example. There are the questions of what kind of men are needed as managers in the new technological environment. What is the best process for developing these new leaders? We do not as yet know.

There are other questions—scores of them. How do we create an atmosphere that is conducive to creative people, for more and more of our businesses must be staffed by more highly educated and creative personnel. Are today's compensation, classification, and organizational schemes appropriate for such conditions?

There are the problems of developing a corporate planning methodology for rapidly changing conditions.

Most important are the human problems. These human questions are related to every single problem we have to face in this field: questions of fear and uneasiness produced by technological changes; questions of education; questions of identification—with the enterprise, with one's profession, with what?

But these are the obvious problems of applying this technology. Let me turn now to some less obvious, but nonetheless important ones.

Changes in What We Manage

The turn toward technology is affecting every aspect of how we manage. But there is a second category of questions in the purely business area concerning what we manage—the question of enterprise.

We all view new developments in different ways. This was brought home to me by a story I heard in Germany some time ago. A farmer, whose fields had been divided by a road, was taking a large load of hay across the road in a cart. The cart was pulled by oxen, and there was a cow tied behind and a helper following. This lumbering procession had just reached the middle of the road when a sports car came over the hill at an impossible speed. Luckily the driver was good, and he was able to swerve out into the field the farmer had just left. Somehow he got back onto the road. The farmer stood still and watched this entire process. Slowly he turned to his helper and said, "We certainly got out of that field in time!"

You see that type of thinking every day in business. In the particular area we are discussing, you can look at new developments and think of them as changing your bookkeeping. Or, you can see in them new areas for business opportunity. Fifteen years ago, when I was trying to write about this, it was very difficult to find any examples. Today, there are many examples of computers used in business, but only a few examples of their affecting the entrepreneurial process which I want very much to dwell upon. I am convinced there will be many more cases fifteen years hence.

Let me begin by citing a few of the specific examples that we do have. Each of the areas I discuss is, or will be, a major new industry brought into existence through information technology.

The first major entrepreneurial opportunity is the obvious one that has already taken form—the industry that supplies the systems and the equipment. This is already a several billion dollar industry, and I will not dwell on it. However, it is well to bear in mind that we have only seen the beginning in this area.

The second example is the as yet nonexistent, but about to bloom, data utility industry. It will become an important basic industry.

The data utility industry is analogous in some way to the electrical utility industry. A large central processor handles information at a very low unit cost, just as a large central generator produces electricity for many customers at a low unit cost. It is cheaper for many people to make use of this central utility than it is for each individual to have his own generator. The same economic reasoning applies to the data utility industry in which many people can use the same machine simultaneously. It will be the technology of real-time processing, time-sharing, and communication which allows this to happen. Small and medium-sized businesses—and, for some purposes, large businesses—will just plug in for data as we now do for electricity.

It is going to be a complete new industry. A very interesting question is, which business institutions are going to be the suppliers for this industry? In a sense, it is up for grabs. Banks are especially well positioned to capitalize upon this new industry. Will they be able to take so fresh a view of their own business service or fundamental nature?

The third new industry is the one now being called the inquiry industry. It is in some ways the publishing field of the future. This development is one which allows the sale of proprietary data over a communication system in answer to a query placed by the customer from a unit on his desk. For instance, you could ask for a selection of stocks, classified by price-earnings ratios. You key this request into the unit on your desk, virtually see the answer on the screen as you ask the question, then go on to ask another question, and so on, through a train of questions. When you get what you want, you can even make a copy of it.

When we use such systems, we are really going to be able to talk about information explosion, for that is when we are going to get an exponential increase in the use of information.

My fourth example is an industry of computer-based educational systems. The technology of which I have been speaking will allow a dynamic or "alive" relationship between a student and a machine system which can answer questions as they are posed and can discern gaps in a student's basic grasp of a subject. Then, the much heralded but, until now, disappointing teaching machines (better, I think, if they were called learning machines) will begin to mean something. Such systems are already at work in some industrial situations—IBM's maintenance training being a good example. Other precursors can be seen in mentally handicapped children's use of computer-driven type-writers to overcome some of their handicaps.

Through this technology of learning systems, we can change the entire world of education. Today, the costs for such systems are pro-hibitive for individual use. However, this may not be true for very long. And, when parents find that their children are learning more rapidly, for the quality and effectiveness will be outstanding, they will demand such systems.

These are just four examples of emerging new industries. There are many others. These are the new types of business which result from this technology.

The real changes in business, from an enterprise standpoint, are the changes that come as a result of social change—and, if there is any one salient fact about information technology, it is that it is going to produce enormous social change.

As the quality of life is changed, as the rate of learning, informa-tion, travel and communications all change, we will see a major change in living patterns, in hopes, and desires—in short, a complete new environment will exist. It is in changes such as these that the real business opportunities have always arisen in the past; the very nature of today's technology insures that this will happen again.

The industrial revolution was revolutionary because it created a whole new environment for mankind—a whole new way of life. What it gave to history was much more than the steam engine and the cotton gin, the railway and the power loom. It gave society a whole new tempo, a whole new outlook. It gave us, as well, a sense of material progress and an itch to get ahead.

It took men off the fields and out of small shops, bringing them into factory life for the first time. Hence, it gave us mass production and, through mass production, the first civilization in history in which luxury was not confined to a few. It gave us, as well, a sense of hurry, of time, which is still unknown in countries that have not gone through an industrial revolution. It gave us a sense of progress which is also unknown to those parts of the world which are still pre-industrial.

In other words, the machines which it produced were agents for enormous social change. No one, least of all Richard Arkwright or James Watt, thought that they were changing civilization itself. Yet, for us, looking back, that is precisely what was revolutionary about the inventions they made.

The current technological revolution promises to have far wider effects than mere technology. Today, we are dealing with machines which have the capacity to change society much more rapidly and much more deeply, because they deal with the very stuff of which society is made. They deal with information and with its communication. Social change is going to be the real meaning of this development to business.

Policy Questions Raised by the Turn Toward Technology

The last area I wish to cover is, in some ways, the least obvious business aspect of the turn toward technology. It is the question of public policy and its relationship and meaning to business.

Who can doubt that this new technology is raising a host of problems that are genuinely problems of *public* policy?

A few moments' reflection upon almost any of the developments I have mentioned makes clear that there is a complete spectrum of other problems, many of which we have no real basis for coping with —moral problems, spiritual problems, legal problems, ethical problems, political problems. Worse still, we do not even debate these questions today.

What about the question of experimentation on humans? It is needed, but do you do it without the knowledge of the patient? We are already beginning to see this happen. The scandal about cancer experimentation in New York brought to public attention the fact that there is experimentation, not related to therapy and without the patient's knowledge, taking place every day in our hospitals.

There is also the problem of our ability to change and to influence human behavior. Experimentation in this area is already widespread.

We are gathering new powers. But who is to decide on their use? Who is to say what form mankind should assume? What conceivable guidelines can we develop for such decisions?

These are just a few of the most fundamental moral problems facing us. But there are many other problems. Think for a moment of the legal problems arising from this new technology. What do you do about copyrights when you have electronic distribution in publishing? What do you do about the problems of property when you can go from a satellite directly into the home with TV, and can skip the local TV stations? What about the property values involved? These and other fundamental legal problems are raised.

One thought I would like to put forward in this area is that, as businessmen, we should accept these as public problems. But we need not sit by and let the public be equated with government. It is all too easy to connect public problems with government action, and to allow government to make the moves and take the steps in handling these problems.

Many of us feel that we, as a society, have too readily relinquished our responsibilities to government. Public policy used to mean that, while government was involved, the private sectors—trade unions, individuals, and private institutions—were all involved too. Should we not make it mean that again, and should we not do this by meeting for discussion in this area? If we leave these new questions of public policy and the need for social innovation purely to government, the response that we find is not likely to be to our liking, nor is it likely to be one that insures the healthiest growth of our country.

Public issues are clearly at stake. We gain nothing by denying it. The complexity, scale and very nature of today's science and technology make this clearer every day. The result of inaction on the part of individuals will be a government solution. The farther this goes, the less likely it is that we are going to have a world in which we have individual freedom and enterprise.

The problems of today are new. The areas of genuine public action are different from those of one hundred years ago when education, public safety, and the like were the extent of necessary public concern. Today, the problems are more sophisticated, more complex, and very much larger. And, it is clear that public action is going to be taken in many areas heretofore private. But we must not abandon the pluralistic nature of our society—this genius of the American system. We must make public policy truly public. Business needs to respond to these new problems as a leader of the private sector.

The new technology is as great a gift as business could give to our society. Until now, we have been fighting a defensive position with respect to it. This need not be the case if we face up to the human problems and lead in social innovation to match the technological innovation.

Only by taking responsible and dynamic action in solving the myriad problems raised by these new and rapidly changing technologies, can we preserve our society as we know it. Here again, I would like to stress the importance to us as individuals and as business leaders of realizing that the human problems facing us are at the core of all the solutions we must make.

Machines have always been important to us, primarily in their role as agents for social change. We speak of the industrial "revolution" because of the changes in society brought about by the process of applying machines to our work. The machines themselves were novel, but for us, looking back, it was the changes they made in our way of living and thinking that led us to the term "revolution." They changed the whole nature of our society. They created a whole new world. That is why we continue to use the term "industrial revolution" long after the machines have lost significance for us—the machines were agents for social change.

Today, we live in an era in which this is happening again. It is happening in a magnified way and on a condensed time scale. The meaning of this new technology is not only that it affects how we manage and what we manage, but, to an increasing extent, that it is changing the world in which we live and in which we manage. It creates important personal, as well as business, problems—and opportunities.

As businessmen, we can play a very important role by insuring that we always focus on the human problems. We should clearly recognize that we do not yet have the moral, ethical, philosophical, legal, or spiritual bases for coping with these new realities. If our children are to live in a world of private enterprise and individual liberty, we, the leaders of business, must express a major concern for the human problems resulting from this technological change. We must insure that capitalism is dynamic, not rigid, in its reaction to this change.

We have left the push-button age. We have already entered the age in which the buttons push themselves. Imaginative and farsighted managers see in this move, not merely the opportunity to decrease operating costs but, in the new world that is being created, the opportunity for new services, new products, and entirely new businesses and industries which will create a new and better environment for us all.

PETER F. DRUCKER

Business and the Quality of Life

6

I

In the late 'forties and early 'fifties, the American automobile industry tried to make the American driving public safety-conscious. Yet when Ford introduced cars with seat belts, sales dropped so catastrophically that the company was forced to abandon the whole idea. But, when fifteen years later, the American driving public suddenly became safety-conscious, the car manufacturers were sharply attacked for being "merchants of death." Similarly, a good many electric power companies tried for years to get the various state utility commissions to approve of their use of low-sulfur fuels and of cleaning devices in the smokestacks. The commissions refused again and again, with the argument that the public was entitled to power at the lowest possible cost, insisting that neither a more expensive fuel nor capital investment to clean the smoke would be permitted in the rate base. Yet when eventually air pollution became a matter of public concern, the power companies were roundly berated for "befouling the environment." Ever since the advent of the "miracle drugs" in the 'forties, the medical profession has been urging the drug companies to respect the independence and knowledge of the physician and not, by word or deed, to interfere in his complete control of the relationship with public and patient. Similarly the druggists have been demanding that the drug companies respect their "professional integrity" and continue to compensate them as if they, rather than the drug companies, were still the compounders of medicines. And yet the same physicians are now attacking the drug companies for making it possible for the slipshod physician to overprescribe highly potent drugs. And the public tends to hold the drug companies responsible for the "spiraling costs of medical care," even though drugs are the only component of medical bills the cost of which has risen less than the general level of prices. For twenty years there has been a campaign to get private businesses to take part in defense production. Businesses that did not bid on defense work have been attacked in Congress, in the press, and in public as unpatriotic. Yet even though the profits on defense business are less than half what the same companies can earn on non-defense business, defense contractors are being criticized for "profiteering" on defense business. And companies that accepted defense contracts under great government pressure find their recruiters chased off college campuses and their offices picketed.

And these are only a few examples of many.

II

When we suddenly realized after the urban riots of 1967 how close we were to explosion and civil war in the Black Ghettoes, the very groups who had always been most contemptuous of business and of the free enterprise system turned as one to the large corporation as the ultimate resource, if not the savior, of the cities. Business is now expected to create overnight a large number of jobs for the least skilled and least trained people in the ghetto and to make employable (and to employ) the very people whom government policy has kept on permanent welfare rolls as "unemployable."

Even staunch believers in free enterprise have long treated low-cost housing, primary and secondary education, and transportation as governmental concerns. Yet as government is proving itself increasingly unable to manage the city, traditional "liberals"—and even a good many "leftists"—now cry for business to take over these functions. It was the late Robert Kennedy, rather than the National Association of Manufacturers, who proposed that the rehabilitation of the slums be taken on by business. The Black Power militants want to make education competitive, with the individual parent deciding whether the tax money available for the schooling of his children should go to the public schools or to private institutions designed and run by the country's major corporations. Columbia University's Frank Tannenbaum, who made his name as a fervent apostle of salvation through industrial unionism, proclaimed in the Spring 1968 issue of the *Journal of World Business* that the multinational corporation was "the last best hope" and the only foundation of a peaceful world order. New York's Mayor Lindsay (according to the *New York Times* of May 11, 1968) now wants Big Business to take over obligations which the welfare agencies were originally created for, that is, to "adopt" whole ghetto neighborhoods—to the point where business, Mayor Lindsay suggests, should make sure that there is a man in the house to look after the Negro family.

It is not my purpose to discuss these specific demands on business and businesses. In any event, the list could be extended indefinitely. What matters is that these demands illustrate a major change in the social environment of business and in society's expectations from business and businessmen. Our society now expects business and its senior executives to take responsibility for the health of society in addition to its traditional accountability for economic performance and results. Society now expects business and businessmen to look ahead and to anticipate the social problems of tomorrow. It expects business to be able to solve these problems when no one else can, if not to prevent their emergence in the first place.

Traditionally, business has been held responsible for quantities: for the supply of goods and of jobs, for costs, prices, wages, hours of work, and standards of living. Now business increasingly is being asked to take on responsibility for the quality of life in our society.

The traditional responses of businessmen and of academicians to such demands have been "public relations" and the "social responsibility of business." These responses are not so much inadequate to meet these new expectations as they are irrelevant to them.

Public relations is concerned with the question whether a business or an industry is "liked" or "understood." Public relations would therefore be worried, because "Black Power" advocates blame the "profit motive" for the ghetto, and they presumably like business just as little as they like any other part of the "white establishment." But what really matters is that the Black Power leaders expect business to perform miracles in respect to ghetto employment, ghetto education, ghetto housing; they expect these miracles virtually overnight.

The relevant questions are: Can business tackle these huge problems? How? Should business tackle them? These are not questions which Public Relations is equipped to handle. Similarly, Public Relations was not able to anticipate the problems of automotive safety and air pollution, or problems of the drug and defense industries. In each of these cases business is in trouble today in large part because it was so very receptive to yesterday's public opinion and did such a good job in its "Public Relations." The great sensitivity of the drug industry to its "publics"—the physicians and the druggists—is a good case in point, and a major reason for the troubles the drug industry finds itself in today.

What has always been meant by "the social responsibility of businessmen" is the way businesses and businessmen spend spare time and spare cash. In a good many cases, the words "social responsibility" were really little more than another way to say "good works." "Social responsibility" meant "Lady Bountiful." But even at its most serious, social responsibility was concerned with events outside of and separate from the day-to-day conduct of business. It was a restraint on business. It never implied responsibility for society and for the quality of life in it.

The new demand is, however, a demand that business and businessmen make concern for society central to the conduct of business itself. It is a demand that the quality of life become the business of business. The traditional approach asks: How can we arrange the making of cars (or of shoes) so as not to impinge on social values and beliefs, on individuals and their freedom, and on the good society altogether? The new demand is for business to *make* social values and beliefs, create freedom for the individual, and altogether produce the good society.

In one way these new expectations are dangerously unrealistic. It is silly to believe, as a great many people seem to believe today, that business is *the* institution of our society and that business is, therefore, the appointed keeper of our society.* The fact is, rather, that every major task of our society is today being discharged in and through an organized and large institution such as the university or the hospital, the government agency, the armed services, the labor union—and, of course, business as well. Each of these must be held fully as accountable as any other for "the quality of life" of our society. Business has a distinct impact on society, distinct capabilities

---

*A good example of this fallacy is Professor J. K. Galbraith's recent book, *The New Industrial State* (Boston and New York, 1967).

and characteristics, and distinct opportunities. But it is not unique, not the only institution, let alone the only one with impact on the society and the community.

At the same time, it is clearly to the self-interest of business and businessmen to accept this responsibility for the quality of life in our society and to build it into businesses and into the vision of senior executives. This is, of course, particularly true for the large corporation.

The quality of life in our society is involved with the self-interest of business for three reasons.

First, the penalty for neglecting this area is so very high. Whenever there has been the kind of crisis which the automobile industry had in respect to automotive safety, the public utilities in respect to air pollution, the drug industry in respect to medical care, or the defense contractors in respect to defense pricing and procurement, the penalty imposed in the end on business has been high indeed. Such a crisis always leads to a scandal in the end. It leads to Congressional inquisition, to angry editorials, and eventually to the loss of confidence in an entire industry and its products by broad sectors of the public. And finally, punitive legislation always follows. The fact that the public today sees no issue is not relevant. Indeed it is not even relevant that the public today—as it did in every single one of the examples above—resists actively any attempts on the part of far-sighted business leaders to prevent a crisis. In the end, there is the scandal, and then business is in the pillory.

On the other hand, the public always in the end accepts an intelligent solution for such a crisis if business works conscientiously to design one. This has been the experience of the Committee for Economic Development (CED) in its twenty years of existence, and of any other business or industry which took responsibility for a crisis and brought to bear the knowledge, the competence, and the seriousness of its best people.

It is, in other words, definitely to the self-interest of business to anticipate social problems, especially those which will be generated by the activity of business itself. And usually these problems can be anticipated. It is not hindsight to say that we should have known that there would be a problem of automotive safety; everyone in the automobile industry knew this twenty years ago. It is not hindsight to say that we should have done something about the smoke from power company smoke stacks; everyone in the public utility industry has known this for twenty years. That the "miracle drug" drastically changed the practice of medicine and made yesterday's pharmacist obsolete, everyone in the drug industry has known for at least fifteen years. And everyone in the defense industry has been saying for twenty years that our defense regulations, written for "temporary emergencies," were increasingly inappropriate for the realities of a permanent, preventive defense establishment. It was, in other words, predictable fifteen to twenty years ago that every one of these problems would become an "issue" in which business would be attacked and penalized. There was only the question how soon this would happen.

A second, even more important reason why responsibility for the quality of life is to the self-interest of business is the obvious fact that a healthy business and a sick society are not compatible. Healthy businesses require a healthy, or at least a functioning, society. The health of the community is a prerequisite for successful and growing business.

This is, of course, not at all new. Sixty years ago this was obvious to such men as Julius Rosenwald and Theodore Vail who built Sears Roebuck and the Bell Telephone System respectively. Indeed Rosenwald, the "city slicker," went so far as to invent—and for years to support single-handedly—the County Agent system through which the work of the land grant colleges first became effective in raising agricultural productivity and with it the farmer's standard of living and purchasing power.

The only new aspect is the demand that business anticipate today what society's central problems will be tomorrow. But to try to do this is better than to wait till the problem is upon us in full force.

Finally, the quality of life of our society should be a tremendous business opportunity. It is, after all, always the job of business to convert the needs of society into profitable business opportunity. It is always the job of business to convert change into "innovation," that is, into new business. And it is a poor businessman who thinks that "innovation" refers to technology alone. Social change and social innovation have throughout business history been at least as important as technology. After all, the major industries of the nineteenth century were, to a very large extent, the result of converting the new social environment—the industrial city—into a business opportunity and into a business market. This practice underlay the rise of lighting, first by gas and then by electricity, the streetcar, and the inter-urban trolley, the telephone, the newspaper, and the department store, to name only a few.

Yet the demand that business take responsibility for the quality of life of our society is a dangerous demand. It needs to be thought through carefully. Shooting from the hip and ad hoc response to yesterday's headlines can only cause havoc. There is grave danger that businessmen will be found inadequate in their vision, that is, that they do not address themselves to the full scope of these demands. This would make business appear irrelevant to society. There is also a danger that business will tackle things it cannot do, or tackle things the wrong way. This leads to failure and to disappointment with business. Yet the cry of "let business do it," is heady wine even for sober heads. It may not be the sincerest form of flattery, but it is a most insidious one.*

III

This whole area will undoubtedly occupy us for many, many years to come. But some guidelines for the approaches to it can already be discerned.

The first thing to say is that business cannot behave like anything else. It can only behave like business. And this is the right way for it to behave.

What this means is that business is an economic institution entrusted with responsibility for the most productive employment of the community's scarce economic resources. If it is untrue to this trust, it is untrue to itself and to the community. It also is not competent, as a rule, to do anything else. This is what businessmen are trained for and tested in. They are likely to perform well only if the tasks can be organized in terms of economic rationality.

---

*A good example of this is Mayor Lindsay's idea that businesses should "adopt" a neighborhood in the ghetto. This is simply another version of something we have tried before with signal failure, namely, community paternalism. This is exactly what the textile industry of New England did in the 1830s when Lowell, Massachusetts was a "model town"—and the result was, thirty or forty years later, deep bitterness which has not yet died down. Patrons of the neighborhood were exactly what the social worker and his community welfare agency were designed to be, and their failure is a major cause of our present discontent. In other words, there is need to think through what the problem really is and how it really should be tackled, rather than sloganeering and flag-waving which makes for impressive headlines and good "public relations," but for serious trouble a little later on.

Specifically, this implies that profitability must be the yardstick for business activity in respect to the quality of life fully as much as it has been the yardstick for business activities in respect to the quantities of life. "Profitability" is simply another word for the economic employment of economic resources. While not a perfect yardstick by any means, it is the only one we have. What is not profitable is subsidized. And businesses, as such, have no right to hand out subsidies —they are trustees for the community's economic resources. Experiments business can support; research and development business must support. Philanthropy business may engage in, up to a point. But in its main thrust, business must behave as a business, that is, must apply economic rationality to whatever it is doing.

Another implication is that business must put to work its specific strength: the market test. The great strength of business as an institution is not that it "makes a profit" but that it is under an objective outside test of performance. The great strength of business as an institution is that it can go out of business if it does not perform. No other institution has any such measurement nor is under such discipline. This is the reason that we now call for business to tackle the problems of the city which no other institution so far has been able to solve. This is the reason, of course, why the communist economies today are all getting back to profitability and the market test— without them there is no measurement of performance and, therefore, ultimately no performance.

Second, business needs to organize for its concern with the quality of life the way it organizes for any other new and dynamically changing area. It needs to organize its "R & D" for society and community fully as much as it has been organizing its "R & D" for technology.* Business has to organize itself to anticipate the issues, the crises, the problems, and the opportunities which tomorrow will bring in society and community. Today's public opinion is largely irrelevant for this, just as yesterday's technology is not too relevant for tomorrow's new products. Where we are likely to go, and above all, where we should be going, are the major questions. For business will have to be ready with the answer when the public finally catches up with the question. Otherwise it will be held to blame for "the mess."

---

*One approach towards this is the new function of "public affairs" that has lately come into fashion, though this is still, only too often, simply a new and fancier name for the old "public relations," if not for political lobbying.

Finally, we know in a general way that responsibility for the quality of life means three kinds of "products," that is, three approaches to the problems of the community:

1. The first and most desirable is an approach in which a "problem" can be converted into an opportunity for profitable, competitive business. I would not rule out the possibility, for instance, that the drug companies, had they gone to work on the problem, might have come up with a solution which might have made the dependence of the physician on drugs he does not understand into a highly profitable business opportunity for the pharmaceutical industry.

The best example of such a solution is the automobile industry. We take the second-hand car for granted. But it actually is a solution to what otherwise would have become a serious social problem. While we worry about housing for the poor, we do not worry about transportation for them; we know they have available serviceable automobiles, at least in the United States. But this they only have because the people who buy new cars willingly take a loss which in effect subsidizes the buyer of an old and used car. Could we not, for instance, work out a similar approach to the housing problem? Unless they are able to buy cheaply the used but highly serviceable goods of the affluent, poor people have never been able to get capital goods of decent quality at a price they can afford. That this is not entirely speculation may be indicated by the fact that "mobile homes" are already the largest single segment of the American housing market, and the fastest growing one.

2. But where a problem cannot be converted into business opportunities, business must then ask: What *regulation* is needed here to enable this problem to become accessible to private, competitive, and profitable business? What standard has to be set by public authority? Automotive safety, for instance, had to be imposed by government regulation once it had proven impossible to convert it into a competitive advantage, that is, once the American public had shown clearly that it was not willing to pay a premium for it (or indeed, to purchase it altogether). Otherwise the irresponsible and opportunistic will always drive out of the market the responsible and far-sighted business. Regulation, in other words, is not an alternative to competitive business. In many areas it is a prerequisite to it. What is needed, however, is a universal standard which applies to everyone and which creates equal burdens as well as equal opportunities for

everyone. At the same time it has to be a standard which accomplishes the needed public purpose at a minimum economic cost. Increasingly it is these public regulations that determine the productivity and with it the competitive position of a country in the world economy. Increasingly, therefore, there is need for a solution which provides the right standards without impeding productivity or imposing costs. And this only businessmen can work out.

3. Finally, if no such regulation can be worked out to create the conditions for competitive business enterprise, the public policy that would enable business to tackle a problem should be thought through. What subsidies might be needed, what guarantees, what forms of public financing or of tax relief and so on would enable business to become effective in a given area, e.g., public education or low-cost housing?

This is a dangerous area. Businessmen are rightly suspect when they discuss the subsidies they should be getting. Yet subsidy is necessary if business is to take over areas in which the market mechanism cannot possibly perform for the time being. It should always be the aim of such a solution therefore to stimulate the creation of a market and of a working market mechanism. This means that subsidies, if needed, should be open. They should be payments by government rather than hidden charges on the community or on the consumer. The goals and objectives should be clearly spelled out, and the results should be evaluated in relation to them in a constant performance review. There should be a definite time limit set for any such subsidy with renewal the exception rather than the rule. Every economist knows the reasons for these safeguards (and every politician tries to conceal them.) It would be singularly unwise for business not to emphasize them, and not to insist on them.

No less an authority than George Champion, the Chairman of the Chase Manhattan Bank (and by no means a "liberal") recently pointed out in the *Harvard Business Review* that many of the "problems" of the city actually offer opportunities for major new industries and new profitable enterprises. I too am hopeful that most of the needs of society and community today can be converted into profitable business opportunity—as were the needs of community and society a century ago. But even if it should turn out that many of them need government and cannot be satisfied through the market mechanism, there is need for business and businessmen to concern themselves with them. The alternative is simply too costly. Business, it is now clear, is both going to bear the blame and pay the price for the inability of other institutions to handle these problems adequately.

Altogether perhaps it might be said that these problems—even that of the black ghetto—are not primarily problems of "failure." It is only because we now take it for granted that the economy can provide the quantities of life that we are becoming conscious of our shortcomings in respect to the quality of life. It is only because business has done such a good job in its traditional areas that it is now, even by its least friendly critics, expected to concern itself with the quality of life in our society.

NEW DIMENSIONS OF BUSINESS

II

EDITOR'S INTRODUCTION

What changes are ahead inside business? What new management tasks will tomorrow's business leader have to be able to perform? What new tools will he have to master to accomplish these tasks? These are the questions considered in Part Two. During the last generation, management has emerged as a major new function and as a major new discipline. Now, as the contributors to Part Two make clear, the scope of management is changing rapidly. It is acquiring new dimensions. But it is also acquiring new tools, fashioned by the behavioral scientist, the economist, and the mathematician. Tomorrow's business leader will both do new things and do old things differently.

FRANKLIN A. LINDSAY

The Entrepreneurial Dimension

7

There is imperative need to inject the entrepreneurial spirit into American business. The problem is most acute in larger corporations—both because they have the greatest tendency toward ossification, and because advancing technology is forcing corporations to become even larger and more complex. This is particularly true in the pioneering fields where we are moving away from single products, which an inventive, small company could often develop better than a larger one, to a major system of integrated families of products which require very substantial resources. So my concern is with the creation of the entrepreneurially-oriented large corporation.

Now, just what is entrepreneurship? Traditionally, it meant combining land, labor, and capital into new productive activities. This definition is too limited for today.

I would define *modern entrepreneurship* as anticipating the future requirements of society, and successfully meeting these needs with new, creative, and imaginative combinations of resources. The classical resources of land, labor, and capital are relatively less important today. The critical resources I would add are information, superior organization, talented and professionally trained people, and lastly, time itself.

Organizations, as well as individuals with the entrepreneurial skills to foresee the future needs of

87

society and to develop new and better ways of fulfilling the needs, must be developed.

One essential ingredient all entrepreneurs must possess is the ability to assemble and assess large amounts of information quickly. Powerful new tools of analysis which will tremendously increase the range of the entrepreneur's creative imagination are in the process of development.

Let me describe one development as an example, and then project how this type of analytical tool can, in the future, contribute to the grasp of the entrepreneur.

A high performance camera lens is not designed by using a mathematical formula that gives the single best design. Rather, a trial and error process is used in which the designer starts by intuitively making certain decisions on the most likely design characteristics that will give the result he wants. He then must go through tremendously detailed computations to determine whether, in fact, his starting assumptions give good, mediocre, or poor results.

Ten years ago, the only computational aids to lens design were the slide rule and the desk calculator. This meant that a single set of calculations might take months to complete. Obviously, a lens designer could not make very many trials before he ran out of time or money.

Today, lens designers have a powerful scientific computer which is programmed to handle more than fifty design variables simultaneously. This means that literally thousands of alternate designs can be tried in a matter of hours or days. Typically, 75 to 100 billion calculations go into the design of a single lens.

But the significance of this example is that for the first time since Newton began to design complex lenses, the lens designer can afford to imagine and to ask over and over, "what if I were to do it differently?" until he is satisfied that he has chosen the best possible combination of these fifty or more variables. He can try a design, get his results back in a few seconds, and then say, "If I were to change this element of the design, would I make it better or worse?" And then he can repeat the cycle a few seconds later.

Earlier lens designers probably never even thought seriously about "what if,"—they knew it was futile.

I used this example of the power of computer models because I think they will have great implications for the entrepreneur of the future. In five years, certainly in less than ten, there will exist large computer models of the population of the United States and of its saving and purchasing habits. Such models will accurately reflect statistically, age distribution and income, family unit characteristics, the present stock of consumer durables such as refrigerators, and the purchasing patterns of each group for food, clothing, entertainment, housing, education, and transportation.

The creative market entrepreneur, and creative government as well, will then be able to ask such questions as, what if unemployment drops to 3 per cent next year? What if the birth rate declines by 5 per cent over the next ten years? What if taxes are increased next year by 10 per cent? And they can ask, what if several of these things happen simultaneously?

Similarly, a future transportation model of the United States, or of the world, could be used by a transportation executive to test out the implications for his company of a variety of possible future developments such as the failure of the government to provide automatic airways control in the 1980's, or the impact of reorganization of the railroads into a few major but competing networks. By asking "what if" he can gain important insights into the payoffs of alternate strategies.

One other thing is certain: more and more entrepreneurial opportunities will exist in big, integrated systems. There will be fewer opportunities for great entrepreneurial success with a single product that is unrelated to such major systems. This means, as I said, that large organizations must increasingly provide the entrepreneurial stimulus. But it also means that systematic knowledge of the expected characteristics of future systems must be provided by those companies who intend to be successful in the high-technology areas of the future.

We are beginning to build such models of future information systems which embody alternate forms and economics of digital and graphic information storage systems, the economic characteristics of alternate electronic communications, and the costs and characteristics of alternate means of getting information into easily usable form (such as microfilm blow backs, computer printout, on-demand book printing, or cathode ray tube display). These models will give us a better backdrop against which to make judgments on investment in this or that research program, on the specific products we put into development, and on the type of marketing organization we will need in the future.

Similarly, we need models of market systems. Tomorrow's new products will not fit into today's markets—neither geographically, nor in terms of market structure, distribution systems, or end-uses. We need to think through what additional innovations and changes are needed to make specific new technology fit existing market conditions.

We may, for instance, have to develop a meter to enable us to calculate and collect royalties for reproduction with duplicating equipment of copyrighted materials.

There is, thus, very great need for the development of new tools of information and analysis to make prompt entrepreneurial decisions in a systems context. But the tools we need are not primarily hardware. They are concepts and disciplines. The hardware we shall need largely exists today.

The entrepreneurial decisions we shall have to make are strategic decisions—decisions on the direction in which we shall proceed into an always unknown and uncertain future. Analysis and information, no matter how good, will never make these decisions for us. The urgency of the opportunities, and the urgency of the dangers from our competitors, will never allow us the time to collect full information before we have to act. Nor can we afford it.

Entrepreneurial decisions must, of necessity, be made on inadequate information. A corporate planner, who sometimes gets no more than two weeks to come up with a conclusion, when confronted with such a short deadline, has asked, "what is the *minimum* amount of information we need to make the right decision?" One of the most needed skills is just that—the ability to quickly determine what the *key* elements of a decision are. I disagree profoundly with those who say, "let's get all the facts before making a decision." If anyone were really to get all the facts before making an entrepreneurial decision, he would be deluged with information. The opportunity would have long vanished by the time he came up for air.

One of the great entrepreneurial decisions of the last few years was the introduction of the 914 copier by Xerox. The existence of a potential new market for convenience copying of good quality was recognized, the technical solution to the problem was found in xerography, and a brilliant marketing plan was devised. Not the least of this creative process was the innovation of the meter by which users paid for copies, rather than for a machine. Yet, I have been told that all the studies preceding the decision to go ahead with the new product indicated that there would be no market for it.

My conclusion is not that we do not need these studies; it is a much more important one. The best tools are useless, are indeed a danger, unless used in and for an *entrepreneurial organization*.

If the entrepreneurial organization is to take the place of the individual entrepreneur of the past, I am convinced that important changes must be made in the typical corporate organizational structure.

The paramount need is to infuse the entrepreneurial spirit into the large organization. The growing enterprise seems to produce—automatically—a towering hierarchy of authority, a multiplying division of responsibility, and a separation and remoteness of functions that prevent all resources from being harnessed to attain a common objective. Individuals and departments tend to become so narrowly oriented that they fail to see their role as an integral part of a larger effort. Instead, their specialty becomes an end in itself.

Coupled with this ossification of organization is the pigeonholing of people. Bright, young, inquiring minds that sparkle with fresh ideas can seldom communicate with the executive office because they often run into intervening barriers of authority encrusted with conventional wisdom. People are discouraged from taking any initiative outside of their designated areas of immediate responsibility, lest they be accused of encroaching on someone else's turf. Thus, the niceties of administration clash with the verve of entrepreneurship.

I am *not* opposed to orderly administration. Indeed, it is essential to a successful entrepreneurial organization. What must be provided is both effective administration *and* successful entrepreneurial activities. We need discipline—but an entrepreneurial, rather than a purely managerial, discipline.

The change to separate divisional profit centers has already been adopted by many companies. It is an important first step in creating a favorable climate for the entrepreneurial organization. This form of organization allows a strong group of divisional managers the opportunity to control nearly all the assets needed to manage their own destiny as a separate enterprise. But decentralization, if carried too far, can result in a rigidly compartmentalized organization in which it becomes difficult to use the resources of the organization as a whole to respond quickly to a new competitive danger or to a new opportunity. This is particularly true in high-technology companies because it is increasingly difficult to predict where the next breakthrough will occur, what branch of science will make the breakthrough, what scientific and engineering disciplines will be needed to convert the breakthrough into practical application, and what markets and marketing organizations will be most involved in exploitation.

A multi-divisional company must, therefore, retain the flexibility to apply whatever resources are needed, no matter where they are located, to the rapid exploitation of a major new opportunity. Flexibility and quick reaction must be central to the organizational philosophy of the company.

The entrepreneurial organization must have an acute sense of timing. If it acts too early, the technical development costs of a new product may be prohibitive and marketing costs may be excessive because the market is not yet ready for the product. On the other hand, the most profitable leading edge of the product life cycle can be missed entirely if the organization acts too late.

A guerilla is taught, for example, to exploit existing forces to the maximum to accomplish his ends. A single pound of explosives or even a few loosened bolts on the outside rail of a curve at the top of an embankment will destroy an entire train. The engine's own momentum as it rounds the curve will carry it off the tracks, then gravity acting on the engine will carry it down the embankment to destruction. Similarly, the entrepreneur must find ways of applying a small leverage to exploit the existing economic forces of the market and the existing forces of technological change.

The conventional layer-cake type of organization in which communications are closely channelled through hierarchical channels, one layer at a time, is not the best entrepreneurial organization. Instead, free communications must be encouraged throughout the organization.

Specifically, several devices can contribute to the strengthening of the entrepreneurial environment.

1. The number of layers or echelons in an organization should be cut to the minimum, and maximum flexibility should be developed.

Itek, for example, (of which I happen to be President) is using the concept of a group executive at both the corporate and divisional levels. By this, we mean that the four or five senior executives who together manage the division, or the corporation as a whole, occupy a single box on the organizational chart. This is not management by committee; each man has specific lead responsibilities. The advantages are that a single staff is used by all and an added layer of management authority is avoided. Most important, it gives us the flexibility to quickly shift one or more of the group to the exploitation of a new opportunity or to the solution of an urgent problem.

2. Corporate technical managers should roam through the technical organizations in order to keep a running inventory of the corpora-

tion's full array of technology and scientific personnel. In this way, the full technical potential is known and is quickly available.

I continue to be surprised by comments such as, "I had no idea that group X had such an advanced capability in that field," or, "if I had only known a year ago that group Y had already solved the problem I've spent the last year resolving." To overcome this lack of internal communication, one of our corporate vice presidents has been given the responsibility of overseeing the transfer of technology from research to product divisions and among product divisions throughout the company. In this way, we expect to appreciably shorten the time from research and development to product introduction.

3. Specific task forces should be used to study a new market area or to plan the applications of new technical breakthroughs.

The advantage of the task force is that people can be pulled together quickly from different scientific, production, and marketing groups without commitment to any final assignment or exploitative responsibility. If a new entrepreneurial element is later decided on, the task force can provide the nucleus of such a permanent organization.

4. In scientific-based companies, a science board composed of outstanding research scientists from universities and research centers can greatly enhance management's ability to concentrate corporate resources on the highest potential programs.

Itek's science board, for example, is composed of leading scientists from Harvard, M. I. T., Princeton, Columbia, and Stanford. Two are Nobel prize winners and one was President Eisenhower's science advisor. This group meets regularly to review progress in our research programs. They make important contributions to the more rapid solution of scientific problems, and to the better selection of high-potential projects.

5. Most importantly, a philosophy of involved management must permeate the entire corporate organization.

Involved management means that senior managers must spend the necessary time with their key people, not only with those at the next level below, to allow for deep exploration of alternatives, for assessment of risks and opportunities, for identification of the *key* factors which will govern the success of each course of action, and for realistically assessing the time and resources that will be required for success. By doing this, senior managers can convey to the organization an entrepreneurial style of doing business and a willingness to accept well calculated risks. They can also identify the innovators in the organization, and see that they are given the sequence of assignments that will absorb their full energies and make them seasoned entrepreneurial managers in the shortest time.

6. Finally, an uncompromising will to succeed must pervade the organization.

There is no substitute for will in any human endeavor. If a corporation is to turn in a superior record of performance, it must have the will to succeed and must be able to sustain this will no matter what happens. A couple of years ago, during a visit to one of our regional sales managers, I inquired why there was such a wide difference in performance among apparently equally intelligent and well-trained salesmen. His response was that the difference in performance was attributable almost entirely to an intense feeling on the part of the successful salesman, when he got up to the point of closing, that he just *had* to make that sale. The indifferent salesman did not have this feeling.

In conclusion, for effective entrepreneurship in the large business we need, a discipline of entrepreneurship that can be taught and can be learned; executives who are trained and developed as entrepreneurs; and an organization built and led for entreprenurial performance.

To develop this discipline, to develop these entrepreneurial executives, and to build and run large entrepreneurial businesses is, I am convinced, the greatest challenge now faced by the American business community—by the scholar, the teacher, and the practitioner of business in America.

HOWARD C. HARDER

The Corporation:
An Educational Institution

8

The role played by the American corporation as the generator of economic growth and the provider of material benefits is widely recognized and generally accepted. But less noticed is another essential role: the corporation as a contributor to social values.

In our society, the ultimate measure of the worth of any institution—and the test of its survival—continues to be the contribution it makes to the welfare of the individual human being. So it is with the corporation.

On the one hand, corporate survival is determined by success in the marketplace, by serving the economic needs of all the groups of people who transact the corporation's business. The corporation, as an economic institution, provides a complex and delicately balanced structure where many individuals join in organized purpose for individual economic gain—each anticipating benefits to himself as an employee, or as an investor, or as a vendor, or as a customer.

On the other hand, the corporation, to survive, must merit the support of all those concerned with the public welfare—the government, the press, the clergy, or the educators—whose criteria in judging the corporation's contribution shift from economic to social values. And rightfully so, because the corporation, as a social institution where people share successes and failures, create ideas, interact and work, can either help or hinder the development and realization of the individual's fullest potential as a human being. In a very real sense then, the corporation is accountable to the individual.

It may be fairly stated, I think, that the corporation has successfully met society's changing economic and social needs as these needs have been felt and expressed by successive generations of individual Americans. Indeed, perhaps the most remarkable trait of the American corporation has been its ability to adjust to change.

Today, a new generation of corporate management faces the challenge of making a difficult adjustment once again—in an era of pervasive and accelerating change and complexity that is unsurpassed in the history of man. As the American business community has repeatedly demonstrated over the years, the challenge of change can only be met by developing new attitudes, by training for new skills, and by instilling new learning—in a word, by education.

Today's educational challenge to the corporation reflects the scope and intensity of the impending changes, and the response must be proportionately immense and penetrating.

A Traditional Role

The corporation evolved a century or so ago as the primary industrial engine of our society. Although the corporation's original goals were solely economic, its powerful accomplishments from the start were also social—and educational.

Consider, for example, the traditional role of industry in America's absorption of the immigrant. The availability of jobs in the New World was the chief attraction to the tidal waves of immigrants. For a century or more, the factory, the mine, and the railroad were, in large part, responsible for the Americanization of the foreigner. The work place was a major socializing influence for millions of new Americans. Work and learning on the job have gone hand in hand ever since.

Consider also, from a purely educational viewpoint, advertising and other forms of corporate communications designed to sell products. Advertising may be laughed at by some, scorned by some, and considered ineffective by others—but the fact is, it created new stimuli and new interests; it has produced a whole process of information which, when distilled by people, manifests itself in changing and educating tastes.

Other, more deliberate business commitments to formal education have emerged such as training programs by industry and conducted at many levels of employment—for the executive, the line supervisor, and the process worker. Most of these outlays for education are regarded by business as an investment in human capital, which is expected to yield returns in future years. The other side of the coin, of course, is the contribution these programs make to helping individuals adjust to change by learning new skills. But the need for upgrading and developing manpower resources from within has been the primary motivation for the growing commitment of business to education.

Today's Manpower Needs

Industry's need for more skilled workers and better-educated managers stems from a variety of causes. Chief among these are scientific and technological advances which add to the complexity of industrial operations and create new demands for highly trained employees, the rate of change at all levels of operation which places a premium on lifelong ability to learn as a virtue in and for itself, and the worldwide scope of business operations today. Sheer size—broadening the impact and enlarging the consequences of a corporation's actions—calls for new, higher levels of executive skill and wisdom.

The United States Department of Labor notes that at least until 1975, the need for training and skill upgrading will not be confined to the most rapidly growing professional and technical fields which require the most education. The need includes other occupational groups as well. Our labor force of over 78 million persons is likely to grow by almost 20 per cent to nearly 94 million in 1975. But an increase of nearly one-third is anticipated for white-collar jobs, as against less than a fifth for blue-collar occupations. By 1975, white-collar jobs may make up nearly 50 per cent of all employed workers.

The rapid development of new knowledge has so drastically changed occupational patterns that a twenty-year old man can be expected to change jobs six or seven times during his work life. Obviously, learning has become a lifelong process.

This was not always so. Until recent years, a man could complete his education and go to work. Or he could learn a trade or vocation and expect to practice it for life.

But now, business and industry are the chief generators of change.

The peril is that the rate of technological obsolescence will be accompanied by a waste of people trained for a disappearing society. Thus, the corporation has a responsibility, as well as an opportunity, to help employees acquire new skills and learn new ideas. Only by adjusting to change can people carry on the corporation's work successfully.

It is this fundamental and continuing need for educated manpower at all organizational levels that accounts for the commitment of the corporation to education on a planned and organized basis—throughout each employee's working career.

Simply to perform its economic role in society, the corporation must find ways to assure the self-development of the individual. It is a truism that no company can move faster than its people let it; every man and woman on every job can work more effectively by learning to live closer to capacity. Thus, the corporation has embarked on a course that promises profound social contributions as well.

The Educational Challenge

Although the requirements of business for trained manpower are growing, a substantial proportion of the labor force enters the job market with little or no education.

Among the unemployed, 16 per cent never completed the seventh grade. In the mid-1960's, some 250,000 teenagers failed to go beyond the fourth grade and were thus classified as functional illiterates.

In the decade ending in 1975, some 30 million children will leave school for work. At least 2 million of these may never enter high school; perhaps 7 million may drop out.

The problem is particularly acute among Negroes. In 1958, two-thirds of young Negroes failed to finish high school; more than half receive diplomas today. Still, among Negro boys eighteen and nineteen years of age, 10 per cent never reach fifth grade (as against 1 per cent for white boys), and 25 per cent end their schooling before ninth grade (compared with a corresponding rate of 8 per cent for whites). It should be recognized, moreover, that the attainment of a particular grade level is not a reliable measure of the quality of learning.

These trends pose new problems to business and industry—and to society as a whole. At the same time that employers require a higher level of educational attainment, large numbers of unqualified young people are entering the job market—and particularly young people from urban ghetto areas. Employers can no longer absorb great numbers of the unskilled and semi-literate. The result tends to be increasing selectivity on the one hand, and waste of human resources on the other.

Fortunately, much has already been done to alleviate the situation. On the part of educators, greater attention is being given in elementary and secondary schooling, and particularly in vocational and adult education, to understanding the world of work itself and to adjustment to the work environment—beyond the provision of skill training. On the part of government, manpower training programs have already had some important effects on the rate of unemployment as a whole, and particularly among the educationally deprived.

But the main job of educating people to adjust to the changing job environment has landed in the lap of industry, where the changes are occurring.

An Emerging Educational Role

At one end of the educational spectrum, the modern corporation has introduced a new capability to overcome illiteracy so that further training can be directed to job mobility—moving people either upwards to a better job or sidewards into a new occupation.

Also at this end of the spectrum, the corporation continues to perform its traditional educational task of the socialization of the American. Work is the great socializing activity, and inherent in work is learning. As more and more Negroes move up the education ladder and into jobs in industry, they become exposed, often for the first time in our society, to the same progressive learning forces that opened doors of opportunity to European immigrants a generation ago and more.

At the other end of the total education approach, corporate executives at the highest level are adapting the business school classroom as an integrated element in human resource development rather than as an independent experience.

A whole world of on-the-job training and management development courses fall in between.

And in the not distant future, much more extensive involvement by the corporation in the nation's educational processes is a distinct possibility.

The corporation's fundamental concern is and should be its own survival. Trademarks, patents, financial resources, technology, and know-how historically have been among the corporate attributes most relied upon by management for economic and psychological reassurance. But they suffice no longer. The survival of the corporation in the future will depend increasingly on the corporate capacity for innovation—the kind of innovation that creative, well-informed, and educated minds can provide. Only the calibre of the corporation's people, then, can promise corporate survival in the future.

First-rate people are educated people. To assure an adequate supply, tomorrow's corporation will not hesitate to join forces with government and with educational institutions in order to get the job done.

Education, it seems, is no longer a compartmentalized undertaking. Education increasingly cuts across those artificial boundaries set in a simpler age—the business mentality on one side, and the educational establishment on the other. In those days, our educational system, as a form of social capital, fully met and satisfied the needs of business. But this source of social capital is no longer adequate. Education today —as a lifelong process—involves the combined resources and motivations of every discipline and calling. The result, I believe, will be progressive change by all participating institutions, with loss of identity by none.

Not the least of the corporation's incentives to share in the knowledge industry, of course, is the realization that the penalties of failure include larger and larger welfare loads—at the cost of higher taxes borne primarily by industry itself.

But the businessmen's basic incentive to rout out poverty and ignorance is practical in another sense. As a leader in society, business shares in the responsibility for society's faults as well as for its strengths. And the urban ghetto represents a failure of the total society in which it occurs. To the extent that businessmen decide to exercise an influence, business will have a key role in solving the problems of the ghetto.

The wise course of business action is to assume responsibility for the development of individuals as whole people—on and off the job.

One Company's Experience

The potential contribution business can make to the educational process is indicated by several programs developed in our own company.

At the lower levels of employment, a Corn Products subsidiary, MIND, Inc., has developed successful new techniques of teaching basic reading, writing, mathematics and other basic skills to the uneducable rejects from our public school systems—and even from military draft calls. Working with high school drop-outs, the low IQs, and the educationally deprived, MIND has achieved remarkable results. In less than eighty hours of training, for example, one group of thirty-eight workers, average age, forty-two, with fourth and fifth grade proficiencies, raised their word knowledge an average of 2.6 grades, their spelling by 2.2 grades and their arithmetic by 3.2 grades. In other words, in each eight hours of MIND training, they gained the equivalent of two or three months in school.

The techniques involve changes in the learning environment, such as the absence of the authority figure of the teacher, the use of programmed instruction materials and audio-visual teaching aids, and the opportunity for individual students to proceed at their own pace. Perhaps the chief factor in MIND's success, however, focuses on motivation of the learner. First, he learns at the work place, where opportunities to put learning to work are apparent to him. Second, he reinforces his learning by applying it immediately. Third, he realizes that learning can lead to a better job. In other words, his motivation is built into the program.

Through our experience with MIND, which has already moved from the experimental stage to that of commercial endeavor, we have been able to develop new ways to satisfy society's need to reclaim the previously unemployable.

At other organizational levels, Corn Products offers a variety of its own training programs—to process workers, middle management and top management.

At the upper levels, moreover, Corn Products has offered outside management development opportunities to selected executives. These programs have been carefully integrated with each man's own development program for improving performance. We have been particularly attracted to the coordinated company-college operation, such as that conducted by the Wabash Institute for Personal Development of Wabash College, Crawfordsville, Indiana.

The three-year program of the Wabash Institute consists of two basic elements: first, seven weeks (over three summers) of on-campus sessions that emphasize the liberal arts and communications skills; and, second, a continuing program of personal development designed by each man, in consultation with staff counselors from the Institute, to fit *his* needs and *his* current and potential roles with our specific company. Each participant's particular staff counselor meets with him *on the job* at least once each year to discuss his progress in implementing his program. At the time of this visit, the counselor also meets with company officials to discuss the man and his program. In this way, the company is a participant in the process; the company's own hopes and plans for each man can be integrated with the college's contributions.

A Look at the Future

Business in general is moving from its traditional passive role of absorbing the educational product of our secondary schools, colleges, and universities toward an active and organized role of supplementing the output of the nation's educational plant and meeting the manpower needs of today's society.

Business, to survive, will continue to seek through its own vigorous initiative an adequate supply of trained manpower to cope with accelerating change and increasing complexity. The corporation has always been an educational institution—by producing knowledge and by encouraging the learning of new skills. In recent years, dramatic technological breakthroughs, growing multi-nationalism, and new management techniques have imposed demands on the corporation for increasing numbers of better-educated workers, technicians and managers. In addition, rapid changes in occupations and industry impose a need for continuing the education of the individual throughout his employment. The task of education is never finished.

To meet the demands, corporations are increasing the scope and intensity of business financed and directed educational programs. In the years ahead, the corporation will deliberately plan, organize and pursue more and more educational activities geared to those intellectual levels—from top to bottom—most needed to fulfill its role in society and enable each individual to realize his fullest potential.

These are the challenges, of course, that lead me to the prediction that business, in learning how to educate its employees, will discover that it has created a new and profitable business for the good of society and the benefit of man.

MICHAEL I. KAMI

Business Planning as Business Opportunity

9 Every business and every organization must be able to master change in order to survive. If it manages change well, it will progress and grow. If it manages it badly or ignores it, it will die. As the rate of change of our environment, both technical and sociological, is constantly increasing, we must find better and new ways to understand, anticipate, cope with, and exploit change. Planning ahead is the key management function for dealing with change in a positive and purposeful way. If planning is not done, changes will "manage" the company. If planning is done poorly, the demise may be even faster than if no planning took place and the management only reacted to circumstances as they came up.

Planning is *not* one of many "functions" of management such as production, marketing, or research. Planning *is* management, an over-all, all-enveloping thought process that cannot be compartmentalized and set in a department.

More and more businesses are beginning to recognize that management does not have a choice whether it wants to plan or not. The only choice is between doing the job systematically or doing it haphazardly. This explains the growing acceptance of planning as a specific task within top management. Yet we are only now beginning to realize the full dimension of the task and its significance. As in everything we do, we first had to make a few false moves. Planning twenty years ago was seen by many people as a way to enable business to foretell the future. We soon learned, however, that systematic ignorance is still ignorance, and that forecasting, however brilliant, is not planning. We soon learned, above all, that planning does not focus on knowledge as such but on action. It does not deal with what will happen in the future. Rather, it deals with what we should and could do today in anticipation of the future.

Then, however, we made a second mistake and defined planning as something "the planners do." In this kind of planning the planners sit in a corporate ivory tower and talk only to themselves, whereas the rest of management blithely concerns itself with the problems of today. But planning only produces results if it leads to drastic changes in what the managers of business do today. Thinking about tomorrow is indeed a separate activity, but its only worthwhile results are changes in the attitudes and actions of operating management.

Finally—and this is the most important lesson from our experience —planning we now know is the organized way to force innovations in the big and successful companies. It is the way to prevent a business from getting stuck in yesterday's ruts. It is the organized method to build tomorrow into today's work. This is done as this essay will explain, by presenting to management the gap between the performance goals of tomorrow and the results that are likely to be produced by continuing today.

Thus, the true definition of planning is *a process of continual selection of actions to deal with the changing environment for the benefit of the corporation.* But this must be further clarified by stressing another obvious point—that there is no absolute best action, there are only alternatives. The selection of one of the many alternatives depends upon the criteria that the top management of the company adopted, or should have adopted. Otherwise planning becomes the impossible task of having to deal with a great number of alternative choices without a means of evaluation or a basis for rejection or selection. This happens particularly in attempts at diversification. "Bring us the best projects you can find" says the President to the Planner. "Best" compared to what? This lack of definition of criteria creates in the long run a total lack of decisions in the midst of a lot of "made work," and contributes to the growing criticism of "ineffectual planning and planners."

There are, therefore, four steps in the process of planning:

1. Establishing criteria
2. Establishing objectives
3. Defining the gap between objectives and expectations, which sets the goals of planning for the business
4. Filling the gap.

Criteria for Planning

The key criteria that have to be established, understood, and agreed upon by all parties concerned, are:

1. Degree of risk
2. What business do we want to be in?
3. Limiting policies

There is a risk in everything we do. The further ahead we plan, the greater will the risk factor be. The aim of the planning process is not to eliminate risk, which is an impossibility, but to select the right risk for the company and its management. But can one establish factually and scientifically the degree of risk for a company? One cannot. Each company has a "personality" of its own. Emotionally, intuitively, its key people have formed an inner criterion of risk-taking, some conservative, some truly extravagant. This risk criterion is quite easily discernible and almost measurable. The planner can attempt to propose a higher or lower risk content for future actions. But it is difficult to change human vision. A company also tends to become more conservative and to demand a lower risk content for actions as it grows and prospers as a result of earlier risky but successful actions. Thus the role of the planner is usually to stimulate risk-taking, rather than to dampen it. It is important to understand that the "psychological" definition of risk-taking is not forecasting a probability of success, but defining the odds a company and its entrepreneurs would accept as representing their standard of daring (two to one, five to one, ten to one or a hundred to one).

The second key criterion is to define "what business are we in and what business do we want to be in in the future?" This is still the most important and the most difficult and soul-searching question a business can ask of itself. What business do we want to be in? determines the selection of the "right" risk for the company. Again, there is no single best answer for any one company; there are many opportunities, and many roads that could lead to great success. But these roads must be in tune with the basic personality of a company and its key people. They emotionally approve of a business, not just through figures for the return on investment and market penetration, etc., but because they "like" the environment, the product, the customers, the "whole bit." A chief executive with a highly technical "frontiers of science" inclination, will emotionally resist guano or potash mining on deserted islands even if all the figures logically point that way. And he should resist, because he is unlikely to make a success out of something he does not truly believe in.

There are a few pitfalls to be avoided in the definition of what business we should be in. It is now well accepted that the definition must be service-oriented and ultimately use-oriented rather than define a product. In the case of IBM the definition became "information handling and processing" rather than the "punch card" business. If IBM had stayed with the old definition, it would not be the leading computer producer of today. Thus, a dishwasher manufacturer has various choices for the definition of his business. He might limit himself to *the business of washing dishes*—this could be done by various other means than conventional water dishwashers—ultrasonics, for instance, can be used, opening a new field of technical knowhow requirements. Or, he might consider *the business of eliminating household chores*—this could mean research and ultimate development of disposable dishes that look as good as china and are cheap enough to be thrown away after use.

But he can go further. If so inclined, he might consider his business to be the *elimination of food preparation and conventional eating*, by replacing the meal as we understand it by a few pills. Then dishwashing ceases to be a problem. But individuals may like the act of sitting at a table and eating several courses to satisfy their gustatory or their social propensities. Thus, a further research and product (pill) to chemically change the personality (likes and dislikes) of a person could be another derivative of the original desire to improve a dishwasher. It is asserted that in the next fifteen years there will be chemical means to alter drastically man's personality. The question is, who will emerge as a leading producer and marketeer? A drug company or an appliance company to protect a multi-billion market of appliances, freezers, refrigerators, stoves, ovens? The planner must be able to envisage either outcome.

It is important to define the ultimate service broadly. But one must know the many subdivisions and functions of that service. One cannot say "we are in the knowledge business" and stop contentedly at that, satisfied that a field has been defined. The "knowledge business" embraces all activities of the human mind. Such a definition is meaningless for taking specific actions unless it is further subdivided.

We can easily see that the risk factor previously discussed is intimately related to the definition of "what business are we going to be in?" The broader the scope, the longer the time span, the more remote the derivation of ultimate service or change of it, the greater the risk to be undertaken by the company. The objective of eliminating the kitchen is certainly more risky than improving the dishwasher, however drastically.

The third criterion to permit practical and meaningful business planning ahead is the definition of "limiting policies." Here again a further subdivision is necessary into self-imposed business ethics and emotional or traditional taboos. In the field of business ethics, some principles are self-evident and others are not. To operate within the "law" is a limiting policy, pretty universally adopted, but certainly restrictive. The Mafia or Cosa Nostra do not abide by such limiting policy and can adopt methods and markets (such as dope or gambling) not open to the rest of us. Other ethical limitations are less easily defined. One company may adopt a "one-price and no commission-cutting" policy, while another may tolerate or even encourage "deals." Certain markets will be closed to the former company because of its policy.

Emotional taboos are very strong. One company has a "limiting policy" of *not* entering the consumer market, but dealing with the industrial market alone. Thus, it would first be necessary to change the "limiting policy" before spending a lot of time and money in developing proposals, services, and products in the consumer field. The reasoning that a good enough proposal will change management's mind may be naive and faulty if we are dealing with human emotions —for example, a deeply held belief that consumer advertising will destroy the company's reputation for scientific leadership in the industrial market is such a taboo. And such taboos are not always purely prejudice; a leading pharmaceutical manufacturer found out to its regret a few years ago that consumer advertising of a proprietary product did indeed seriously hurt the company's standing with its main consumer, the prescribing physician.

Other important limiting policies may be the maintenance of full employment, i.e. eliminating seasonal fluctuations, no unions, avoiding large urban centers, or maintaining 100% ownership and control of foreign subsidiaries (which may eliminate most of the world market).

Objectives of the Corporation

At this point objectives for the company can and should be set.

The objectives have to be quantitative and qualitative. The quantitative objectives are absolutely necessary for the measurement process and the reiteration process, to be discussed later. Typical quantitative objectives are the desired rate of annual growth of sales, the profitability ratio of net income to sales, the return on investment, and a turn-over index for money in the business.

Here again, the personality of a company plays a role. There are no formulae, no market research, no competitive data, no share-of-market index that will yield "scientific" objectives for a company. You can have go-go, swinging super-growth businesses in a conservative market (for example, the growth of discount stores in retailing, or the success of some railroads in a decaying environment). You can have "winners" in regulated and almost protected industries (some airlines are so much better than others, and yet they fly the same planes at the same fares almost at the same time to the same cities). You can have "losers" in fast growing markets of enormous potential (such as the failure of the electronics giants like RCA, GE, and Westinghouse to penetrate the computer market). Management decides on quantitative goals and motivates the team to achieve them. It is a question of leadership and motivation for innovation and not a derivation from scientific numbers.

High quantitative objectives automatically impose high qualitative objectives. A high growth objective requires fast penetration of the market. Therefore there is an implicit objective to search for new and virgin markets and replace rapidly existing products and services by radically new and different approaches. If we have a saturated market potential, growing at the rate of GNP, better marketing, better production or better "anything" with the basically identical product or service will *not* produce super-growth and drastic changes in share-of-the-market percentages. For example, the gasoline companies or the soap companies compete for fractions of a percent. But introduction of a different fuel or an electronic cleanser would permit a fast rate of penetration into the existing potentials. On the other hand, television created a brand new market, as did space technology, and as oceanographic services may do in the future.

Defining the Gap

Where are we today and where are we going to be if we continue as we are? This is the crucial question.

We may well accept the theory that accelerated progress produces an increased rate of obsolescence, and that our products and services are going to die faster than previously expected. Unless we replace them ourselves, competition will do it for us. We accept all this for others, but not for our own company. The planners' decreasing curves for the future of the present products and businesses are often dismissed as prophecies of doom and gloom. "All we need," management may say, "is an energetic marketing effort" (or "lower manufacturing costs" or "a new advertising agency"). But a realistic projection of the results of "business as usual" will usually come out well below the objectives which the executives have set themselves.

This area of as-yet-unfulfilled business is the quantitatively measurable *gap* that has to be filled to compensate for the attrition of the existing business and to create additional growth. The more ambitious a management, the greater the gap.

The Gap-filling Process

How do we fill the gap?

First, we have to remember once again that new things require risk, and therefore there will be false starts, unsuccessful attempts, and even utter failures on the road to the ultimate objective. We also must understand that there is no ultimate objective, but a moving target which keeps retreating and increasing each year as we succeed in meeting the yearly sub-objectives. We have to motivate people, departments, and outsiders to present to top management a series of ideas and proposals to fill the gap.

To expect that the gap will be filled if the total revenue projected from the sum of the proposals is equal to the *gap* is therefore naïvely unrealistic. Even with moderate risk we need enough new starts to promise, if successful, at least three times the amount of gap. If the sum of all proposals and projects does not come up to three times the gap, we know immediately that either the organization is not trying to reach the objectives or that the objectives are unrealistic under the existing circumstances. Management has then to make an important and immediate decision: do we reduce our goals or do we improve our creativity—by changing people, by motivating them better, or by modifying the organizational structure? But we *know* we will not meet our objectives unless we do something.

Above all such a shortfall in proposals for the new and different always signifies that top management does not allocate properly its own time and energies, the company's good people, and the available money. There is a disproportion between what is allocated for today and what is allocated for the future.

The first action result of planning is therefore always a change in the priorities of key-resource allocation in the present, the existing business. It is always a shift in risk—we take more risk today, in the known and going business to have a greater chance of success tomorrow, in the uncertain but different future. It is always a change in values— defending yesterday and solving problems becomes less meaningful than making tomorrow and optimizing opportunities. We still have to learn a great deal about planning. But we know enough already to allow us to say that planning gives us a discipline for building the future into the present organization.

The deficiency of "return on investment" and of similar financial measurements is not, as is said so often, the failure to include the "intangibles," especially the human and social results of business. A financial measurement does not, after all, pretend to such competence. To fault it for not doing what it is not designed to do makes about as much sense as to criticize a tape measure because it does not tell us whether a person's eyes are blue or brown.

But the financial yardsticks are seriously deficient as measurements of what they pretend to measure, that is, as measurements of economic performance. They only measure past economic performance. There is, however, no such time dimension as the "past." Economic performance consists after all in the commitment of resources to future expectations. Unless we can therefore build an appraisal of the future into our financial measurement system, we misdirect ourselves constantly. Opinions—all we have had so far—are of little use. We need quantitative, systematic, and reasonably rigorous measurements which show the businessman whether he is meeting the "costs" of the future, that is, the cost of staying in business in a changing and growing environment, or whether he is eating up economic resources at the expense of the future.

Planning as it is developing today brings the future as an economic dimension into our economic measurement system. At least it indicates the magnitude of the job to be done today to deserve a future. But like all instruments in business, this one does not do its job by itself. For business is a human activity. The central purpose of planning must therefore be to create motivation for managers to do the work needed and to liberate human energies to get the work done. Planning, therefore, changes the job of the manager. It adds the dimension of performance for the future to every important managerial position.

DALE E. ZAND

Managing the Knowledge
Organization

10

The future of management will be affected by one development in our culture that stands out above all others: we are becoming a knowledge society, and business enterprises are becoming knowledge-processing organizations.

A massive system of public education guides the knowledge development of more than 60 million children and adults. We employ more than 2 million educators in this country. Adult education, once considered a pastime, has become "continuing education" —a necessity for simply keeping up with the explosive growth of knowledge; project "head start" reaches back to the cradle; the "job corps" and "teacher corps" are in hot educational pursuit of the "high school drop-out"; and a comprehensive system of scholarships, student loans, and tuition-free public universities practically assures a college education and even graduate studies to every student with sufficient ability and motivation.

Although unheralded in the public press, business organizations have been a major stimulant of the quest for knowledge. Increasingly, they demand well-educated, knowledgeable new employees—in many firms a college education is a minimum condition for employment. After a person is employed, the firm provides tuition support to those who wish to continue their education. Many firms give full-time

scholarships to employees. Universities receive from businesses unre-
stricted donations as well as substantial grants for specific research
projects. In addition, many large firms are directly engaged in disseminating and generating knowledge. For example, organizations
like General Electric, General Motors, and IBM not only send
managers and professional employees to university programs, they
also maintain educational facilities and operate educational programs
that rival the largest universities.

This evolution in the basic quality of our society portends significant
changes for managers. We can get a glimpse of the magnitude of what
lies ahead by reviewing some of the socio-economic effects of earlier
transitions.

Three hundred years ago we were an agricultural society. Men
worked in family units—physically and socially remote from each
other. Life's major activity was to sow and harvest the fruits of the
soil. Markets were primitive, and management as we know it today
did not exist—indeed, could not exist.

One hundred and fifty years ago we began the transition to an industrial, capital society. Industrial organizations erupted on the social
landscape. In time they became key institutions. They mobilized great
masses of men, contributed to the economic well-being of citizens far
beyond the factory gates, and influenced social patterns more than the
governments of the largest cities and states.

These transitions, although imperceptible to most of the people who
lived through them, had dramatic, far-reaching effects. Some were
highly desirable: the standard of living increased; the quantity, quality,
and variety of goods available increased; leisure time increased. Other
effects were not so desirable: land was stripped; forests were laid
waste; air was polluted; rivers were fouled; and men devised a subtle,
new form of social indenture—dedicated conformity to the employing
organization.

Now we stand on the threshold of another transition—the emergence of the knowledge society. Production of the necessities of life,
food, shelter, clothing, and other common material goods will require
the labor of a smaller and smaller percentage of the population. Even
now less than 3 per cent of the population works on farms, less than
12 per cent produces all of our industrial out-put, while more than 30
per cent goes to school. These developments are in the penumbra—
the dimly lit half shadow of the future that managers will have to
contend with. Although it may be difficult to predict the exact shape

and form organizations will take, it is clear that managers will be concerned with what can best be described as a knowledge organization.

The Knowledge Organization

What is the character of a knowledge organization? On the surface several features are evident. (1) The ratio of knowledge workers to production workers increases rapidly. (2) The relationship between the two groups changes. Whereas in the past the knowledge workers were supported by the production workers, this reverses and the production workers are increasingly dependent on the output of the knowledge workers. (3) Knowledge becomes the leading edge of the competitive effort. How knowledge is applied to products and markets determines the long-term expansion or contraction of the firm's production work force.

Less evident but equally important in the knowledge organization, managers are aware that their firm is under unrelenting pressure to acquire and to use knowledge. They know that it is increasingly difficult if not foolish, to base survival and growth on the ownership of scarce materials, on the ownership of patents, or on a temporary superiority in a market. They understand that product discoveries and marketing decisions made more than five years ago rapidly lose their ability to sustain the firm. Managers in a knowledge organization acutely sense that the major basis for economic growth and profitability lies in developing future managers who know how to guide an organization in the acquisition and use of knowledge.

Finally, the essence of the knowledge organization is that work is done in the head. This means that knowledge work can't be seen. It does not fit into discrete, neatly separable units and it is difficult to measure. Generally, managers with a traditional production, marketing, or accounting orientation find this difficult to comprehend.

Perhaps what most annoys and frustrates traditional managers is that knowledge work is non-linear. It doesn't make sense to insist that a man should produce twice as many bright ideas in two hours as he produces in one hour. We can't insist that the quality of a decision arrived at after seven men deliberate should be seven times as good as the decision made by one man. If we seem to be half way toward the solution of a problem after two days, should we expect the complete solution in two more days? If we have worked ninety-nine hours and the problem still seems muddled, does this mean that we will need another ninety-nine hours? Will we need more than ninety-nine hours? Or, will the dilemma fall into place and will sensible solutions emerge in the next two hours?

The manager in a knowledge organization thus faces a life in which productivity is intangible and resolution is uncertain. It is hard for him to know when his people are working. It is also extremely difficult for him to know when he has accomplished something. His knowledge has been fused with the contributions of so many others that it is fruitless to identify his contribution.

Traditional methods of supervision emphasize regularity, measurement of work in process, and orderly appearance. When this form of supervision is rigidly enforced in the knowledge organization it may not only be ineffective but actually obstructive.

The Knowledge System

When we view the knowledge organization as a system, we can see four processes that should concern managers:

1. Collecting and disseminating knowledge that already exists in the organization;
2. Acquiring and creating new knowledge;
3. Converting knowledge to profitable products and services;
4. Managing people who work with knowledge.

Let us examine each of these in turn.

Existing Knowledge

The first job of a manager is to assemble and use the knowledge that already exists in his organization. A major difficulty is that existing knowledge simply does not move to the people who should get it. For many years, as a consultant to various organizations, I have been struck by how much people know and have thought about the problems and needs of their organizations. But I have been saddened by how difficult it is for this knowledge to flow freely from where it is to where it can be used.

There are innumerable examples of the failures and near catastrophes that have followed from management's inability to use existing information. One case that received wide publicity is that of a well-known aircraft manufacturer who decided to build planes for the highly-competitive, commercial jet transport market. Top management felt that the opportunities for profit more than offset the high risk in this venture. As engineering design and model testing proceeded, it became clear to several members of middle management that the original cost estimates for the venture had been underestimated by a factor of no less than four, and possibly as high as ten. Moreover, the company's lack of design experience with jet aircraft caused innumerable difficulties and departures from the original time schedule for completion of the first test aircraft. This information, which already existed within the organization, was diverted before it could reach top management. By the time it was allowed to reach top management, a major failure was in the making. The information was no longer news; it simply confirmed what no longer could be hidden. The company suffered a severe economic setback, and losses were so great that the company was on the brink of insolvency. There was widespread contraction in employment, and confidence in top management was shaken.

In another company, a research organization, several managers estimated that it costs more than two million dollars and it takes about two years to stop a project that is failing. It takes that long for people in the organization to "leak" negative information to top management.

In still another situation, a long-range plan had been developed to guide the future of a major food growing and marketing company. Top management refused to follow the plan, apparently because it would have involved fundamental changes in the company's competitive strategy and in its top organizational structure. The company suffered economic decline for several years until, in desperation, the board of directors brought in several new top managers. The long-range plans that existed were dusted off and put into operation. The company's competitive strategy was redirected from growing and transporting products to developing new food products and to creative marketing. Over a period of four years the company became a highly effective, profitable organization.

Organizations today can be viewed as cauldrons of knowledge—rich with ideas about new products, new processes, new approaches to markets and new ways to improve management's effectiveness.

In such organizations withholding, diverting, or ridiculing existing knowledge becomes the greatest source of current error. Isolating, ostracizing, or punishing those who present adverse information and analysis becomes the major source of future error.

Recognition of the organization's dependence on knowledge is an essential managerial attitude. In addition, however, managers should be asking a number of hard-nosed questions about existing knowledge:

1. What knowledge is worthwhile?
2. Who in the organization has, or should have it?
3. Who should receive this knowledge? Why? What are they expected to do with it?
4. How can we improve the way we collect and disseminate existing knowledge?

The question "what knowledge is worthwhile?" deserves further discussion. It is particularly troublesome for most managers. Some find themselves uninformed on one hand and overinformed with useless data on the other hand. The manager in the knowledge organization must understand the various qualities that make knowledge valuable. Worthwhile knowledge reduces uncertainty when making a decision. Knowledge that does not reduce uncertainty is either redundant or irrelevant. Worthwhile knowledge may also have a different quality: it may clarify where uncertainty cannot be reduced. It is extremely important for the manager to know what cannot be known. Also, the manager should know what knowledge is so costly that for decision-making purposes it must be treated as an area of uncertainty.

Rather than seek knowledge in general, however, as if by amassing a great enough quantity a decision will emerge, the manager must be able to pinpoint the kind of knowledge that is needed. Two simple questions can guide the manager to vital information: (1) How much would current conditions have to change for me to change my decision? (2) What information or conditions, not presently known, would cause me to change my decision?

Worthwhile knowledge may also have the quality of suggesting additional areas for search. In other words, worthwhile knowledge will describe the limits of its usefulness. It will clearly point out that beyond these limits we do not know whether or not all, part, or none of our current knowledge is usable.

Interestingly, knowledge does not come only in the form of answers and objective data. In management, there are few things as dangerous as a comprehensive, accurate answer to the wrong question. This is pseudo-knowledge. It easily misleads management into erroneous actions. Pseudo-knowledge has mushroomed with the advent of computers which have made available masses of data that answer questions managers found too costly to ask before. In far too many instances, however, the data are collected but not used because they answer irrelevant questions.

It is vital to understand that in the knowledge organization, worthwhile knowledge may take its highest form in the framing of relevant questions. Formulating the right questions becomes increasingly a crucial function of the manager.

There is one final point about knowledge that I feel has been over-emphasized—the psychological value of redundant knowledge. Many managers gain an increased sense of confidence and comfort from data that continually confirms what they already know. They frequently want "all the data" so they can "get a feel for" the trends and irregularities. Actually, their decisions rarely change as a result of these additional data. In the knowledge organization, supplying managers with redundant data can become an unbelievable burden. In one organization an executive estimated that he and his colleagues spend no less than 80 per cent of their time preparing and polishing reports that tell upper managers what they already know.

New Knowledge

It is evident to insightful managers that knowledge is rapidly becoming the firm's primary instrument of progress and competition. Existing knowledge defines our productivity and competitive skill in the present; new knowledge determines our productivity and competitive skill in the future. Acquiring and generating new knowledge, however, is one of the great uncharted areas of management and human behavior. Indeed, if there is one place we need new knowledge, it is in the area of how to get new knowledge. Managers, for example, need to study how they themselves generate new knowledge. In addition, they should be supporting research on the whole process of how we obtain and discover new knowledge.

Knowledge is new in two different senses, and it is important to distinguish these. (1) Knowledge may be new to one firm but known to others; (2) Knowledge may be new to one firm and not known to others.

This distinction between "new only to me" and "new to all others including me" suggests different approaches to getting new knowledge. The first indicates a strategy of acquisition. Search of literature, meetings with others, and negotiation are ways to obtain knowledge which already exists for others but which is new only to me. The second indicates a strategy of creation. Speculative thinking, imaginative leap, and original insight are needed to invent knowledge that is "new to all including me." From a managerial point of view these are two very different processes. Often they can be performed only by completely different people.

All new knowledge has "stress potential." Conventional ways of thinking, well established relationships among people, and the power to make decisions may be severely disturbed by new knowledge. Two extreme—but particularly dramatic—examples of how new knowledge can be upsetting are Columbus' concept that the earth was round when everyone believed it was flat and Copernicus' concept that the earth revolved around the sun when everyone believed that the sun revolved around the earth. Acceptance of the idea of a round earth stimulated an era of exploration. It made possible a national strategy of colonialism, it upset economic relations among nations, and it shifted competition to naval efficiency. Copernicus' concept raised so many questions about theologies founded on the idea that the earth is the center of the universe that the well established relation between people and the Church and the distribution of power between governments and the Church could never again be the same.

Managers favor new knowledge. Like most of us, however, they want its promise but not its dislocations. Hence, the strategy of acquiring new knowledge possessed by others is fraught with mixed motivations. On the surface this strategy is deceptively straightforward. It simply says search out and get from others the new knowledge they have.

Of course, competing corporations deliberately want to conceal new knowledge from each other. But in the same corporation, divisions are often more dedicated to concealing new knowledge from each other than from competing corporations.

Managers should understand that efforts to acquire new knowledge arouse strong resisting and accepting forces. At the outset it is not clear which set of forces will prevail. When we lack knowledge and attempt to acquire it from others, four types of resisting forces may be triggered:

1. We did not invent the new knowledge, therefore, it is suspect—not relevant, not applicable.

2. Disdain for the organization (or division) that originated the new knowledge may prevent us from seeing the merits of the new knowledge—to do so would require us to change our unfavorable image of the originator.

3. We may fear that accepting the new knowledge will be seen by higher management as evidence of our inadequacy.

4. We may fear that disruptions may follow use of the new knowledge —possibly decreased need for my capabilities, adverse changes in the organizational structure, reduction of my influence.

Thus, the simple intention to acquire new knowledge can stimulate a deep core of resistance.

On the other hand, awareness that knowledge exists that we do not have can arouse strong accepting forces. Probably the greatest motivator is management's concern that if we lag behind our competitor too much, too long, we may not survive. Second, some people in the organization will see in the use of the new knowledge benefits for themselves—greater responsibility, increased influence. Finally, the originator may have an established reputation as a capable, forward-thinking organization (or person)—doubts tend to be resolved in favor of the new knowledge; the reasoning usually is as follows, "There must be something in it we don't understand otherwise someone as smart as Mr. X (or organization X) wouldn't be doing it."

In any case, the manager plays a crucial role in efforts to acquire new knowledge. It is his job to encourage his people to search, to sense, to scan, to expose themselves to as many sources of new knowledge as possible. Failure to reach out regularly for existing new knowledge leaves an organization vulnerable. It greatly increases the probability that management will be unaware of significant trends in new knowledge, will be making inappropriate decisions, and will not know how to look for new knowledge even when it wants to. Consider the case of American Woolen Company, once king of the woolen fabric business. The company earned peak profits by meeting delayed demand for woolen fabric during the five years after World War II. Then, after steadfastly ignoring knowledge about weaving synthetic fibers and blends for thirty years, it declined into bankruptcy. By the time management wanted to reach for new knowledge, it didn't know how.

When it comes to creating new knowledge, the manager confronts a strange and different world. Gone is the stability, order, and reliability so essential to the daily recurring activities of the corporation. Instead there is the unusual, wondrous world of discovery and unpredictability.

The creation of new knowledge depends on several supporting conditions. Managers will find their concepts and skills severely tested when they attempt to provide these necessary conditions. Outstanding among them are:

1. Support for creative deviance
2. Immersion in existing knowledge
3. Unstructured time
4. New perspectives
5. Unusual groupings

Let us look briefly at each of these.

First, to create new knowledge means to depart—often radically—from conventional knowledge. Many half-formed concepts and irrelevant ideas have to be cast up before we can sift out an occasional nugget of worthwhile new knowledge. In any effort to create new knowledge, the manager's first task is to develop a climate that supports creative forays. These ventures in imaginative thought must be departures from the known, the accepted. New concepts will deviate from the commonplace—indeed, they must if they are to be meaningful additions to the known.

The creative process is different from its final output—the creative product. The process flourishes in a climate that encourages deviant ideas—a climate in which it is understood that many ideas will be generated but few will pass the test of rigorous critical analysis. The manager must expect false starts. He must be prepared for vigorous argument today for concepts that are discarded as worthless tomorrow.

Second, creating new knowledge depends on being familiar with what exists—that is, if one wishes to avoid laborious rediscovery of what is already known. Robert Oppenheimer, the noted atomic physicist, would often say that adding to our knowledge in physics was not as difficult as most people thought. He said that first one must learn the language of the subject—the mathematics, the concepts, and the experiments, all of which were available knowledge. This might take a great deal of time and dedication, but after it had been done he said that the process of adding to knowledge in physics was about the same as it would be in any other field. Although Oppenheimer, with characteristic modesty, understated his talents and his unique contribution to new knowledge, his point still stands: immersion in and absorption of existing knowledge is an important precondition for the creation of new knowledge.

Third, people engaged in creative activity need unstructured time. They need adequate freedom from routine, repetitive activities that dull the senses, use energy, and occupy the mind with trivia. This is not to say that a regular schedule of work time is inappropriate. Quite the contrary. Productive discoverers of new knowledge follow a fairly regular work schedule, regardless of whether or not they feel creative. They tend to work excessively long hours when they think they are on the brink of a breakthrough; usually they need time to recuperate and to rearrange their thinking after these intense episodes that often turn out to have been false starts. Unstructured time doesn't mean time without work—it simply means time in which structure (possible goals and possible methods) emerges as one tries to work.

The creation of new knowledge depends on guarding unstructured time—keeping it free of routine, programmed activities. Here managers in knowledge organizations can create great difficulties for themselves. If they completely succumb to the pressures of short-term, measurable output and do not preserve some unstructured time for themselves and their work team, they are in all probability efficiently managing the decline of their activity.

Fourth, new knowledge is often discovered by systematically taking different positions (roles, locations) when viewing a problem. For example, it is well known that the same situation will elicit different problem definitions and different solutions when seen from the different viewpoints of managers in production, marketing, finance, or personnel. In the quest for new knowledge the idea is to capitalize on these differences, not suppress them. New knowledge is frequently lost to an organization because managers do not encourage the taking of unusual points of view.

Managers have made some of the greatest advances in new knowledge when they began to think from the point of view of people who were not even in the corporation. One great leap occurred when they asked, "How would I see this product if I were a consumer?" This was quickly followed by, "How would I see this product if I had to service it? If I had to install it?" In this mass consumption society, with its growing population, managers will someday realize that they ought to ask, "How would I see this product if I had to dispose of it?"

Taking unusual points of view can be systematically encouraged. *Synectics,* a method intended to encourage creativity, does just this. For example, it asks people to explore military and political analogies to the problem being considered. It asks them to think as if they were something in nature with characteristics similar to those in the problem —an animal, a tree, a geyser. The method asks people to imagine that they are the real object. Consider this illustration from a team working on new products for a surgical manufacturer. "If you were an open wound what would you see? How would you feel? What would you want?"

Behavioral research long ago established that difficult problems are more likely to be solved by people who alter their points of view. It is now a matter of implementing this in the management of knowledge organizations.

Finally, the discovery of new knowledge is stimulated by exchanging ideas with people who think differently than we do. As a matter of fact, in a knowledge organization the manager makes an important contribution by taking the lead in establishing unconventional groupings. People with different systems for conceptualizing problems tend to stimulate new approaches to knowledge in each other. Research discloses that the most productive scientists gain new perspectives by regularly discussing their ideas and problems with experts in fields different from their own.

The manager in the knowledge organization must understand how to encourage and guide unusual groups. Such groups pose a difficult opportunity: how to capture the creativity that inevitably resides in diverse views? The search for new knowledge by groups composed of different specialists is increasingly common. We refer to these intellectually high-powered groups as "brain trusts" and "think tanks." But, regardless of the irreverent names, they are an unusually rich source of new knowledge.

Converting Knowledge

The corporation is a social instrument. It exists to perform an economic function for society, to provide desired goods and services, and to earn a profit. Ultimately, a corporation must use knowledge; it must convert knowledge into new, or better, or less costly products;

into more efficient marketing; into more effective use of its capital, and of its material and human resources.

Most managers are conversion-oriented. They tend to be impatient and uncomfortable with knowledge that is in the form of theory. They usually consider theories that do not prescribe unequivocal answers or simple methods to be irrelevant or pretentious abstractions. They tend to view the pursuit of knowledge with suspicion—a tolerable distraction when the firm is profitable and an impractical luxury when the firm is not profitable.

The process of converting knowledge to activity is vital and difficult. Although managers may know intellectually that knowledge unconverted to action is of little economic value, they continually face the problem of selecting what knowledge is worth converting and what knowledge is not. Consider the following case. Shortly after World War II, the top management of a firm that was a leading producer of soap flake products for home laundering was asked to approve a project for the development of a home laundry detergent. Much was known about the physical and chemical properties of detergents, but up to that time they had been used almost exclusively in industrial processes. A major use was in separating and concentrating ore particles by "flotation"—a process in which detergent-laden water is mixed with pulverized ore, and as a result the ore particles adhere to bubbles formed by the detergent, float to the top, and then concentrate in the broth that flows over the side of the tank. At the time there was no home laundry detergent. Because of the company's long, successful history with laundry soap flakes, top management decided against the development project—a clear decision not to convert existing knowledge. About the same time another soap manufacturer, with a much smaller share of the market, decided in favor of conversion. Approximately two years later it introduced the first detergent for use in home laundering. The results are well known—the detergent manufacturer swept the market, displaced soap flakes, and kept a major share of the market for at least a decade.

Very often knowledge is available, but for many reasons it is not converted to action. Sometimes the reasons are social and cultural. For example, knowledge about how to improve productivity in underdeveloped countries is readily available, but there is strong resistance to converting this knowledge into action when it may upset ancient power relationships between fathers and sons, women and men, village elders and family heads. In our own culture knowledge frequently will not be converted in a firm when it may upset ancient power relationships among managers. Also, knowledge conversion may require altering customary beliefs about the place and role of work in the scheme of life—a current problem in not-so-underdeveloped England.

The conversion or utilization of knowledge is a separate, distinct process about which we need more information. The process involves a transition, a crossover from the realm of thoughts and information to the realm of action and things. The manager's growing dilemma, because of the accelerating rate of knowledge acquisition in the knowledge organization, is to determine what knowledge to convert to action and how to convert it.

The fact that the corporation has an economic purpose provides, at best, some modest guidelines for conversion analysis. The following difficult questions and rejoinders are a framework for the conversion decision. (1) What are the customer's needs? This assumes "the customer" can be identified and his relevant needs can be described. (2) How will this knowledge conversion contribute to the organization's goals? This assumes that organizational goals which are more than vague generalizations have been articulated and that one can predict quite specifically the consequences of the conversion decision. (3) What is the economic efficiency of this conversion proposal? How does it fit into the organization's over-all plan for economic growth? This assumes unusual ability to forecast economic results, behavior of competitors, and general economic conditions. It assumes existence of a comprehensive plan for growth. (4) Finally, what are the human and social costs and benefits of the conversion proposal? This assumes that we can make explicit the personal motives of managers and the moral consequences of their actions, which ordinarily tend to be ignored or disguised in highly rational statements about economic efficiency.

In spite of these difficulties, knowledge conversion decisions must be made and are made. As a matter of fact, the manager can be thought of as continually making conversion decisions. Organizations differ in their knowledge conversion methods. Consider the different roles of American banks in international banking. America's deficit balance of payments currently restricts the outflow of credit; nevertheless, international banking is the fastest growing department in many banks. Some American banks have developed themselves into well informed sources about business, politics, and finance in foreign countries—a tremendous aid to American corporations with foreign branches or affiliates. Other banks are experimenting with management science methods to guide the management of their foreign assets. Some banks have converted established knowledge into ingenious financial arrangements that make loans to European customers possible without violating credit restrictions.

One question that arises about knowledge conversion is: what relationships best aid the conversion of knowledge to action? Corporations are generally organized into a chain of command and into divisions that separate knowledge people from operating people. Difficulties in the conversion of knowledge most often emerge in the form of an "interface" problem. The people who "know" are in one group, while the people who "do" are in another group; the face between the two groups is a boundary under constant pressure as each attempts to influence the other. Thus "staff" people may be uncoupled from "line" people; functional experts may be ambiguously linked to operating managers. Knowledge conversion activity in this type of organization increases stress at group boundaries. It tends to precipitate conflict. Unfortunately, the conflict frequently gets distorted into a battle over the question of final authority. The real issues are: what are the right questions and what are the best answers?

One approach to the interface symptom in knowledge conversion has been to appoint coordinators or liaison agents. The people in this intermediary role must be extremely competent in the social process of knowledge conversion; otherwise, they will introduce an additional barrier. If they are not competent, they are likely to be ignored or at best humored by both camps. If they are not competent and in addition have formal power, they can so complicate and obstruct knowledge conversion as to bring it to a complete stop. In one organization, for example, a "coordinator" was appointed with formal authority over a research group and a development group. At first each group attempted to form a coalition with the coordinator against the other group. In the interests of harmony the coordinator gave each group the impression that he was on its side. Unwittingly, his behavior confirmed the idea that there were "sides," and each group increased its intransigence, believing that it was simply a matter of getting the coordinator to "straighten out" the other group. This continued for several months. In an effort to extricate himself, the coordinator practically eliminated all meetings between the groups and ordered that all communication go directly to him; he would decide how differences would be resolved. Both groups were frustrated and angry. They communicated only the information he asked for, which frequently was not adequate or relevant for the knowledge conversion decisions that had to be made. Unfortunately, the reorganization that had been intended to aid knowledge conversion deteriorated into an impediment.

The basic question still remains: how can we bring knowledge conversion closer to knowledge acquisition? Approaches that build people with knowledge conversion orientation into the early stages of a knowledge acquisition project probably will be more successful in bridging the knowledge conversion gap. On more than one occasion the presence on a team of a single member who considers resource allocation, commercial feasibility, and organizational implications significantly eases the knowledge conversion process. Managers will also have to consider how to train themselves and selected knowledge workers in the intricacies of knowledge conversion. As a start, one major corporation uses exchange assignments—selected managers in the research division exchange positions with selected managers in the production and marketing divisions. In another case, product development managers and marketing research managers exchange positions with production and sales managers. Although rather primitive, these methods at least show a concern for knowledge conversion.

Knowledge conversion is a continual process. Different aspects of the organization's knowledge are being converted into action simultaneously. Thus, while top management is attempting to plan and budget for the next year, managers and shop foremen are converting current product plans into action. In knowledge conversion there is a need to review continually the relationship between current activity and the knowledge intended to guide that activity. Historically, when the knowledge received from higher authorities is not relevant or appropriate to the current environment, this has to be referred up the chain of command. In production, to give a common example, a problem with parts that should fit together according to engineering design but do not in production must be referred up the authority ladder in manufacturing. The organization operates in a way that primarily guards the chain of command and secondarily deals with the problem. For knowledge conversion this may be unnecessarily complex, even restrictive. A promising development in organizational behavior, variously referred to as the *all-connected network* or the *matrix organization*, indicates there are better ways to deal with this type of knowledge conversion problem.

The operation of this recent development is simple: when a manager has a significant action that involves knowledge given to him by others, he may initiate a meeting without passing the issue up the chain of command. In the production example, the shop foreman could deal with his problem by calling a meeting with representatives of engineering, quality control, and purchasing. This immediate access to the other appropriate individuals is even more useful at higher levels of management where divergence between knowledge, understanding, and action tends to be greater. Matrix behavior accepts the formal hierarchy as well defined and stable; it does not believe that the hierarchy is endangered every time managers work directly with each other to resolve knowledge conversion problems.

Up to this point we have assumed that knowledge is available. The problem has been to convert it to economically useful activity. Now let us look at how demand for knowledge to convert may affect the generation of new knowledge. Two major hypotheses have been advanced to explain the generation of new knowledge: (1) The *serendipity hypothesis*—new knowledge results from active analysis of accidental events, like Charles Goodyear's discovery of vulcanization by accidentally dropping rubber into a fire; (2) The *demand hypothesis*—new knowledge results from research programs in response to specific demands for knowledge.

The serendipity hypothesis may have been valid when our society had few large organizations, but students of this subject are of the opinion that the demand hypothesis properly describes the process in our society now. This means that the manager's demand for convertible knowledge is the major determinant of the generation of new knowledge in an organization. The issue is not "what don't we know?" but rather, given our limited resources, "what do we want to know?" The knowledge organization thus confronts the manager with an awesome question: what new knowledge do we want?

Managing People in the Knowledge Organization

Although we have introduced examples of human behavior that illustrate some difficulties in acquiring, generating, and converting knowledge, we have treated people as incidental to the processing of knowledge. Now we will reverse the perspective and treat the processing of knowledge as incidental to people.

The knowledge organization is an unusual social system—quite different in several subtle ways from the hierarchial production organization that spawned it. These differences introduce new human stresses and require new human responses. Foremost, and with the most penetrating effects on human relationships, is an implicit change in the bases people use to attribute power to each other. A manager, by virtue of his formal role in the production organization, not only has the power to *reward* his subordinate managers with merit increases and attractive job assignments, but he also has the power to *direct* and is expected to do so in even the most minor aspects of the work. Indeed, if the manager does not firmly and regularly assert this supervisory right, he often believes he might be considered weak or incompetent. Strangely, in the knowledge organization a manager who does firmly and forcefully assert his supervisory right to direct, will undoubtedly be seen as weak and incompetent. He appears to his subordinates as incapable of using their knowledge capabilities.

The reward and penalty power of the manager still exists in the knowledge organization, but the exercise of straightforward directive power to determine goals and methods is greatly diminished. This occurs because in the knowledge organization the ultimate foundation of power shifts to the relevance and correctness of knowledge. Although hierarchial power continues to exist, it is used basically as a last resort to resolve conflict deadlocks. Otherwise the authority of knowledge guides the organization. This sounds simple, but in practice there is constant tension in the knowledge organization between authority based on position and authority based on knowledge.

Another characteristic with pervasive effects is the rapid formation of work teams and components of the organizational structure to cope with a knowledge project, and the equally rapid dissolution of these organizational contrivances when the project is completed. The knowledge organization is a stream of temporary social systems coming into and going out of existence. In such an organization, managers and knowledge people are centrally involved in some projects, moderately involved in others, and peripherally involved in still others. But regardless of centrality, each person is a vital contributor to the project.

These changes introduce new forms of human stress. In the production organization, stresses take the form of physical fatigue, monotony, and boredom. In the knowledge organization, they take the form of mental fatigue, overwhelming variety, and unrelenting demand for complete psychological alertness. The production organization used man's muscles and neglected his mind; the knowledge organization uses his mind and neglects his muscles. The production worker seeks mental stimulation and spectator entertainment as a relief; the knowledge worker seeks physical stimulation and muscular activity as a relief.

Psychologists are increasingly concerned about man's ability to cope with the stresses of modern life. The knowledge organization is one arena in which man's capabilities are being severely tested. Managers in the knowledge organization are asked to cope with the following demands, each of which alone is stressful; in combination they are potentially lethal. (1) Situational complexity: Goals must be defined and selected; there are many possible; no one goal is sufficient; priorities of goals continually change with accomplishments; alternative courses of action must be created; rarely is there an alternative without some undesirable consequences; final results frequently depend on the actions of many others with goals that differ from ours. (2) Ambiguity: It is difficult to connect results with actions; some accomplishments are because of what we have done, others are in spite of what we have done. Which is which is often a matter of speculation forcing managers to face the next decision situation either uninformed or, worse, misinformed. (3) Multiple supervision: In addition to his hierarchal superior each manager must contend with many other temporary but equally influential superiors, because of the authority of their knowledge. (4) Membership in many groups: Each manager will have to establish, maintain, and sever competent membership in rapidly-formed and dissolved project teams. (5) Conflicts of ideas and egos: Since knowledge is the fundamental commodity of the knowledge organization, it becomes difficult to separate the value of an idea from the value of the person, as one can separate a product from a person. Yet this must be done because even the worthiest of managers have their share of poor ideas.

These sources of human stress, which are part and parcel of the knowledge organization, cannot be eliminated—they can only be managed. They highlight for us the fact that managing a knowledge organization essentially consists of managing a complex human network. Human problems will not be less important than in a production organization; if anything, they have the potential to be far more disruptive.

What behavioral knowledge and skills will be required of the manager? These I believe will be particularly important:

1. An understanding of limitations and the uses of formal power in a knowledge organization.

2. Concepts of structure and of how people may interact that are different from the customary hierarchical, authority-obedience pattern.

3. Behavioral competence—behavior that encourages search, creativity and commitment will be important.

4. Insight into the attitudes and concerns of knowledge workers.

Understanding the Limitations and Uses of Formal Power

In a knowledge organization, although a manager has formal power to make decisions, this power is limited by his ability to understand the implications of the knowledge communicated to him by subordinates, peers, and superiors. The rapid development of knowledge makes managers obsolescent if they do not continually update their knowledge. A production worker who lags in knowledge limits his own opportunities, but a manager who lags in knowledge exacts a greater toll: his power multiplies the consequences of his deficiency because he can impede the development of a major segment of the corporation.

Here is a typical case in point. The vice-president of finance in a manufacturing organization specializing in electronic test equipment had not kept up with new developments in financial theory and electronic data processing. His department employed several bright young men with graduate degrees in business administration and with working experience in the use of computers in financial analysis. The knowledge that these men attempted to use for the company's benefit made little sense to the vice-president. He resisted changes in financial reporting and data processing that were by then commonplace in many competing organizations. Turnover was high among the knowledge competents. The vice-president's decisions not only limited sophistication in the finance area, but also contributed to poor inventory decisions, inappropriate pricing, and misdirected market development expenditures. The company was subsequently purchased by a larger organization. Management of the finance area was gradually assumed by the parent organization as the incompetence of the financial vice-president became clear.

The knowledge organization is particularly vulnerable to managers who wield formal power and who are knowledge incompetents. This is not to say that every manager should be more knowledgeable than his subordinates and peers. As knowledge develops, the manager must expect to lag behind others. Indeed, if he does not, the chances are that he is settling for mediocrity in his subordinates and is probably inhibiting their knowledge growth.

The manager's task is to continue his personal development in order to keep the gap in knowledge between himself and his team within workable bounds. He must be able to understand the consequences and the implications of the advice and information he receives. In a knowledge organization few things are more destructive than the manager who uses his power to cut himself off from others to avoid exposure to knowledge he may not understand.

With the diffusion of knowledge people in an organization, however, managers must confront a new phenomenon—the arrogance of knowledge. Knowledge people at times ascribe a degree of certainty to their models of the world that can baffle and offend managers. Too often the complexity of the world cannot be reduced to abstractions that make sense to managers. Managers who demand a simple one-to-one correspondence between the real world and each element in the model are disappointed.

This conceptual gap strains the relationship between knowledge people and managers. Managers often consider knowledge workers to be naïve, insensitive and arrogant. Knowledge workers often consider managers to be intellectually unsophisticated, defensive, and self-protective. Each obstructs and frustrates the other. What was intended to be an infusion of knowledge degenerates into a series of skirmishes. It is important that the manager be alert to this process.

The manager has a right to ask for explanations of assumptions and theories behind knowledge. But he also has an obligation to use his powers to encourage pilot testing of knowledge that he does not have the conceptual training to understand. Consider the following illustration. Management of a major bank decided to build into its organization a "management science" group. The group received continual encouragement to study and if possible to improve asset—management policies and decisions. Over a period of several years the group developed decision models that significantly assisted management. To this day it is doubtful that any of the managers whose decisions determine the continued existence of the group understand, except in the most general terms, how the decision models are designed, tested, and used. Yet they clamor for the analytical outputs that come from the group and are delighted to propose additional decision situations for study.

Although the manager's knowledge competence subtly limits use of his formal power and affects his relations with others, he must expect many situations in which he will have to use his formal power. The advent of knowledge should clarify and sharpen situations in which there is no knowledge. It is important that the manager with his team identify what is not known. When knowledge is not reliable or comprehensive, it may be insufficient to indicate a decision. Here the manager must resort to intuition, judgment, and creative insight. He has the power to make a decision, and make it he must.

New Concepts of Structure and Interaction

The manager's job in the knowledge organization will be to find ways to go beyond the knowledge limitations of the single human being. Organizations have become large in terms of people employed and complex in terms of structure. Knowledge, intricate and rich with different meanings, is a neglected third dimension of organizations. It is a major complicating factor that has yet to be portrayed on a chart like an organizational structure.

The knowledge that the president of a large organization needs is increasingly beyond the energy and the capability of one human being. Traditionally, the president is served by layers of subordinates and buttressed with supporting committees. Several organizations (e.g., Union Carbide, General Electric, Borden) are using a different structural approach to extend the capability of the president. They have a President's Office, populated by several top managers, each complementing the other's knowledge. Here is a concept that departs from the single superior notion. It is an attempt to deal creatively with the need for expanded capability in knowledge processing. Of course, this complicates interactions, but the alternative is to restrict knowledge flow at a crucial decision level—a price that fewer and fewer organizations are willing to pay.

Not only presidents, but managers at all levels can expect organizational structures to loosen. They can expect increased interaction to aid the flow of knowledge. The entire organization will be considered one big manpower pool. Managers will simply clarify goals and criteria. Once goals have been defined, a temporary system—or whatever name you wish to give to a group with transient membership and limited purpose—will be formed. People, regardless of their level of authority, continually will be joining temporary groups as knowledge goals are identified and then leaving them when goals are accomplished. This phenomenon has been called *free-form* organization. It would have little use in repetitive production activities, but in the quest for knowledge about, for example, how to improve production, it is remarkably useful.

Managers tend to misunderstand the free-form concept. It is not a substitute for the formal organization, but rather a supplement, intended to deal with knowledge tasks.

Behavioral Competence

The free-form character of the knowledge organization will place heavy demands on the manager's behavioral competence. He will constantly have to adapt to the situation of working with many different people on unfamiliar tasks. Solutions to technical problems may suffer not because of a lack of knowledge, but because managers and knowledge workers may not have adequate behavioral skills. For example, a headquarters staff marketing consultant had been invited by a regional sales manager to review plans and methods in his region. The consultant unwittingly offended the regional manager on his first visit by publicly criticizing the region's performance and by implying that the manager was at fault. It was not then politic to dismiss the consultant, so the manager and his staff spent the better part of a year compiling evidence to prove to headquarters that the consultant was technically incompetent. Actually, he was very competent. However, having failed to obtain adoption of any of his recommendations, he was on the verge of being expelled from the region. A behavioral specialist who had been working with the regional manager suggested a meeting of the region's top management with the marketing consultant to consider how they might better work together. At the meeting the marketing consultant described his disappointment over his inability to influence the organization. The regional manager discussed the development of the relationship with the marketing consultant and gradually came around to the "insult" of the first day. The marketing consultant was astounded. He had been completely unaware of the defensiveness his remarks had aroused. He thought that a little criticism would show people that he knew the field and that he would not "soft pedal" any adverse findings. With this unfortunate incident out in the open, the group was finally able to begin to work on the marketing consultant's recommendations.

To improve their skills in working with groups, managers will want to consider the contributions of the behavioral sciences. In the field of group behavior, significant knowledge has been amassed. Substantially improved methods (such as "laboratory education") have been developed to enable managers to become more effective member-contributors. Because relationships in a free-form organization are more consultative than directive, managers will need to develop better skills in giving and receiving help. A manager will need increased awareness of his feelings, his expression of feelings, and his style for dealing with conflict. In general, the manager must learn about how unintentionally he may be precipitating defensiveness that interferes with the search, creativity, and commitment he is trying to encourage.

Attitudes and Concerns of Knowledge Workers

The current generation of recruits coming into knowledge organizations are bringing new attitudes and concerns. They are changing the culture of organizations. On one hand they seem almost belligerent. Their training has emphasized freedom of inquiry. Brought up on the discovery method—if you don't know, find out for yourself, develop and test your own theory, use your own reasoning skills, find your own way out of dilemmas—they question teachers, analyze the pronouncements of authorities, and are quick to find the disparities between what people say and what they do. For them no question is unaskable, no theory or authority is inviolate.

On the other hand, they are anxious. They feel a sense of guilt if they are not actively involved in socially responsible uses of the advance in knowledge. They have witnessed wide public dissent: labor strikes that violate existing laws, civil rights demonstrations, pro- and anti-war protests. They have had to decide when they personally would or would not participate in some form of active protest. There have also been opportunities for increased self-responsibility. New recruits have been involved in student self-government programs that encouraged responsible self-direction in affairs that traditionally had been left to parents, to public officials, or to school authorities. As a result, they have learned how to dissent constructively and with responsibility. For example, students at the New York University School of Law decided that a course in the consequences of military justice upon civil liberties was needed. The faculty was not enthusiastic, so the students arranged the course themselves, obtaining the services of several of the best authorities in the field. Although the course is not given for credit, it was continued, and additional non-credit courses are being designed by the students.

Opportunities for personal growth, for variety, for new challenges and a need for accomplishment are continuing concerns for knowledge workers. As if in direct violation of these concerns, knowledge workers are often introduced into an organization by a process of negative assimilation rather than positive stimulation. The recruit or the transferee is given a picture of great opportunities, but when he starts to work he gets miniscule, repetitive activities. If a manager were to attempt deliberately to demotivate a knowledge worker, it is doubtful that he could design a better method. The knowledge worker needs continued new education. He may have to go back to some form of schooling every two years. He needs assignments that stretch his capabilities. He may complain about overwork, but deep down he would not want it any other way.

The morality of how knowledge is used is also a major concern of people in a knowledge organization. They are aware of social inequities and international difficulties. They question whether man was designed to become a slave to the organizations he has created to be his servants. They have theories of political economy, of social welfare, of government, of international strategy, and of economic values. They do not stop thinking about these matters when they come to work. They have become increasingly aware that government and its agencies need guidance and help in correcting injustices and in controlling destructive practices. They see knowledge organizations as effective, productive social instruments. They want to find more ways for these organizations to take direct action in dealing with inequities.

In sum, future knowledge workers will be quite different from their predecessors. They will be better informed, more skeptical, more questioning, more accustomed to dissent and protest, more personally involved, and more inclined to action. How to manage by liberating these drives for self-direction for creative response, for action, and at the same time constructively to use the many conflicts that are bound to occur—that is the challenge.

GERALD J. GLASSER

Systematic Decision-Making

11 This chapter is about decision-making—decision-making in a world of uncertainty and complexity, two words which fairly well describe the world of business. The chapter discusses a particular approach to decision-making, namely a quantitative approach. It is my strong belief that this approach will become increasingly important. Certainly tomorrow's manager, or for that matter, the manager of today, needs to be familiar with it.

The theme underlying this discussion is that the quantitative approach provides much more than a set of tools and methods. It is *a way of thinking*.

For what levels of management does this way of thinking offer the most opportunity and challenge? At any and all levels where decision-making authority rests, but especially at the highest levels of management, where the less routinized problems of business must be resolved. This statement implies my belief that the influences of quantification, currently strongest in middle management, will be moving upward at a rapid rate in the near future to top management levels.

What is the current state of the art of quantification in business? As is well known, an important trend in the field of business in recent years has been represented by increasing attention to the use of mathematics and statistics in the solution of business problems. In many business firms, the applications of quantitative methods are widespread. However, many of these applications have, underlying their use, the objective of providing better information for management decisions. Let me say that one who has seen such applications of mathematics and statistics, and the enormous gains that accrue from them, cannot be less than wildly enthusiastic about them. The fact is, however, that the phrase "better information for management decisions" connotes, at least to me, a cleavage between the scientific processes of gathering facts and figures, and the subjective judgmental processes of translating these facts and figures into management decisions. Fortunately, in recent years there has been an attempt to close any such division between the two processes, be it real or apparent. Increasing attention has been given by many academicians and many practitioners to decision-making, especially decision-making under uncertainty and complexity. This *behavioralistic* philosophy, as it has been called, has led to the formulation of a quantitative theory of decision-making—a theory of how to make decisions in the face of uncertainty and complexity.

This theory of decision-making is the subject of this chapter.

Nature of the Theory

The phrase "quantitative decision-making" may appear forbidding. The suggestion that mathematics and statistics can be used to make decisions may appear arrogant. The fact is, however, that statistical decision theory is not designed to replace managerial judgment. It is designed to use managerial judgment—in the most effective way possible. Furthermore, the main ingredients are not so much formulae and the like. The main characteristic of this philosophy is formalization of one's thinking, designed to replace careless, seat-of-the-pants, informal reasoning. Often the main contribution of the quantitative approach is not so much to solve a problem, but to enable a statement of the problem so that it is capable of solution.

Statistical decision theory is a theory how to approach management problems, and other problems, in a systematic manner. It provides a conceptual framework within which a decision-maker can operate to recognize problems, to analyze problems, and to solve problems.

There is another important aspect of the theory. In a sense it is an assumption, or even a limitation. That is, one must be forewarned that this quantitative theory of decisions, as it has been developed, is merely a theory of consistency in decision-making. The primary aim of the theory is to help a decision-maker reach rational decisions—rational in the sense that he chooses the course of action that seems most reasonable in view of what he knows, and what he believes, about his problem situation. That is, statistical decision theory provides a method of logical and consistent reasoning in the face of uncertainty and complexity.

The decisions that one reaches by means of decision theory may or may not be wise. To repeat, the theory is designed to lead a decision-maker to adopt decisions that seem wise in view of what he knows and believes. Whether the decisions reached by this method of logical analysis are, in fact, wise, will depend on whether the decision-maker started his logical analysis knowing and believing correct facts.

However, it seems quite likely that most decision-makers would find that they make wiser decisions with decision theory than without it. This should be true simply because decision theory provides them with a way of using what they know in the most effective manner.

A few other preliminary words on uncertainty and complexity, the key words of this chapter, are in order. The first point to make is that uncertainty and complexity are merely states of mind. Often, all of the pertinent facts are not known in a given decision problem, and often, it is not feasible to research a problem sufficiently to obtain all the facts. This means that uncertainty about what will result from a given decision exists. Virtually all business decisions are subject to some degree of uncertainty, and some persons feel this limits the applicability of the quantitative approach to business decision-making. Nothing could be more incorrect. Uncertainty is the statistician's specialty, and instead of merely bemoaning its existence, he threats it in terms of the mathematical theory of probability. In fact, an integral part of decision theory is the treatment of uncertainty.

Very many business problems are complex. Some persons may think that this precludes the use of a statistical theory of decisions. They argue that our problems are too complex to be solved in this way. On the contrary, I believe that the more complex a businessman regards a problem, the more important it is to look at it from the point of view of statistical decision theory. Application of this theory forces the businessman to structure his problems, which in itself eliminates much of the supposed complexity. They are then more capable of rational solution.

Areas of Application

When can statistical decision theory be applied? In my opinion, it can be applied any time when there is a decision to make with no answer immediately obvious, and when the decision-maker is competent to use the theory. On the lighter side, one may use the theory in personal life to decide what to order for lunch, what time to get up in the morning to make an appointment, at what stop to get off the subway, and to resolve many of the less frivolous problems of life. More serious applications of statistical decision theory are continuously being developed in agriculture, medicine, science, government, and business. Any present listing of applications will increase rapidly over the next few years as businessmen become more familiar with this quantitative approach, and as they discover new applications for it.

Some of the important applications in business one finds in current practice include problems of industrial inspection which involves deciding how much inspection to use on incoming raw materials, on goods in process, and on finished products. Decisions on scheduling production and inventory are being made with the aid of the theory. So are decisions on the choice of advertising copy and media by agencies and their clients, on the composition of financial portfolios, on the acceptability of credit risks, and on personnel. A very important area of application of statistical decision theory in which some companies have had success is capital budgeting problems. Another such area is the one of decision-making regarding the marketing of new products.

In all of these areas, the general aim of application is the same: to structure the problem, to quantify the available facts and judgments in a specified way, and to resolve the problem by a logical procedure. We shall elaborate on these various phases of the decision-theory approach in the remainder of this chapter.

Overview of the Subject

It may be helpful to think of the subject of decision theory as being composed of three interrelated, though distinct, topics. First of all, the theory develops a general form for decision problems. This topic involves description—that is, it provides a general means of describing decision problems in a formal way.

A second integral part of the theory is a general procedure for analyzing a problem and deciding upon a course of action. This decision-making procedure, together with the general description, make up the basic framework of decision theory. Our discussion will focus on these parts of the subject.

The remaining topic involves techniques that a decision-maker may find helpful in analyzing a problem. These techniques are statistical methods (some old and some new) and, more generally, the mathematical theory of probability. This last topic may be, and often is, called *Bayesian analysis* because it frequently utilizes Bayes' theorem —merely a particular rule of computation from probability theory. Some persons like to use the term "Bayesian analysis" to describe all of decision theory. However, the name used in this connection sometimes leads to misunderstanding.

General Model of a Decision Problem

As pointed out earlier, the first part of decision theory is a general and very formal mathematical description of a decision problem. While it is clear that every decision problem has its own unique characteristics, it is equally clear that all problems have certain general characteristics. For one thing, in every decision problem there must exist at least two alternative courses of action. In decision theory, each alternative is supposed to be a complete description of some way in which the problem may be resolved. Decision-making involves making a choice among these alternatives.

In our theory, we adopt certain conventions in defining alternatives. They should be mutually exclusive so that a decision is a choice of one and only one alternative. They should also be collectively exhaustive so that one of them must be chosen.

Thus in any problem, we have a set of acts to be denoted

$$a = \{a_1, a_2, \ldots, a_m\}$$

For example, in problems of industrial inspection of a manufactured product there are often two alternative courses of action: (1) Pass (accept) the lot of products without inspection; (2) Inspect all of the items in the lot, screening out defectives. In this case, a_1: accept or a_2: inspect.

Another frequent problem, in advertising, requires the choice from among various advertisements. If there are three advertisements (A, B, C) and one is to be selected, we may define a_1: (A), a_2: (B), a_3: (C). If the problem is to decide on two advertisements for use, we should define a_1: (A and B), a_2: (A and C), a_3: (B and C), so that the alternatives are mutually exclusive and collectively exhaustive.

A common problem in the credit field involves two alternatives a_1: extend credit, and a_2: do not extend credit. Another common decision problem involves deciding on a credit limit for a customer. If we view this problem formally, alternatives are represented by the various possible dollar limits, and the decision problem is to choose one of these limits.

An important type of capital budgeting problem involves a decision on whether to lease or to buy a piece of equipment, or perhaps a complete industrial plant. In its simplest form, the problem presents two alternatives: a_1: lease, and a_2: buy. In more complicated versions, there may be several possible leasing agreements, and each may be regarded as an alternative.

Another type of capital budgeting problem might involve the general question of plant expansion. Alternatives might be a_1: maintain existing plant capacity now and expand only as the market grows in order to maintain existing share of the market, and a_2: build new plant now and attempt greater penetration of the market.

In some problems, there may be a large number of alternatives. For example, in an inventory problem in which orders must be placed periodically (e.g., every Monday), alternatives may be thought of as different order quantities. Thus, these alternatives may be identified by the expression

where $x = 0, 1, 2, \ldots.$

$$a_i: x$$

Any problem in portfolio selection also presents a huge number of alternative courses of action. Each alternative is a particular combination of stocks and bonds and cash. It can be appreciated that even if the purchase date and holding period for the portfolio are known, the list of candidate securities has been preselected (e.g. is a legal list for a trust), and the total size of portfolio is known, the number of potential portfolios is extremely large.

So the first lesson, or principle, of statistical decision theory is to begin by facing each problem by thinking in terms of what you can do; by thinking in terms of alternative courses of action.

States of the Problem

In every decision problem, the consequences of a decision will depend on certain variables. A "state" of the problem is a set of values that may be assumed by those variables that determine profit and loss (and other results, whatever they may be). In brief, a state is a *possible* set of facts describing the problem situation.

In those cases in which we know the value of each of these profit-and-loss determining variables, we have a decision to be made under certainty. Under certainty, by definition, we recognize only one possible state: all pertinent facts are known to the decision-maker.

The second step in formulating a decision problem formally, is to specify those variables that are pertinent in the given problem, and to consider the possible states of the problem.

If some pertinent facts are not known exactly, we have a decision problem under uncertainty. This means that the values of some of the basic variables are not known exactly (to the decision-maker), and that they may equal any of several different values. Under uncertainty, there are many possible states of the problem, to be denoted

$$s: \{s_1, s_2, \ldots, s_k\} \qquad k \geq 2.$$

We adopt the convention that these states be mutually exclusive and collectively exhaustive.

For example, reconsider the industrial inspection problem in which the alternative acts are accept, or inspect, a lot of products. The pertinent variables that we would consider are the per unit cost of inspection, k, the per unit cost of passing a defective, K, the number of units in a lot, N, and the proportion defective in the lot, π. In many problems, we may treat k, K, and N as known with certainty, but for a particular lot, the value π is uncertain. In any event, a state of the problem may be described by four values as

$$s_j: \{k, K, N, \pi\}$$

There are a number of these states, each including a different value π. The problem requires a decision under uncertainty.

Similarly, there will be several pertinent variables in a capital budgeting decision problem of whether to lease or to buy. These may include (1) the cash outlay required to buy; (2) the life of the equipment under consideration; (3) the rates of interest that will prevail over the term of the lease under consideration; (4) the tax rates that will prevail over this same period. To the extent that one or several of these pertinent variables cannot be forecast exactly, the problem is one of decision under uncertainty. A capital budgeting decision problem of plant expansion contains at least two additional variables of importance, because the decision to do nothing is considered one alternative. These new variables include market demand over the life of the old and new plant, and the investment decisions of the rest of the industry.

Consider a problem in competitive bidding for a construction award. A firm's alternatives are represented by possible bids

$$a_i: x$$
$$\text{where } x \geqq 0$$

We may regard the pertinent facts in the problem as the lowest competing bid that will be made, y, and the total cost to us to do the job, K. Neither of these values would be known exactly. The decision is under uncertainty and each of the many states would be of the form

$$s_j: \{y, K\}$$

Finally, consider a portfolio problem. The relevant variables may be considered to be the rate of growth of national income, g, during the period over which the portfolio is to be held, and the level of interest rates at the end of this period, k. If neither of these variables can be forecasted exactly, then we again have a decision problem under uncertainty with states of the form

$$s_j: \{g, k\}$$

Note that in this example, an unlimited number of states are possible.

Conditional Consequences

Our general description of a decision problem must include one other ingredient in addition to alternatives and states, namely, the possible results or consequences. For each alternative, a_i, that one might adopt, and for each possible state, s_j, there will be a set of results.

These results are conditional upon the particular a_i and s_j. To describe a decision problem completely we must consider the results of all possible combinations of a_i and s_j. A particular set of results may be denoted c_{ij}. In some problems, it is possible to measure c_{ij} solely in terms of profit and loss. In others, of course, at least part of the results that we wish to consider will be of a non-monetary nature.

For example, as we have previously formulated the problem of industrial inspection for a lot of manufactured products, the alternatives are a_1: accept, and a_2: inspect, while states are described by s_j: $\{k, K, N, \pi\}$. Results or consequences are represented by total costs and equal

$$c_{1j} = N\pi K$$
$$c_{2j} = Nk$$

The first expression equals the number of defectives passed times the per unit cost of passing one, while the second equals the number of parts in a lot times the per unit cost of inspecting a part.

In the competitive bidding problem we formulated above, alternatives were possible bids a_i: x where $x \geqq 0$. States were defined in terms of two variables: y, the lowest competing bid that would be made and K, the cost to us of the job. Conditional consequences may be measured in terms of revenues as follows:

$$c_{ij} = \begin{cases} x\text{-}K & \text{if } x < y \\ 0 & \text{if } x > y \end{cases}$$

The top part of this function gives the profit if our bid is lower than the lowest competing bid, while the bottom part reflects the possibility that we are underbid and lose the contract.

To summarize, there are three things that a decision-maker must specify to formulate a decision problem in the formal terms that we have been discussing. These are: (1) his set of alternatives, a; (2) the variables pertinent to the problem and the set of possible states, s; (3) the complete set of conditional consequences, c_{ij}. Given these facts, any decision problem may be thought of as a matrix or "payoff" table of the kind shown in Table 1.

For another example, consider again a plant expansion decision, and assume that the main variable which cannot be forecast exactly is the investment decision of competing firms. If the relevant states are

Table 1

Act	State					
	s_1	s_2	...	s_j	...	s_k
a_1	c_{11}	c_{12}	...	c_{1j}	...	c_{1k}
a_2	c_{21}	c_{22}	...	c_{2j}	...	c_{2k}
.						
.	...	...	...	...	...	...
.						
a_i	c_{i1}	c_{i2}	...	c_{ij}	...	c_{ik}
.						
.	...	...	...	...	...	...
.						
a_m	c_{m1}	c_{m2}	...	c_{mj}	...	c_{mk}

(a) competition maintains existing capacity and (b) competition increases capacity by, say, half with the construction of new facilities, we have a 2×2 payoff table. Rather than express consequences in terms of dollar profits, suppose we scale these in terms of invested capital so that the entries in the table represent rates of return on the capital invested in the firm subsequent to the capital budget decision. Hypothetically, we might have the following;

	States	
Alternatives	*Competition Maintains Capacity*	*Competition Builds New Plant*
Maintain capacity	.10	.04
Build new plant	.15	.02

Comments on Formulating the Problem

Thus far, our discussion has been limited to describing a decision problem in a rather formal way. We have said nothing about how to reach a decision about a problem. Nevertheless, this mode of formal description is itself a powerful tool. It provides a way of thinking about problems.

Clearly, a good deal of preliminary work may be needed to formulate a particular problem. Identification of alternative courses of action that are worthy of consideration, and recognition that certain facts are useful as a basis for evaluating alternatives, is largely an art. In any event, decision theory starts with the formal description of a problem that we have discussed and it presumes that such a description is feasible.

The formal description is sometimes referred to as a mathematical model of the problem. The model presumably incorporates those facts that the decision-maker considers pertinent, and also includes the assumptions that he wishes to make, or has to make. The problem, as formulated, is a model of the real problem to the extent that in some ways it may ignore or assume away certain real complexities.

The word "model" causes apprehension among some business people. To them, it suggests a lack of reality. It should not do so. It is true that most models of decision problems are simplifications of the real problems that they supposedly represent. However, informal (non-mathematical) analyses of the same decision problems that are faced every day by business people or scientists, also require simplifications, omissions, and assumptions in synthesizing pertinent facts. Human minds are capable of weighing only a limited number of factors in an analysis of any complex problem, whether the analysis is mathematical or not. And at least mathematical models make simplifications, omissions, and assumptions quite explicit.

For example, in the portfolio selection problem, the predetermination of a holding period may be patently unrealistic by itself, but repeated analysis for alternative holding periods will then explicitly demonstrate the effect of this variable upon portfolio composition.

A decision-maker rarely, if ever, analyzes a real problem. He merely analyzes his own version of the real problem.

Decisions Under Certainty

We now turn to methods of solving decision problems. A solution to a decision problem, of course, is a choice of one of the available alternatives.

Under-certainty solutions are conceptually simple, though in any given problem, the solution may be quite burdensome to actually work out (*a la* mathematical programming). An example of such a problem is determining what schedule of coupon rates a bidding syndicate should assign to an issue of municipal serial bonds. The general aim of the problem may be straightforward and simple: minimize net interest cost. But the computations required to accomplish this objective may be somewhat tedious (particularly without an electronic computer).

Decisions under certainty are conceptually simple because presumably, the decision-maker is certain what the consequences of his act will be. The decision-maker may, therefore, solve a problem under certainty merely by determining which alternative course of action will lead to what he, the decision-maker, considers the most desirable result. This may, for example, be represented by maximum revenue or minimum cost.

Furthermore, some decisions under uncertainty may be transformed into certainty decisions if the decision-maker is willing to assume, for example, that his forecasts as to states of nature are reasonably accurate. Although some extensions have been made in recent years to incorporate uncertainty, the highly developed apparatus of linear programming, for example, assumes implicitly that all of the relevant states of nature are known in advance.

Decisions Under Uncertainty

However, uncertain conditions mean that the decision-maker is not sure exactly what the consequences of any action will be because he is not exactly sure of his facts—there are several possible states of his problem. The choice of any particular act will lead to results that differ with the state that actually happens to apply.

Uncertainty, *per se*, is not new. Decisions under uncertain conditions are made in informal ways every day. In general, what is a reasonable way to analyze such a problem? First of all, a decision-maker should want to consider the likelihood of each of the possible states of the problem. Secondly, he would want to consider the relative desirability of the various consequences. Finally, he should choose the act that, in his judgment, provides the best bet, considering the likelihood and the desirability of the consequences that a given act might lead to.

Decision Theory

We shall now consider a formal method for analyzing a decision problem under uncertain conditions that incorporates the informal ideas just discussed. The method is a quantitative approach to decisions under uncertainty in the sense that it requires a decision-maker to quantify his aims and his judgement in any given problem. The approach is sometimes called statistical decision theory and sometimes Bayesian analysis, as already explained.

Decision theory requires a decision-maker to take two preliminary steps in the analysis of a decision problem: (1) He must scale his preferences for the possible consequences in risky (uncertain) situations in terms of a so-called "utility measure." (2) He must express his judgments on the likelihood of the different states of the problem in terms of a so-called "probability measure."

The subsequent steps involved in decision theory are simply (a) the computation of expected (average) utility for each act and, (b) the choice of that act with the largest expected utility. All of this follows from the fact that utility is defined and measured in such a way that a decision-maker should logically want to act on the basis of expected utility.

Thus, given stated preferences and judgments, decision theory provides a framework within which a decision-maker can analyze a complex problem and deduce what course of action he should rationally adopt. Hence, the theory merely offers a method of logical and consistent analysis. If a decision-maker can supply the two basic inputs in quantitative form, he can solve any decision problem by subsequent numerical computation.

It is to be stressed that decision theory merely offers a decision-maker ways of formally expressing his preferences and judgments about the details of his problem (namely, consequences and states). Focusing on these basic factors explicitly will presumably lead to better decisions than attempting to synthesize preferences and judgments without the aid of a formal approach.

Personal Probability

It should not be surprising that a great deal of the theory of decisions under uncertainty is involved with probability theory and probabilistic concepts. This has led to a reappraisal of these concepts. As we have already noted, one part of the analysis called for by decision theory requires a decision-maker to express his judgment about the likelihood of the various possible states of the problem in terms of a probability measure. However, most decision theorists feel it is more meaningful to view probability differently from the way classical statisticians have. In the past, virtually all statisticians have defined probability to mean long-run relative frequency. The people who have developed decision theory, however, feel probabilistic concepts are more useful if probability is interpreted to represent personal betting odds. This approach gives rise to the terms "subjective probability" or "personal probability."

It is to be stressed that even according to the subjective approach, we expect a decision-maker, in assessing probabilities, to be influenced by his past experience with related events and, where it is available, by the frequency with which he has observed comparable events in the past. Irrespective of his basis, however, decision theory is based on the assumption that the decision-maker can express his judgments probabilistically. He is to reach these judgments, according to the theory, by introspection.

According to the subjectivist theory, the process of introspection involves comparison with a standard lottery of one type or another. Thus, to assess his personal betting odds for some event, E, a decision-maker may imagine himself being in the position of trying to win a large amount of money (or some other valuable prize). He wins if (a) the event E occurs, or if (b) a red bead is drawn from a supply of beads which includes a known proportion of red beads equal to p. For what value of p would he be indifferent between his alternative vehicles for winning? This value is defined as his personal probability of the event E actually occurring.

The point of a lottery is merely to fix a personal standard against which to measure one's personal probability. The standard need not involve selection of beads. Other, perhaps more meaningful, forms for this standard may be designed. In fact, the decision-maker may wish to think in terms of long-run relative frequencies rather than a standard lottery in assessing his personal probabilities.

In any event, objective evidence on the relative frequency with which comparable events have occured in the past provides useful information to anyone who must assess personal probabilities. What information is relevant, and how much weight to give to different types of evidence, is up to the individual. His final judgments are, of course, reflected in his personal probability.

For example, consider a credit manager's decision problem on whether or not to extend credit to an applicant for a loan to purchase an automobile. The alternative acts are simply a_1: extend credit, and a_2: do not extend credit. States might be defined in terms of whether or not the applicant will successfully complete the required payments, so that s_1: complete repayment, and s_2: repossession necessary.

For a given applicant, what is the probability that all payments will be made? From the point of view of personal probability, this is a question for the decision-maker. It is to be stressed that different credit managers with different backgrounds of experience may tend to give varying weight to different factors and might well assess a given applicant's chances for repayment somewhat differently.

Any credit manager would consider the nature of the proposed transaction itself and the applicant's personal qualifications. He could then resort to introspection, including consideration of a standard lottery, to assess the probability of repayment. If he determines that a value of $p = .75$ in the standard lottery is his indifference point, then .75 is the probability he assigns to the possible state, s_1. Because probabilities are defined to sum to one over mutually exclusive and collectively exhaustive outcomes, the probability of the state s_2 would then be $1 - .75 = .25$.

The process of assessing personal probabilities, as we have discussed it, is abstract to the point where many practitioners may find it difficult to employ, at least formally. Two points may be made in this connection. First of all, in a great many problems, the probabilities that one assigns to states of the problem can be based directly on objective evidence in the form of historical relative frequencies. For example, if in the selection problem the holding period is indefinite, then it might be entirely appropriate to estimate probabilities for interest rate levels and natural income growth rates on the basis of historical relative frequencies. Nevertheless, in all of these problems in which past data is used, some thought must be given to the comparability of these data and the extent to which the available objective facts do reflect one's personal betting odds. Thus, the formal process involving a standard lottery is useful as a way of checking out the applicability of the available facts.

Secondly, it may be remarked that the mathematical theory of probability provides a number of tools to help a decision-maker assess probabilities to states of the problem. We shall discuss the role of probability theory in the decision-making process in more detail below.

Utility Theory

Actually, even before he assesses personal probabilities to the various states of his problem, a decision-maker should attend to one other preliminary. This first task is to express his preferences for the possible consequences in risky or uncertain situations in terms of a utility measure. This measure is intended to reflect the decision-maker's preferences in quantitative terms. Utility is measured in a way that requires a decision-maker to act on the basis of average (expected) utility; that is, on the basis of the average utility of all consequences that might occur for a given act, these utilities being weighted according to the probabilities assigned to the possible states of the problem.

With respect to a measuring scale, we may first note that this utility measure must be unique only to the extent of a linear transformation. Therefore, we can always set the minimum and maximum values of the utility measure arbitrarily. If in a given problem, c^* is the most desirable consequence and c_* is the least desirable consequence, we shall denote the utilities assigned to these consequences by u^* and u_*, respectively. As noted, u^* and u_* can be set arbitrarily, except that $u^* > u_*$.

A decision-maker determines the utility of any other set of consequences, c_{ij}, by introspection—in particular, by answering the following question: suppose that you were offered a choice between the two sets of consequences (a) c_{ij} with certainty and (b) c^* with probability p and c_* with probability $1\text{-}p$. For what value of $p = p'$ would you be indifferent between the two alternatives? (Presumably for $p < p'$, c_{ij} would be preferred, while for $p > p'$, the $c^* = c_*$ combinations would be preferred.) Given the answer to this question, the utility of c_{ij} is, by definition,

$$u_{ij} = p' u^* + (1\text{-}p') u_*$$

(If we adopt the convention that $u^* = 1$ and $u_* = 0$, then $u_{ij} = p'$ and our measuring scale is simplified.) This utility measure is to be evaluated for all sets of possible consequences.

Can a businessman actually assess a utility function? The best answer, probably, is that some can for some problems, and some cannot for any problem. A person has to train himself to think in quantitative terms, and this is not easily developed. However, in many problems where consequences can be measured in monetary terms, a decision-maker is willing to act on the basis of expected monetary value. This means that his utility measure is linearly related to money. If so, the application of decision theory is simplified because a ready-made scale of preferences is available for use in the analysis. Use of expected monetary value will usually be reasonable when the amounts of money involved are not viewed as extremely large by the decision-maker. With respect to the ticket problem, it is extremely likely that most commuters would want to act on the basis of expected monetary value.

On the other hand, if outcomes in the portfolio problem are defined as current yield plus rate of capital appreciation, utilities might be linearly related to expected monetary outcomes only for relatively small total dollar portfolios.

For another example, the utility measure in the plant expansion problem would not be, in all likelihood, a linear function of rates of return for a number of reasons. First, the total dollar commitment may differ greatly between maintaining expanding plant; second, the owner-manager (or stockholder) may be contemplating alternative uses of the funds (dividends, government bonds) which have some value; and third, the tax status of the owner-manager (or stockholder) may not be linearly related to the various outcomes of the capital budgeting decision.

In those cases where abnormally large amounts are at stake, or where non-monetary consequences play an important role, a utility measure must be constructed explicitly if decision theory is to be applied.

Summary of the Procedure

In summary, then, statistical decision theory requires three steps in the analysis of a decision problem: (1) The decision-maker scales his preferences for the possible consequences in terms of a utility measure, u_{ij}. (2) He assesses his personal probabilities for the various possible states of the problem, to be denoted $P(s_j)$. (3) He calculates, for each act, the expected utility over all possible states, weighting according to the likelihood of those states,

$$E\ (u_{ij}) = \sum_j \{u_{ij} P(s_j)\}$$

The act with the largest expected utility is the one chosen.

The Role of Probability Theory

Now that we have completed our discussion of the basic framework of decision theory, we shall turn to the other part of the subject—statistical and mathematical techniques. We will deal with the general nature of the techniques and with the role they play in the theory. We shall not discuss specific methods.

In particular, we shall consider the role of the mathematical theory of probability and the use of statistical information in the decision-making process.

In general, the mathematical theory of probability helps develop the answers to somewhat complicated questions, with which one has had little direct experience, based on answers to the simpler questions one has had more experience with. It is a method of logical thinking. It provides a businessman or scientist with the opportunity to use his judgment and experience most effectively, because it allows him to answer questions to which his judgment and experience apply most directly.

Probability theory can often play this same kind of role in decision problems. Thus, probability theory will provide a tool for use by a decision-maker in assigning personal probabilities to states of a problem. That is, in some problems, the decision-maker may answer questions on which his past experience and judgment bear most directly, and then use these answers, together with appropriate probability theory, to calculate the probabilities of the various states of the problem.

Bayes' Theorem and Statistical Information

One formula of probability theory that is particularly useful in assessing the probabilities assigned to states of a problem is called Bayes' theorem. From a mathematical point of view, Bayes' theorem is merely a special way of writing out the standard formula for calculating conditional probabilities. It does, however, have great significance in decision theory as is indicated by frequent references in the literature to Bayesian analysis.

Bayes' formula may be written as

$$P(s_j|x) = \frac{P(x|s_j)\,P(s_j)}{\sum_i P(x|s_i)\,P(s_i)}$$

This formula is particularly useful for decision problems in which additional evidence in the form of sample information is made available to the decision-maker. (As the formula is written here, x represents a set of sample results.) The decision-maker must then revise the probabilities that he assigned to the states of the problem, prior to learning the sample results. In the formula, $P(s_j)$ represents these prior probabilities, and $P(s_j|x)$ represents the revised or posterior probabilities—that is, the probabilities to be assigned to the states of the problem given the additional information, x.

In order to use Bayes' theorem, one must have prior probabilities $P(s_j)$ and conditional probabilities $P(x|s_j)$. It is usually easier to assess these probabilities from past experience and judgment rather than to assess $P(s_j|x)$ directly. (If it is not easier, one should assess $P(s_j|x)$ directly.) Thus, Bayes' theorem—like every other formula from probability theory—merely provides a means to answer complicated questions on the basis of answers to simpler questions.

In brief then, Bayes' theorem provides a basis by which sample information may be incorporated in the decision-making process—hence the term, "Bayesian analysis."

Expected Cost of Uncertainty

A decision made under uncertainty is subject to the risk of turning out to be, after the actual state of the problem is known with certainty, the wrong decision—in the sense that a better alternative is available for the correct state. Some measure of the expected loss from incorrect decisions that are risked under uncertainty is desirable. Among other things, it guides the decision-maker in deciding whether or not to try to reduce uncertainty by gathering additional information.

To define such a measure, we first note that the expected utility of the optimal act in a problem may be written

$$\max_{i} \left\{ \underset{j}{E}(u_{ij}) \right\}$$

because the act for which expected utility is a maximum is the one adopted. Next, suppose that the correct state could be ascertained before choosing an alternative. For a given state, the act for which u_{ij} was a maximum would be adopted. The expected value of this maximum u_{ij} over all states is called expected utility under certainty, and may be written as

$$\underset{j}{E} \left\{ \max_{i} u_{ij} \right\}$$

This expected maximum will be larger than (or equal to) the maximum expectation written above, and the difference between them is called the expected cost of uncertainty,

$$
E_j \left\{ \max_i u_{ij} \right\} - \max_i \left\{ E_j (u_{ij}) \right\}
$$

This quantity is of considerable interest in decision theory. For example, it represents the maximum value one would attach to perfect information. Imperfect information is, of course, less valuable.

Design of Statistical Studies

A special topic of interest to statisticians is the design of statistical studies. In the simplest cases, this merely involves a decision on the size sample that is required. In other cases, decisions must be made on allocating a sample among strata and on choosing levels of variables in an experiment.

The problem of statistical design of studies may be regarded, conceptually, as a particular type of decision problem. Alternatives are represented by different possible designs, such as random samples of different sizes.

The value of any sample result is the amount by which it reduces the expected cost of uncertainty, as we previously defined it. In the planning stage of a study, there are, of course, many possible sample results—the actual result that will occur is uncertain. Each result will change the expected cost of uncertainty by some given amount. The value of a particular sample design is the expected value of these changes. The aim of the statistician working on a problem is to maximize the difference between the value and the cost of a sample design.

The process of evaluating the value of a sample design is sometimes called preposterior analysis. Much of the current research in the field of decision theory is concerned with this topic.

Implications for the Future

In the past few years, great interest in statistical decision theory and Bayesian analysis has developed in the business world. What implications does it have for the man in business? In my opinion, the theory's main contribution is that it provides a new and important philosophy of management decision-making, whether or not the specific details of the theory are formally applied. There is little doubt that over the next several years, statistical decision theory will have a major impact on business decision-making practices.

DAVID B. HERTZ

New Management Concepts
and Tools

12 Management science techniques—including the imaginative and effective use of computer systems—have already given many firms decisive advantages over competitors. These techniques have revolutionized management processes by changing not only the information inputs on which major business decisions are based, but also the kinds of decisions made and even the key factors for success in these decisions.

Specific applications of management science—such as operations research, critical-path scheduling techniques and PERT, business model-building, and the emerging systems analysis approaches—have gained renown through their use by large corporations and government agencies. One major foods processor, for example, initially applied management science techniques to develop a model that would aid in routing shipments of one of its products from some six plants to 70 warehouses. The new system cut direct shipping costs by many hundreds of thousands of dollars each year, and this same company later planned its entire national system of warehousing for all products with management science methods.

One of the largest paper products companies has developed a special variety of systems analysis for evaluating proposed new products, and consequently its performance is significantly better than the 75 per cent to 95 per cent failure rate for new-product introductions characteristic of the nation's 200 leading packaged-goods manufacturers. A major aircraft corporation applies management science extensively in its long-range economic and sales forecasting. PERT is used to control enormously complex manufacturing development operations in one highly diversified organization, while a leading oil company gets hard data on the risks and returns of its major capital investment opportunities through management science.

But management science is by no means limited to the nation's biggest businesses. In fact, seasoned practitioners have found that the profit ratio for the smaller company is likely to be higher than it is for the large corporation. One firm of modest size, for instance, manufactured 20 different kitchen sink models for which it frequently changed its single assembly line. Changeover costs ate deeply into profits, so the company put a management science team to work on reducing the costs. The team produced a set of production scheduling rules that resulted in cutting costs by one third.

Another small company sold a line of portable machines to industrial users, and its concern lay in a completely different area—marketing. It assigned a management science group to examine routine sales visits. Salesmen were calling only on about two-fifths of their accounts in any one quarter by rule of thumb, but the company had no idea whether this was too many or too few. The researchers first determined that an account had, on the average, a 30 per cent chance of becoming inactive if it was not called on in a quarter; even if active, the account would produce only 70 per cent of the business that a sales call would otherwise realize. The combined difference came to about 50 per cent more business from an account if called on. However, the group looked further into the effect of rising volume on manufacturing and distribution costs, and worked out a detailed plan for maximum profit (at the level of highest sales consistent with economical costs). The firm's management thus obtained a really solid justification for increasing routine sales calls on accounts by 50 per cent, and reaped a six-figure increase in annual gross sales with a spectacular rise in net profits.

Clearly, management science has demonstrated its effectiveness and has become sufficiently widespread so that no executive can afford to ignore its opportunities or its pitfalls. Any executive who has failed thus far to develop a general understanding of what it is and how to take advantage of it may now be endangering not only his company's future, but his own. On the other hand, management science is still just at the beginning of its development and application, and managers at almost all levels and in virtually any kind of business function can find many opportunities for increasing their success.

First, a brief review of the general character and very recent origin of management science should prove helpful. What has already been said indicates why management science has become one of the fastest growing new approaches to problem solving. Almost every graduate business school or school of industrial administration or engineering now gives or is actively planning courses in management science or in operations research, quantitative methods, computer systems, or mathematical programming—terms for various areas of management science.

Management science applications today can be likened to those of accounting 30 years ago and of statistical quality control twenty years ago. Even now, not all firms use good cost accounting methods; not all businesses use, nor do all need, statistical quality control. Yet both these tools are unquestionably accepted as a part of sound management. Each had to displace gradually more primitive methods and concepts; slowly, company by company, school by school, course by course, each had to develop adaptations and applications for all kinds of businesses, large and small—for manufacturing firms of all varieties, extraction enterprises, service organizations, and marketing concerns. For all these types we now have cost accounting and quality control approaches to fit every need and every purse.

Management science, being so much younger, has just begun to develop similar universally applicable approaches. Authorities generally agree that it started in the late 1930's* and came into large-scale use as the "operations research" or "operations analysis" of World War II, in which military staffs were faced with enormously complex new problems of strategic and tactical decision. In 1939 Winston Churchill called upon some of the leading scientists in England to help figure out what would *probably* be the most effective way to use the just-invented radar devices (which were in critically limited supply) to protect England. You can visualize the problem if you mentally picture the map of England, the possible attacking routes of German aircraft, the multitude of targets, the defending airfields, and the mere 20 radar sets with specified capabilities of probable detection. The very best

---

*A pre-World War II application was the use of mathematical techniques at a large department store—Bamberger's in Newark, New Jersey—under the direction of Harold Levenson, a former astronomer and then treasurer of the company, and Dr. Arthur Brown, a mathematician, to help determine the best patterns of store evening hours, advertising effectiveness, and so forth.

mathematical and scientific brains were able to work out a close-to-optimum placement of those twenty sets, and the German attackers felt their effects decisively in the historic aerial Battle of Britain.

The radar problem thus presented a number of new and complicated technical and operational variables and relationships that the military men were not used to handling and could not "optimize" with standard techniques. Operations research gave them a basis for decision by quantitatively weighing the consequences of the enormous number of alternatives and sorting them into manageable categories.

This quantitative evaluation of the consequences of proposed actions still remains as the key contribution of today's management science to the executive or decision maker. Many other assignments were undertaken during the war, some with more success than others, but all had as common features the collaboration of scientists with military men and the statement of results as quantitative evaluations of alternative ways to deal with the practical, operational problems at hand.

It became clear even in the early days that there was something new and useful here, but it took several years for a clear statement of the new approach to evolve.* Today the term "management science" has begun to seem more appropriate for the techniques of operations research and similar tools starting to emerge; it signifies, essentially, the various ways in which scientists may analyze problems of management.

One large body of today's management science techniques that continues the military OR tradition consists of developing analytical models for determining, analyzing, and presenting information about the likely costs and revenues (or benefits) that will accrue from alternative decisions in complex or uncertain business or government problems. Such work is variously called operations research, operations analysis, systems analysis, or cost-benefit analysis, depending on who is doing it and where it is being done. The purpose is improved performance through quantitatively and analytically informed decision making. The key words to remember in this area of management science are:

---

*During those years the Operations Research Society of America was founded (1953), as was the Institute of Management Sciences (1954). Both flourish and publish professional and managerial journals in the field. Many universities began to offer courses and degrees in operations research and management science, among them Case Institute of Technology, Columbia University, Carnegie University, University of Pennsylvania, Northwestern, Stanford, University of California, and Massachusetts Institute of Technology.

1. Improved analytical methods
2. Complex or uncertain business problems
3. Alternative decisions
4. Information about costs and revenues (or benefits).

Analytical models for dealing with uncertainty and complexity are thus fundamental to management science. Underlying many such applications are two branches of mathematics: *probability and statistical inference* and *higher algebra*. Because of their key role and frequent use, it will be helpful to know a bit about their contribution to the objective.

Probability and statistical mathematics are powerful and proven logical tools for helping to describe uncertainty and the outcomes of actions taken in the face of uncertainty. The future is always uncertain, and critical decisions, the results of which hinge upon the outcome of extremely variable events, must often be made. Things never happen exactly the same way twice—they fluctuate more or less widely. On the other hand, this very uncertainty provides the enterprising entrepreneur with his opportunities to introduce new products and build new business through taking risks. Sales vary from week to week; equipment breakdowns occur at different times; products come off the production line at irregular rates. Uncertainty is universal and lies at the heart of every planning and scheduling problem. The businessman's solution is to provide margins of safety or to try to anticipate uncertain opportunities—inventory in the warehouse to meet unexpected demand, spare parts to guard against equipment failure, standby labor to keep production lines from becoming bottlenecked, research staffs to develop and market new products.

But margins of safety are expensive, and risk-taking can be dangerous as well as profitable. Uncertainty is the manager's enemy as well as his opportunity. This is an ideal problem for the logic of probability—the measurement and determination of the limits of uncertainty. What are the odds on tossing ten heads in a row? This is perhaps similar to asking about the chances of getting ten customers per day for an item with a usual demand of one per day. Management science uses statistical methods to evaluate the size of the safety margin that must be provided for a given probability of serving customers within specified costs. The cost of carrying extra inventory is balanced against the cost of special handling or loss of sales, through statistics that provide means for determining the probability of running out of stock for any given inventory level.

There are many other problems in which statistical methods are useful as a management science tool. For example, how many check-out counters should be provided in supermarkets to avoid excess waiting lines, or how many truck-loading positions are required at shipping platforms? The best sizes and locations of warehouses and other material-handling facilities can also often be determined through the use of these techniques. And the concepts of probability and statistical methods play a large role in risk analyses of investment alternatives.

The second type of frequently used mathematical logic—the solution of complex sets of equations that describe a given situation (and specifically, what are called linear programming and mathematical programming)—deals with problems combining many variables or factors to give combinations that best achieve a specific objective. For example, the best combination of feed stocks and process methods, to yield the most profitable mix of products at a petroleum refinery, is today invariably determined by linear programming methods. As can be imagined, such methods help businessmen solve problems of great complexity. Management of a modern business involves the need to select from a great many possible courses of action some particular combination that will satisfy in the most profitable way a variety of simultaneous conditions, constraints on resources, or output requirements.

Thus, a producer of animal feeds can use any number of combinations of ingredients, each costing different amounts and perhaps subject to daily changes, to meet the nutrient and bulk requirements of the feeds he markets. The requirements are known, as are the costs; the objective is to produce each feed at its lowest cost to meet his demand, and at the same time to satisfy the nutritional and other objectives. Through the tool of linear programming this problem can be solved directly and simply—and when it has been done, the very best answers, as well as the costs of any alternatives to the best answer, are clearly spelled out. In addition, linear programming provides the answer to an oft-times puzzling problem: what is the value of relieving a restraint? Given that ingredient X is available in limited quantity at price Y, how much more X is it worth buying and substituting into the feed formula at the higher price? Or, given that the demand for feed A at price B is limited, how great will be the benefit of reducing the price to increase demand? These and many other questions are clearly and explicitly answered by linear programs.

As a tool for determining the best allocation of resources to activities or operations to accomplish an objective, linear programming is amazingly versatile. It can be used to determine what products should be made on which machines in a machine shop, how paper rolls should be most economically cut into strips of specified sizes, or how to schedule the most efficient order of steps in building a house, an office building, or a group of houses in a development. For the businessman, linear programming has provided a means which helps to solve not only such complex problems as these, but also problems of keeping costs of production, shipping, or storage at a minimum; or of maintaining the lowest inventory consistent with customer-service requirements; or of combinations of problems like these.

Thus, to help make business choices in the best manner, management science attempts to provide the businessman with improved methods or systems for obtaining and using information on the cost and revenue relationships in his business. These systems relate to problem areas in which every businessman must have definite ideas and make decisions, whether he does so systematically or not. The areas for improvement in information will provide the basis for decisions across many problems.

Every businessman—whether his business is large or small—must take a long-range view of the future. (This is true even if he wishes to ignore the future completely by assuming it to be a total blank; even this approach can be systematized by some of the methods of management science.) Many of the businessman's decisions will, of course, be influenced by the way in which he assembles and analyzes information about the long-range future. The information he must deal with for this long-range view includes product demands, competition, price changes, and cost patterns, among others. The management scientist helps assemble such key information effectively to provide the basis for determining the likely consequences of alternative courses of action.

Working backwards from the long-range future, a businessman must develop ways of looking at the short range—tomorrow, next week, or next month. Once again, no matter how he does it, he has to have some way of deciding how much inventory to stock, how many people to hire, how much cash he needs. It will be recognized that many accounting and control methods are used to this end. It is when the situation is complicated by many factors and by uncertainty that management science comes to his aid, as, for example, in setting inventory levels to meet desired customer service when demand is uncertain.

Another problem area in which everyone has some kind of system is that of the allocation of resources to requirements. As we have already seen, management science has been particularly helpful in this area—in the assignment of repair crews to minimize the costs of labor, materials, and downtime; in the release of orders to plants or machines; in the distribution of raw materials among processing units; and in countless similar functions.

The businessman must also decide on the sequence of activities which he, his machines, and his personnel will carry out. And he would like to do this at the best level of profitability. In other words, he must specify who does what, and when. Routing of trucks, control of construction and maintenance projects, salesmen's routes, scheduling of machine operations—all these represent a few of the innumerable applications of management science methods for sequencing activities.

Another kind of problem that businessmen face is the acquisition of resources, be they raw materials, machines, spare parts, or people. Often efficiency can be improved through the use of the new techniques in providing cost and benefit information for such purposes as commodity buying, replacement of equipment, and determination of relative efficiencies of various combinations of new machines or even new plants.

A moment's reflection will indicate that these areas are far from unrelated. For example, both short-range and long-range forecasting are unquestionably involved in resource balancing, activity sequencing, and resource acquisition. With this in mind one can appreciate how the introduction of new and improved techniques in any of these areas can spread a beneficial influence throughout a firm.

Thus, management science can successfully build models to aid decision makers in large and small firms in answering a variety of questions such as the following:

1. What capital investment projects should be accepted?
2. How much money should the company tie up in inventory?
3. To what extent should larger orders be used to take advantage of quantity discounts?
4. How can plant capacity be utilized in combination with fluctuating demand to maintain lowest overall production cost?
5. How should production be scheduled—by machine or by process?
6. How should a construction or maintenance project be scheduled?
7. How does the cost of maintenance and repairs change over the

life of a piece of equipment, and how will its resale value probably change?

8. What is the best transportation, warehouse, and delivery routing
combination?

The result of management science applied to such a problem is an
information structure specifying the cost and revenue consequences
of alternative operating decisions under given sets of management
policies and external conditions. In addition, such a system should
predict performance under alternative policies, external conditions,
and contingent plans. These studies provide insight into the relations
between operating conditions, business performance, and the related
decision-making processes. In practice, they often identify, beyond
any question, the course that will minimize costs and maximize income.

How may a company go about employing these new techniques?
First, a note of caution: there is no magic here. Sound results require
sound data. The information house must be in order if anything significant is to be accomplished by detailed analyses. On the other hand,
starting management science studies of critical problem areas can
lead to the pinpointing of weaknesses and information requirements.

Once a solid information base is assured, a company should take
either of two initial steps and then a second step. As a first step, key
executives should do a little boning up on management science; they
should try to decide on problem areas; and they should have at least
one good man ready to start the work. They must then be patient,
because studies take time—time to obtain data, to develop relationships,
to let events begin to jell for implementation, and so forth.

An alternative first step is to train (in special university courses and
readily available seminars) an able man from the company's own
staff in the techniques of management science—preferably one who
is himself already trained in physical science and mathematics. After
his special training, the company should let him start off slowly on
relatively easy projects; he should report to a sympathetic high-level
executive sponsor who will give him a chance to learn and develop.
A variant of this step would be to hire a graduate of one of the management science programs offered at business schools or engineering
colleges—and give him perhaps still longer to learn and develop.

As a virtually essential second step, the company's chief executive
(or another key executive) should take an interest in the venture and
support it fully at the very top of the company. Lack of wholehearted

support by top management severely reduces the chance of success for any mangement science program.

Management science techniques, in sum, are practical ones that apply to problems faced by most companies regardless of size. They can no longer be viewed in any sense as merely "blue sky" theorizing. Their wide and successful use puts this question squarely before each executive: are the data and information on which you base your decisions the best you can get—particularly if you know of better methods readily available to your competitors?

In conclusion we can say that the systems provided by management science do not, in themselves, create a capability for overall planning and control; they only provide the tools. Thus, another very important part of this kind of activity is to determine how a complex modern organization can develop the capability for *using* integrated management science approaches and the associated new techniques effectively. This naturally raises the question, what does modern management *capability* really mean? It means that an organization must meet five basic requirements:

1. It must understand and accept the need for the modern tools necessary to do its key tasks.

2. It must have, or design, these needed tools.

3. It must implant the skills and get the people required to use these tools effectively.

4. It must establish the motivation in all those who are important in the development and implementation processes to do the job agreed upon.

5. Finally, it must get at the key problem of making all these new procedures, new techniques, and new hardware tools a part of its everyday administrative and decision-making processes.

In other words, the new approach to management must become a way of life in an organization. Thus, to a large complex enterprise, which cuts across many scientific, management, and industrial boundaries, having a management science capability implies that an understanding or acceptance of new ideas exists, that tools are to be developed, that skills are to be established, that motivation is to be implanted, and that use is to be ensured.

As management science moves forward, it will continue to change management's environment. Decision making will move to a new and perhaps more difficult level. We have already increased our theoretical understanding of the economics of decision making, and we have developed some methods to apply such understanding to specific problems. We now face the job of making choices among methods and improving our use of these new tools.

The answer to the question of whether management decision making can be automated seems to be that if a decision can be automated, it is no longer a management function. Management will continue to "make decisions" no matter what algorithms are supplied by the management scientist. Effective leadership will lie in the area of decision-making. This will be apparent both to the decision-maker and to those who are affected by the decisions. Management will retain the sense of making choices, of having and using preferences, and of forming resolutions to action. These will continue to be as real as they are today, or, in an artistic sense, even more real—for the deeper one's understanding, the more meaning can be deduced or inferred from a situation.

In fact, by the use of these new decision-making tools and concepts, the environment in which management operates is changed and the language which management speaks is changed. Events are seen through eyes so different that they take on a virtually new character. The competitive advantage of increasing understanding and increasing ability to measure, quantify, and analyze is so great that we will all be caught up by it, just as, nearly seven hundred years ago, the business world was revolutionized by double-entry bookkeeping.

INTERNATIONAL
BUSINESS

III

EDITOR'S INTRODUCTION

Since World War II, business has become multi-national. And so has the work of the business leader and thus his systematic preparation and schooling. Yet business is a social institution, and management always takes place within a cultural setting. Part Three, therefore, examines the trends of business management in several major areas outside the United States—Britain, Continental Europe, Latin America, and Japan. It also examines the multi-national corporation and the multi-national executive. What emerges is the view that the tasks of management are increasingly becoming "non-national." It is the same task everywhere. Similarly the economic and social role of the executive assumes very much the same aspect everywhere. The tools too are "non-national," and apply as well in Japan as in Western Europe or in the United States. At the same time, the specific social and cultural traditions of major areas are increasingly being made to serve effective business management. While the discipline of management is becoming truly worldwide, the practice of management is increasingly coming to be a specific cultural and social asset. Management, the six essays of Part Three seem to conclude, is pluralism in the best tradition—diversity generating organic unity.

JOHN J. POWERS, JR.

The Multi-National
Corporation

13

I

All during 1967, the best-selling book in France—
and indeed in all of continental Europe—was a book
on business. *Le Defi Americain* (*The American Challenge*), by a well-known French political journalist.
Jean-Jacques Servan-Schreiber predicted that fifteen
years hence, in the early nineteen-eighties, the world's
third-largest industrial power will be the American-
owned, multi-national companies in Europe.

The only thing wrong with this prediction is that
it has already become fact today. In 1966, the overseas production of United States-based companies
amounted to about 125 billion—a little larger than
the Gross National Products of Germany or Japan
which, in the traditional count of industrial countries,
are vying for third place behind the United States and
the Soviet Union.

At that, multi-national developments are by no
means confined to United States corporations. Indeed,
while many American companies have long operated
all over the world—Singer Sewing Machines and
International Harvester have been multi-national for
well over a century, for instance—the pioneers of the
modern multi-national corporation have been companies headquartered in the smaller European countries that were forced early by the narrowness of their

171

home market into operations beyond the national boundaries of their mother country. Unilever and Philips, both starting out in the Netherlands, are well known examples, as are the Swiss chemical and pharmaceutical companies.

Even during the last twenty years, some non-American economies have gone multi-national at least as fast as have the American companies.

Sweden, at the end of World War II, was still largely an extractive and raw-materials-producing economy. Her manufacturing industry, while technically excellent, confined itself largely to supplying the Scandinavian markets. But since 1950, the direct investment of Swedish manufacturing industry—electrical machinery, precision mechanics, advanced engineering, and so on—has grown more rapidly even than that of United States manufacturing industry, especially if figures for the investment of the United States petroleum industry abroad are taken out of the figures for total United States direct foreign investment. Total United States direct investment abroad has grown from about $12 billion in 1950, to about $60 billion in 1966—roughly doubling every six years. Total Swedish direct investment abroad in multi-national operations has grown, during the same period, from less than $100 million to about $1 billion—doubling roughly every four years. And there is reason to believe that Swiss-based multi-national investment may have grown at a similar speed.

The development of the multi-national corporation is world-wide, therefore. Still, it is the United States-based company that is leading the parade. Within less than twenty years, American business has, so to speak, built a second United States economy outside our own political boundaries.

II

What is behind this enormous growth of direct investments and consequent production in overseas markets by American-based companies?

M. Servan-Schreiber, whose book I mentioned earlier, shows one major reason: modern technology, modern transportation, and modern management require large, integrated markets. Even the largest European country is too small a market for the effective utilization of the resources required in today's large business. Indeed, even the American market, despite its continental scope and wealth, is increasingly a local market. Yet—as Servan-Schreiber points out—the governments of the larger European countries, France and Germany in particular, restrained their large companies from becoming European businesses. It was left, therefore, to the American company to convert the European "Common Market" into business opportunity and business reality.

But, equally important, has been the growing equalization of purchasing power, of tastes, of common demands. Even the poorest nation today is under pressure to provide its citizens with the health care which the modern pharmaceutical industry and its products are making available. And even in areas that are considered underdeveloped—e.g., Latin America or India—there have emerged urban mass-markets with aggregate demands that require large producing and distributing organizations equipped with highly skilled, specialized, flexible managements and with tools of analysis and control of the large business and of the advanced industrial areas.

Of course, these developments also encourage trade. And world trade has indeed grown fast. From 1950 to 1966, United States exports tripled—from $10 a year to about $29 billions. And the trade of other countries, notably Japan, grew even faster.

But in the first place, export trade and direct investment abroad are not alternatives, let alone mutually exclusive. On the contrary, they are complementary. Indeed, there is good reason to believe that the capacity to export of a highly developed industrial country such as the United States will depend increasingly on investing in manufacturing subsidiaries abroad.

Secondly, however, trade, while freer than it used to be in the nationalist thirties, is still far from free. Government regulations in the host countries may require local production by cutting off, or heavily taxing, imports of finished goods, or even of some basic materials. But, regardless of this, to compete effectively for a good share of any major market requires direct investment in that marketplace in the form of sales offices and warehouses and, at least, packaging and assembly plants, if not basic production units. It is just not possible for a mere exporter to become a major, long-term factor in a market in this second half of the twentieth century.

It is still true that many American companies are primarily oriented to the domestic market. And if there is an international division in such companies, it probably has junior status in the allocation of managerial and financial resources. Many companies have little incentive to take on the complexities of international business operations. The domestic market seems to offer sufficient opportunity. They react, therefore, somewhat negatively to the proposal to move into distant and unknown places, and to make sizeable expenditures beyond the immediate supervision of American management. It may well be that many of these companies are right in such an attitude. Their resources are limited and, with adequate potential for growth in the United States and without the depth in management that would permit a breakthrough into international operations, concentration on the domestic market may well be prudent.

However, for a company which has already realized a good share of its potential in the United States marketplace, or for a less mature company which discovers an outstanding new product that will attract strong demand everywhere, the case for worldwide marketing seems almost irresistible. To allow competitors to enjoy the growth potentialities abroad would be to concede to them substantial earnings which they can use to compete more effectively everywhere, including the domestic market. For such a company, a beginning is made with exports. But more importantly, the company will inevitably be drawn into making direct investments, first in marketing facilities, sales offices, and warehouses, and then, as necessary, with plants. And so a company, keyed to expansion under American conditions, will be drawn out of its shell. In a decade or so, a domestically-oriented management will find that it has a large proportion of its assets deployed around the world, that many of its employees are foreign citizens, that a large amount of its earnings are in foreign currencies, and that it is operating, to an important extent, outside the jurisdiction of the United States.

In these circumstances, the company finds it has not just grown—it has been transformed. In making direct investments abroad, it has become multi-national. In such a situation, though the headquarters of the company is in the United States, and though it has the large United States market at hand, it must now be organized as a world enterprise. The company's assets and efforts must now be managed multi-nationally, in accordance with market opportunities wherever they may be.

There is an immense amount of thinking going on as to the best form of organization for multi-national companies. Whatever specific solution is arrived at, it is clear that we are struggling to find patterns that will reflect new relationships within the enterprise. Most broadly, we are striving to establish appropriate relationships between the parent company and the international divisions, and between parent company management and domestic operations. Indeed, it occurs to me that one crucial test of the maturity of a multi-national company might be whether the domestic operating organization and the parent company are separate, functional entities.

But the change is not only in the organization chart. Again to the degree that the multi-national organization is mature, there will be found a change in the attitudes of its people towards a more international viewpoint. The development of an international viewpoint, however, does not take place rapidly. It must be learned, and it must be continuously emphasized. Many people at higher, as well as at lower, levels must be exposed to new experiences. There must be a continuing supply of men who have participated in both international and domestic operations. And as a continuing part of management development, these men must be given the opportunity to stretch their minds and, from varied experiences, to develop a truly worldwide view.

In addition to these organizational and personnel changes, we find that when a domestically-oriented company has gradually evolved to the point at which it can truly be described as multi-national, it must cope with some totally new issues in its new environment. Prior to World War II, to all but a very few Americans, international business meant exports-imports. The situation now is very different. As I have already pointed out, American multi-national companies have found it necessary to go abroad to do the job themselves. They put roots down in a country. They add foreign identities to their American identity. They buy land. They hire and train people. They borrow money locally. They negotiate with governments. Their operations stimulate other industries. They bring about developments in housing and education. They may become a part of a national economic development plan, or participate in a national program for the expansion of exports or reduction in imports. In other words, multi-national companies become committed to their host countries and inevitably play a significant role in their future growth.

It is obvious that a few large investments can have revolutionary effects on the developing societies of small countries. Even in developed countries, however, the cumulative impact of American investments can be considerable. They stimulate competition. They change financial institutions and practices. They transform labor-management relations. They alter social habits. They break down class barriers. Abroad as in the United States, the American company offers opportunities for talented people to get ahead without reference to social background, and thus, adds considerably to social mobility. We are accustomed to this in the United States, but abroad, where class divisions have been more rigid, this social impact of the multi-national company has been, and will be, even more dramatic.

In these circumstances, multi-national companies generate tensions. They are agents of change—socially, economically, and culturally. They are pacesetters. They reach across geographic boundaries and overlap political jurisdictions. It is not surprising, then, that the reception in host countries of multi-national companies is often mixed. For some reasons, they are welcome; for others, they are resented. They bring employment, but they also bring competition. They import technology and skills, but the foreign connections of these corporations sometimes offend national sensitivities. The dilemma is evident. All countries want to raise their standards of living, but they fear some loss of independence if foreign investment is part of the process.

But is this a realistic view? It is true that modernization has a price. But it is not so much the loss of independence as the *growth of interdependence*. The economic, as well as the political, history of nations is converging, and the multi-national company plays an important role in that convergence. Though countries may be in different stages of development, modern economies show similar characteristics. Computer plants, supermarkets, telephone systems, automobile assembly lines, and pharmaceutical production facilities are local expressions of an industrial technology that is not national, but supra-national. They would quickly become obsolete without constant feeding with new techniques and new products from abroad, and this process is, to a large extent, the work of multi-national companies.

III

But, as I have suggested, multi-national companies have not always been welcome by their host countries abroad, and because of national sensitivities, this is not completely surprising. What is surprising is that these enterprises are not infrequently regarded with some hostility by their home governments. It is a curious fact that many men in government and in universities who have done much to build up international governmental institutions in the political and financial fields, have, at the same time, failed to see the unique benefits of worldwide private industrial and financial enterprises. As Lord Cromer, former Governor of the Bank of England, said so aptly in a recent address at New York University, "Although the world has moved forward in international cooperation particularly since the last world war, governmental thinking on international investment has lagged behind that of the business and financial communities."

In the field of international direct investment, practice is clearly ahead of theory and policy, and the gap is becoming troublesome. There is a growing number of problem areas requiring that the laws and policies affecting world business be reviewed in the light of multi-national corporate operations. Multi-national companies are urged—and wish—to become good citizens of the countries in which they operate, but it is sometimes difficult for them to satisfy the political and economic demands of conflicting jurisdictions. American-based multi-national companies owe allegiance to the laws and policies of the United States, but their operating affiliates are spread across the globe and are equally subject to the laws and policies of the countries which they inhabit. Thus, at times, conflict will arise—with the multi-national corporation unwittingly caught in the middle.

It is relevant to raise a question as to how far it is always in the interests of the United States to press jurisdiction over the operations of American subsidiaries abroad. In 1961, for example, there was an effort by the United States government, partially successful, to make the foreign earnings of multi-national companies subject to United States taxes, even when these earnings never leave the host countries. Some foreign commentators have suggested that under the voluntary Balance of Payments program, the United States government reaches across national boundaries to control local business operations to their detriment. Existing United States laws governing trade with communist countries, including trade by foreign subsidiaries of American corporations, have been criticized, most noticeably in Canada. And to pose a final difficult issue, to what extent should the United States anti-trust laws, confusing as they sometimes can be to us at home, apply to actions of American-based companies overseas where such actions fit within the laws and the mores of host countries?

But the greatest threat to the multi-national corporation comes, paradoxically, from the government of the one country that has both led the development and benefited from it the most: the United States government. The voluntary restrictions of 1965 on foreign investment of American companies, and now the Mandatory Program to improve the United States balance of payments, may not even help the balance of payments in the short run. In the long run—and this may be less than three years—they are bound to do grievous, perhaps irreparable, harm to the United States balance of payments. For United States direct investment has been the goose that laid the golden eggs of foreign-exchange income all these years—in the form of exports to American subsidiaries, in the form of dividends from profits abroad, and, increasingly, in the form of purchases by foreigners of securities in the American companies which, because of their becoming multi-national businesses, grew fast and became attractive investments.

During these fifteen years, Europeans have actually invested more in American securities than American industry has invested in European manufacturing subsidiaries. And this European preference for American companies is in large part due to many of them being multi-national businesses European companies should have become, but did not.

Above all, direct investment itself has been producing a payments surplus. The flow of dividends and capital payments from subsidiaries abroad has consistently been exceeding the flow of investment funds from the United States into subsidiaries abroad. If aid-financed exports are deducted, the United States now has a deficit in its balance of trade, while net inflows from direct investments continue to be substantial.

The surplus on investment account is now the largest positive factor in the United States balance of payments. Yet, it is investment abroad that is being prohibited now in the name of improving our balance of payments. And the essential balance of payments problem is not even touched by this dangerous maneuver. For our balance of payments deficit is, of course, entirely in the public sector, and not in the private sector at all.

IV

The fundamental problem goes much deeper, however, than United States economic figures. It concerns the structure of the world economy.

It has been said that the function of the entrepreneur is to bring about new and more effective combinations of economic resources. This role involves more than passively reacting to new business conditions. It involves initiative; it involves looking ahead and acting now in the light of things to come. In a speech made in Tokyo recently, George W. Ball, former Under Secretary of State, now permanent representative to the United Nations was asked what objective we should work toward. His answer was that we must work toward the construction of a true world economy. "This is no idealistic pipe dream," he went on, "but a hard-headed prediction; it is a role into which we are being pushed by the imperatives of our own technology."

Essential to such an economy is the multi-national corporation. Indeed, the multi-national business is both the builder of a true world economy of integration and independence, and its specific institution. The growth, the freedom, and the prosperity of the multi-national corporation should therefore be a major goal of United States policy, both at home and abroad. The multi-national corporation is not only the most significant managerial achievement of the period since World War II, it is also the most significant fruit of the long American struggle for a growing and dynamic world economy and a free world community.

CHRISTIAN GASSER

The European Manager
of Tomorrow

14

Is there a "European manager?" I can claim to have worked with business executives all over the European continent, but I do not know a single one who would call himself a "European executive." There are Germans and Italians, Swiss and Danes, French and Englishmen—all proud of their nationality. There may be a European economy. But there surely is no "European manager."

The management style of the large corporations, wherever they are, might be called "international" or "cosmopolitan"—similar to the "international style" of the large office buildings whether they are located on New York's Park Avenue, in London, in Tokyo, or in Sao Paulo. Just as differences in style and structure of the large buildings reflect, as a rule, external restraints, e.g., the composition of the soil or zoning regulations, differences in the style and structure of management in the large corporations tend similarly to reflect external restraints, such as governmental pressures, laws, or limitations of the capital markets, rather than differences in managerial policies or principles. The American executive who moves from New York to Minneapolis simply moves from one suburb to another. But the Italian executive who lives in Rome but works for a multi-national corporation is likely to be reluctant to move to Copenhagen or to London and thus become an expatriate. This makes for considerable rigidity in personnel policy, but it does not make for a distinctly European management.

However, there may be one area in which one can meaningfully speak of a "European manager": the owner-manager of small-to-medium-sized businesses. In Europe such businesses still are the main source of entrepreneurship, creative design, and innovation in many areas. Here the diversity of Europe, her small scale, and her emphasis on local roots become sources of strength. Here, I believe, lies a European distinction and a European advantage. And this specific European feature is likely to become more rather than less pronounced.

These thoughts were crystallized for me last fall when I visited the European Machine Tool Exhibition in Hanover. I was greatly impressed by the diversity, the entrepreneurial vitality, and the ingenuity of the small-to-medium-sized machine tool companies which this exhibition made visible. But I took this for granted, knowing the industry rather well after many years in it. On the return trip, however, I found myself sitting next to an American machine tool manufacturer. I expected him to belittle the European performance in comparison to his own. But instead he confessed himself to be totally overwhelmed. "This European show was four to five times as large as any of our machine tool exhibitions in Chicago," he said, "and this is supposedly an old and tired industry in Europe."

We hear a good deal about the "technological gap" between America and Europe. I see no evidence of it except in those areas where the American defense and space budgets have pumped billions into research and development, e.g., in aviation, computers, and some areas of electronics. But otherwise the "gap" may run the other way. Since we in Europe do not have the lush research funds of American companies, we have had to learn to husband our resources and to make each penny do the job of two. We have, of course, a lot to learn about research. I would be the last person to admit satisfaction with our research work. We do poorly, for instance, in translating research results into marketable products, especially when compared to our American colleagues and competitors. We Europeans do not however, suffer from a "technological gap." But we do suffer from a "gap" between our scientists and engineers and our businessmen where there should be the closest cooperation. We also are still focused too much on techniques and are far too prone to consider quality to be what the design engineer likes rather than what the customer needs.

But the quality of technical work done in Europe and its results compare with the best done any place else. As a Swiss I may be forgiven for using as a proof the innovative performance of our pharmaceutical companies in Basel—Geigy, Hoffman-LaRoche, CIBA and Sandoz.

I am also rather skeptical when I hear people speak of the "management gap" between the United States and Europe. In the large American company one often finds at the top men of greater vision, courage, and drive than are commonly to be found in the—often rather bureaucratic—top echelons of the large European businesses. But at the same time, one often finds in the large American companies a lack of initiative just below the top, in important middle management positions, where the same level in Europe tends to show self-reliance and strength. I know a good many European companies where the senior functional managers can be depended upon to lead their company effectively even though top management sound an uncertain trumpet. And that Europe still retains a good deal of pride in craftsmanship makes many a good European prefer to remain an outstanding engineer rather than to become a weak president.

There also is a European tendency to use local traditions going back centuries as an excuse to stand still rather than to change. It is not always easy for the European to say yes to the dynamism of science, technology, and economy when it threatens cultural traditions that mean a great deal to him. Every European businessman needs to remind himself again and again: "Business survival and success demand of you the acceptance, indeed the encouragement, of change." But in America one finds often a faddism which embraces the new just because it is new—and sometimes, I suspect, because slogans are easier than accomplishment.

But these are differences in emphasis rather than in substance. And the differences in managerial attitudes and methods between various industries—for example, compare the steel industry with the pharmaceutical industry or the department stores—are more pronounced, I believe, than the differences between the same industries on either side of the Atlantic.

The structural requirements of the large business determine in large measure the management it develops rather than geography or history.

But the *role* of the small-to-medium-sized business is indeed specifically European. Of course, there are many such businesses in the United States—I myself have been working in close contact with quite a few of them for years. But the typical small-to-medium-sized American business exists in symbiosis with a large business, as a supplier or distributor. The typical European business of this kind is autonomous. The American small or medium-sized business wants to become big. It feels that its size is a reflection on management competence. The typical European business of this kind does no more want to become big business than the grasshopper wants to become an elephant. It wants rather to become the best business of its kind. The small and medium-sized business in America tends to see itself as a "follower," but the typical small-to-medium-sized European business is the leader, if only in a narrow segment of industry or technology. The small-to-medium-sized American business tends to be local, but in Europe it is often the medium-sized business that is world-wide. Surprisingly, it is the large European business, especially in the major countries, that is under constant government pressure to be purely national, that is French, German, or British. The small, independent businessman of Europe may have a narrow focus, but his range tends to be world-wide. To give some typical examples: a family-owned company employing barely 200 people, yet the world leader in an important segment of the instrument industry; a quite small Austrian company—perhaps no more than 400 employees—and located in a small town tucked away in the mountains, with world-wide leadership in cutting tools for haying: sickles, scythes, and cutting blades that are being used wherever haying goes on; a firm in Switzerland producing miniature ball bearings, which exports 95 per cent of its production all over the world, yet employs no more than 300 people.

The American business traveller in remote corners of the world more often than not works for one of the "multi-national" giants. His European counterpart on the airplane seat next to him is more likely to be one of the top men of an Austrian sickle manufacturer, a French or Swiss maker of specialized textile machinery, or an English manufacturer of automatic ovens for bakeries—all small businesses, yet all world-wide and all leaders. Where the traditions of Europe are restraints on the large business, they are sources of strength for the small entrepreneur.

Switzerland for instance, one of the smallest countries of Europe, is divided into three cultures and speaks four languages. Politically it consists of 25 separate sovereignties and 3,000 municipalities enjoying substantial local autonomy. We do not consider this diversity a source of weakness but a source of strength. It creates an atmosphere in which the independence and diversity of the small or medium-sized business and its voluntary concentration on a segment of technology and market, are sources of strength and of pride and an attraction to good people. Similarly, what is a great weakness for large business in our capital market is strength for the independent small business. In America the capital market "pushes" a business to be large, because the capital market is based on a multitude of individuals looking for equity investments, and therefore for businesses large enough to "go public." We in Europe lack this kind of capital market. Instead, the European banker—simultaneously a commercial and an investment banker—channels the capital of the economy into investments. He tends to encourage businesses that are vigorous enough to deserve financial support and yet still so small as not to absorb a large share of the bank's resources.

I expect rapid growth of large business in Europe. But I expect the small-to-medium-sized business to further develop its own strength and to become even more important. The question, what does the independent middle-sized business need in management, I therefore see as central to the future of business and management in Europe. Let me offer these general observations.

1. We do need better management. Large companies, whether European or American, seem to me to require above all, entrepreneurial spark. This the medium-sized business must have or it does not last long. But it often lags behind in using new management principles. One still finds the belief that "management is for the big ones; we can get by with disorganized improvisation." In the European medium-sized business this is readily apparent in manufacturing. Here our American competitors are way ahead of us on the average. The American plant operates at half the lead-time of our plants, especially for long runs. When I visit an American company I find myself full of admiration. In the past European labor costs were low enough to let us get away with slipshod production management—but no longer.

Similarly, the European medium-sized business has to do much better in marketing. We know our customers, but rarely have we even tried to know markets, especially markets we are not yet serving.

Altogether there is not yet adequate recognition of the fact that managerial principles are needed more in the small business than in the giant one. The small business cannot afford the sizable overhead of staffs and controls which in a large business may take the place of clear objectives, defined responsibilities, and purposeful direction— at least for a while. In the small or medium-sized business, managerial confusion immediately saps even the best entrepreneurial performance. This, however, the European owner-manager still has to learn in many cases.

2. We need younger people in top positions. Today's top managements in a great many medium-sized companies in Europe tend to be overaged. This applies particularly to the boards of directors, since old men on the board are unlikely to retire old men in management or to advance young men. Tomorrow's economy requires, however, from the management of today the initiative, the courage, and the flexibility of young people. Far too many of us in management are still living in the past and will have to be replaced by young people who reach for tomorrow.

3. Finally, we require a profound change in education. The schools of Europe tend to define knowledge as "whatever has no applicability." A by-product of this is the tremendous gulf between the university and the economy, and indeed, between professors and students.

At the same time educated men will have to learn that education does not stop when they get a diploma. There is no "final exam for life" any more. Continuing postgraduate studies should be practically compulsory for executives. But in Europe it is still far from common to see adults back in school.

During these last twenty years Western Europe has increasingly organized postgraduate institutes for management development. In many of these organizations the level of work is high. Still, most of it is done outside of the university and with little contact with university faculties. Far too much also is done in traditional and unimaginative ways, with the canned lecture still the rule rather than the rarest of exceptions. And the top men from medium-sized businesses rarely attend. They do not even, as a rule, send their good young people to advanced manager courses. Yet it is the medium-sized business which is likely to benefit the most from continuing management education.

The European manager of tomorrow faces a high challenge. He will be expected to create a new economy and technology while maintaining the values of old pre-industrial traditions. He will have to be a creative entrepreneur and a systematic manager at the same firm. He will have to be imaginative and yet know and apply rigorous quantification. He will have to be multi-national in his vision and operations, and yet local and diverse in his characteristics.

Similar requirements, I am sure face the manager everywhere else, in the United States as well as in Europe. The difference may well be that in Europe it is the owner-manager of small-to-medium sized businesses who is most likely to turn these challenges into opportunity and achievement.

H. F. R. CATHERWOOD

Tomorrow's British Manager

15 Britain today faces problems very similar to those of the United States but with far more slender resources. Both countries have put a high proportion of their resources into the defense of the free world, both have made the overwhelming contribution to the investment and economic growth of the free world, and both have enabled world trade to grow by maintaining reserve currencies. This accumulation of burdens, however vital for the peace and development of the free world, brings problems, and these problems impose more strain on Britain with its scarce natural resources and low liquidity ratio than on the United States with its higher monetary reserves and abundant natural resources. And although both countries are committed to the development of world trade, Britain, because of its minute natural resources, is more dependent on the successful development of world trade than the United States.

The first requirement of Britain's manager of tomorrow is not just competence or knowledge of the current management techniques, but ability to exploit the strength of Britain's international position in world trade and finance.

Britain has built up considerable goodwill and reputation around the world, and our experience of the affairs of other countries is immense. Up to now a great deal of British talent and energy has gone into the maintenance of international peace and the promotion of international order. We have fought and helped to win two world wars in this century. In addition, we have kept the peace with limited resources over a great area of the world. We have done this with goodwill and are still welcome in most of the countries we ruled. The best of British talent has gone into this effort. The British educational system turned out district officers who by their integrity, diplomacy, and judgment were able to keep order among alien populations who outnumbered them 100,000 to one. British shipping and British trading companies built up vast businesses in Africa, India, Southeast Asia, Hong Kong, Australasia, the West Indies, and elsewhere. The British judicial system was recognized all over the world, and the final court of appeal throughout the British Empire and later for some time, even in the Commonwealth, was in London. The whole of this apparatus was backed up by a superb Civil Service strongly weighted towards Britain's overseas commitments and by the financial services of the City of London, which also faced outwards towards the world. Indeed, British finance not only went to British-controlled territories, but also, to a very large extent, to the United States where British investments still have a value of over ten billion dollars.

Up to now the consensus for future British strategy has been a redeployment from the far-flung outposts to a future within an enlarged European Common Market. In many ways this seemed to make sense. Our share of trade with our former dependent territories was declining as they set up their own infant industries, and our share of trade with our industralised neighbours in Europe and in the United States was fast expanding. We already have a free trading area in Europe covering a hundred million people, including many of the wealthiest European countries. We could with our European Free Trade Area partners contribute to the rest of Europe not only this enlarged market, but all of Britain's international trading expertise and our more advanced technology. If this enlarged Europe wanted to build international companies capable of matching the resources of the great companies of the United States, then we alone of the major European nations had the experience of putting together international consortia and of operating international companies. The two great diarchies of Shell and Unilever are just the tip of the iceberg of British international operations. We have the expertise of the City of London to help to deploy the savings of Europe internally and externally. Europe, with its marginally under-valued currencies and its receipts from Anglo-American defense expenditure, has accumulated cash surpluses which could greatly help the short-term liquidity of sterling. To a majority in Britain and Europe, this has seemed the right course for Britain. It would give British management a thoroughly worthwhile task, and would be a tremendous contribution to the prosperity and stability of the western world. But this grand design requires goodwill, requires a recognition that our trading surplus was put into deficit solely by the contributions it made to other nations, and that its resulting weakness requires not the maximum exploitation of bargaining power against it, but the kind of help which Britain has always given to others when they were in need.

Meantime, Britain is stretched between obligations actual and potential to Europe and largely unrequited continuing obligations to its former sphere of influence. In military terms we retain troops in Southeast Asia for the defense of Malaysia and Australia and troops in Germany for the defense of Western Europe. Our balance of payments at the old exchange rate might have borne one of these burdens, but could not bear both. We were on the one hand attempting to get the rate of industrial investment in Britain to the proportion of GNP required to maintain our share of a united European market, and on the other hand maintaining an enormous investment program in the overseas sterling area and, to some extent, even outside it. It was open to a prospective partner to strengthen us and to help us to continue to make a contribution to world liquidity, investment, and trade and world peace. Or we could be pressured to abandon this role as a price for partnership. This was a choice we were and are reluctant to make.

If Britain were, in fact, to become part of a continental economy, the requirements for British management for the future would be fairly straight-forward. It would probably be right to adapt itself as nearly as possible to the management techniques of North America which serve the great continental economy of over two hundred million people. Our exports outside the European continental economy would possibly be as marginal as American exports are to the gross national product of the United States. There would be specialization and a greater scale of production with interchange of components between Coventry and Cologne, between Manchester and Milan. Although dedicated Europeans still see this as the future for Britain and cannot conceive of any other, I myself feel that we will not become part of a continental bloc, but will remain a salty maritime nation, the sailor with friends in every port. This will leave British management with a much more complex and difficult job, but one probably much more suited to our national character and to our traditional skills. It will mean especially that we will continue to earn our keep in the world more by our contribution to the development of world trade and investment and less by our contribution to a continental economy.

If this were to happen, it does not necessarily mean that we should be entirely on our own. To go it alone would mean a heavy withdrawal from international commitments of all kinds. If, however, we did not have to go it alone on trade, if some sort of wider and more liberal trading area were possible, including our EFTA partners and perhaps Australia and New Zealand as well as Canada and the United States, then our improved trading position would probably enable us to continue to share our partnership with the United States in defense outside Europe, and would also enable us to maintain our overseas investment without further sales of our United States portfolio investment.

How then can British management best exploit our international expertise and our reputation as honest traders and bankers? The City of London has already shown its very high degree of adaptability to the changing conditions of international finance. It has shown beyond a doubt that the decline of the sterling area does not mean the decline of British merchant banking as an institution. The Euro-dollar market centers not in the three great countries of the Common Market (which might have been expected to develop the financing of Common Market transactions), but on London. The British banks have shown their ability to deal in deposits of whatever currency happens to have a surplus of deposits. It is reckoned that British banking contributes about £200 million to our balance of trading surplus, and it is vital to us that this should continue—and vital, therefore, that we should continue to build on the management skills which we have acquired in international banking and finance. British insurance companies and investment trusts manage 10 billion dollars worth of overseas portfolio investment, which also contributes a substantial surplus to our balance of payments. Direct British overseas investment controlled by British parent companies amounts to a further $20 billion, and despite our over-all balance of payment deficit, it has been growing at the rate of about a billion dollars a year. This is a high proportion of our national resources, higher than almost any other country, and with it comes a high degree of skill in international operations. For many an American executive, an overseas post is exile from the mainstream of the company's work and doom to his prospects of promotion. In British companies like Shell, Unilever, Rio Tinto, British American Tobacco, it is the route to the top. This is an expertise which tomorrow's British manager must have.

Not only is there considerable outward investment, but foreign investment in Britain, especially from the United States, has been very high. About 10 per cent of British manufacturing industry is now owned by United States corporations. These companies depend heavily on British management, and many of them use Britain as a base for their international operations. It is generally reckoned that the average American-owned company in Britain has no more than one resident American manager. British management has, therefore, increasing experience not only in running international companies controlled in Britain, but in running companies controlled in Cleveland, Cincinnati, Detroit, San Francisco, and New York. The profitability of American investment is good, and the alliance of British and American skill seems, in most markets, to be an unbeatable combination. The ability to work with overseas owners, to put to use American skill and technology, is likely to be of increasing importance for tomorrow's British manager.

If Britain is not going to be part of a continental economy with the scale and specialization which this brings to the individual company, then it will probably have to exploit even more its expertise in international joint ventures. Britain has been a highly inventive country, but has not had a secure and homogenous market which is large enough to bring all the potential winners into really profitable volume production. Yet Britain must compete against continental economies which already have this kind of secure market base. One way of keeping in the "big league" is the international joint venture. I have been involved in my time in at least eight major international joint ventures. These require management with a very highly developed professional sense, capable because of their integrity and of their competence of commanding the trust of people from different nationalities and different backgrounds. It is interesting just to look, for example, at the eight with which I have been involved to see the variety of contribution. The largest was the British Aluminum Company, which was Anglo-American with mainly British management. Allied to this was Canadian-British Aluminum, which was Anglo-American with a mainly Canadian management. There was FRIA in Guinea, which was American, French, British, German, and Swiss with a French management. There was DNN in Norway, which was Anglo-Canadian with a Norwegian management, and there was Australuco, which was Anglo-Canadian with an Australian management. There was Costain Blankenvoort, Anglo-Dutch with a Dutch management; Costain Raymond International, which was Anglo-American with a management which alternated for each major project between Britain and America; and Costain West Africa, which was Anglo-Nigerian with a British management and a Nigerian chairman. This must only be a very small sector of a vast web of joint venturing. The common strand is usually a British partner who, whatever else he puts in, almost always contributes expertise in joint venturing. What was common to these joint ventures was: (1) a clear-cut understanding between the partners as to who did what, and, in particular, who contributed respectively the technical expertise, the management, the money, and the marketing; (2) a clear delimitation of the market in which the joint venture operated, and an agreement between the partners which avoided clashes between the partners' main interests and the joint venture; (3) a very clear understanding of the objectives of the joint venture, and (4) a negotiating procedure (and, no less important, a will to negotiate), which enabled the partners to resolve very quickly, and with a minimum of fuss, conflicts of interest between them. These joint ventures did not succeed without pain and trouble. But when there were difficulties we were almost always able in Britain to lay hands on someone who was expert in international negotiation, someone who could devise an arrangement which was capable of being agreed to and operated by all the partners. This is a relatively rare expertise, but it is one which is very much in the British tradition and one which we will have to exploit for all we are worth.

However adept we may be at creating business by overseas investment and by international joint ventures, we will still be dependent for a very long time to come on direct exports to a great variety of countries over tariff barriers and against local preferences and restrictions. A quarter of our manufacturing production goes to export markets, and the home market has been small relative to the continental economies. It has also been slow growing, because of the weight of our international commitments. Faced with the exploitation of volume production in the great continental economies, British management will have to learn how to adapt the requirements of the markets which it serves to the economies of bulk production. It will, of course, be helped by the reduction of tariff barriers under the Kennedy Round, and the slightly lower parity will also help it over remaining tariff barriers. But, in the long run, it must be able to match volume for volume, despite the variety of the market.

In terms of straight marketing this will require a switch by many more British companies from passive selling through agents to active marketing by the company's own staff in foreign markets. The agent picks up whatever business is going, but the staff of the company tries to look for business which will fit best with the company's production. Those who have made the switch from agents to direct sales find that the overhead of direct marketing is wiped out by additional profit in a very short time. There is a good deal of evidence that direct marketing would produce not only lower costs of production but higher prices. The agency system seems to have its roots in Britain's widely-scattered Commonwealth markets, but almost two-thirds of Britain's markets now are in the developed industrial countries where British goods are competing not against other foreign imports sold through agents, but against local production sold by sophisticated marketing techniques. One symptom of agency selling is evident in Prince Philip's complaint that British goods are not advertised in the countries he visits.

The higher profitability of exports following devaluation will make it much more worthwhile for a British company to start direct selling. Once started, the company is most unlikely to go back to agency selling. The home sales and export sales operation will tend to become part of one coordinated marketing system, and the matching of the production process with the needs of the market will become feasible for the whole volume of the company sales.

But, whatever Professor Galbraith may say, companies do not control their markets, and customers will always want more variety than is strictly economic. Pilkingtons, the British inventors of the float-glass process, made another important breakthrough when they adapted this new process to give short runs without losing the economies of the bulk process. Tomorrow's British production manager is going to have to become very expert in getting economies of bulk production out of small and specialized orders. The computer makes it easier to bulk orders and hold stock, but a high degree of production skill will be needed too.

In foreign markets British salesmen will have to learn to exploit the opportunities available to the underdog. The local producer is usually the price leader. He has most to lose from an across-the-board cut in prices. It may even pay him to lose some volume in order to maintain price in the market as a whole. He will not, therefore, match the price cuts of every importer. Britain has suffered from shrewdly aimed commercial raids which have exploited the anomalies in an industry pricing structure and have offered cut prices for the plums; or, alternatively, cut prices for a limited range of goods which happen to fit the foreign supplier's production process. Britain must, in turn, learn to exploit the ability of the underdog to live well on 10 per cent of the market, and the British manager of tomorrow will have to understand the whole gambit of pricing and costing techniques if he is to find the most profitable outlets for British goods.

All of this will involve tomorrow's British manager in a degree of concentration on entrepreneurial skill. It is a cliché that British industry is production-oriented. In some ways there is nothing wrong with this; it is better to undersell a well engineered product than it is to create an artificial market for a poorly engineered product. But entrepreneurial management does not consist in the promotion of marginally useful products; it consists in the skillful direction of scarce resources for the maximum revenue. The entrepreneur is perhaps above all the man who is prepared to make harsh commercial choices. He cuts his losses ahead of time. He slims his product line again and again, until all his products are making the maximum contribution. He understands the structure of markets, knows when to trade price for volume and when to trade volume for price. He not only understands his own economics, but the economics of his customer and of his supplier. He takes enormous care and trouble to see that his distributors make money by selling his products and that his customers make money by buying them. He will choose his suppliers with the utmost care and patience and will then take great trouble to build them up so that they can make money for him and for themselves by progressively reducing their costs. One such entrepreneurial company is Britain's retail chain, Marks and Spencer. British diplomats returning on leave will stock up with five years' clothing for the family at Marks and Spencer's Oxford Street store. Dutch, Belgian, French, and even Russian housewives make special expeditions to London to shop at Marks and Spencer. In the commodity markets, in sugar, for instance, and in the London Metal Exchange, Britain has tremendous entrepreneurial skill. This skill in retailing and in commodity dealing needs to be applied by tomorrow's British manager to manufacturing and especially, perhaps, to engineering.

Whether or not Britain remains outside the continental trading blocs, its dependence on world trade means that its companies must match the resources of the companies operating in international trade. This means that many industries may well end up with one major company in a dominant position in the domestic market, and the balance of the industry will become either suppliers and sub-contractors to the giants or independent specialists. Two years ago the Industrial Reorganization Corporation, with a financial backing of $375 million, was set up to promote just this kind of merger. Britain now has two major electrical engineering companies instead of three, three or four big shipbuilding companies instead of a dozen or more, and there are probably more big mergers on the way in electronics and other industries. These giant companies are not only more likely to be successful in finding the finance to develop British inventions, but are also more likely to devote a higher-than-average proportion of their output to exports. The bulk of Britain's export effort rests on about 150 major companies.

All this means that more British managers will have to learn to manage the very large company. We do, of course, have our share of giant corporations. ICI, as well as Shell and Unilever, is in the first league internationally, and so are the nationalized Coal and Power industries. Britain is well up in the lists of large companies outside the United States. And, of course, apart from industry, Britain has always had a large number of men trained in operating very large organizations. These are now finding a place in industry. The Colonial Service and the Armed Services have been running down over the last ten or fifteen years, and many of the district officers, the judges, the colonels, and captains who came out of them have transferred to industry and have brought with them the professional discipline which is necessary in the very large organization.

I would say on any straight comparison that top management in Britain is probably as good as, if not somewhat better than, top management elsewhere in the world. But good middle managers are much thinner on the ground. The newly-fledged British giant will probably have great gaps for the next decade or even longer to be filled by good industrial engineers, metallurgists, shift superintendents, assistant warehouse managers, operational researchers, works accountants, sales engineers, research chemists, and all the other jobs advertised in page after page of our Sunday newspapers. This gap may partly be the fault of our educational system which still tends to turn out an elite, and which leaves rather a large gap between the elite and the rest. By contrast, the American system seems to turn out a far greater number of potential managers, and the large companies seem to drill these effectively in doing a fairly limited job. British company training tends to produce "officer material" capable of taking on any situation. If the candidate fails to become "officer material," he is then unceremoniously returned to the ranks. The American company training system by contrast seems to be geared much more closely to the needs of the particular company. It seems to me that for Britain something between the American and British education system and somewhere between the American and British training system is about right for tomorrow's British manager. For although we need more bodies, companies selling in world markets will require their men to be more versatile and to have a higher individual initiative than companies selling in a continental economy. Individual initiative has always been a strong part of the British character, whether in industry or on the battlefield. So we should make sure we keep it and exploit it.

Britain's industry is currently much more labor-intensive than American industry and requires, therefore, much more weight of first-line supervision for a given output. Although wage-price guidelines and then devaluation have been aimed at making British labor cheaper internationally, Britain must in the long run regard its labor as scarce and, therefore, as an expensive resource. For this reason, we must put far more skill into the actual organization and direction of our labor on the shop floor. Some companies have already experimented by giving the young, trained engineer a job of first-line supervision, instead of giving such a job to the traditional foreman upgraded from chargehand or operative. The engineer has a trained and flexible mind and a far greater knowledge of the process than is possible for a traditional foreman. This is just one way of tackling the problem. But it is a problem which will have to be tackled. The symptoms are in the British newspapers every day of the week and tend to be exaggerated in transmission abroad until there arises an image of the British working man which is quite unreal. The symptoms may be wild-cat strikes, arguments about tea-breaks, knocking off early and arriving late, arguments about the manning of machinery, inflexibility in the transfer from one machine to another and so on. Behind almost every one of these arguments, however, I suspect lies weakness in first-line supervision. But take two companies in the same town and with roughly the same unions and the same kind of labor force; the one will have all these troubles and the other will have none. If the labor force and the unions are common to both plants (as they almost always are), then the trouble must lie not in the men but in the management. Indeed, my American colleagues who have worked both in Britain and America tell me that British labor is a good deal easier to talk to, more adaptable and flexible than American labor. But it is my impression that the first-line supervision in America is more concentrated, more professional, and tougher. It may be true that because more men have to be supervised in a British plant, the management of the shop floor is more hierarchical than it need be. While labor is relatively cheap it will tend to be used too lavishly. But even if we have just lowered its cost internationally by devaluation, its scarcity will eventually be felt, and tomorrow's British manager from first-line supervisor upwards must be able to organize it and use it to optimum effect.

One of the great tasks which Britain faces in the next decade is the redeployment of labor from declining to expanding industries. Britain's coal mining industry used to be one of its largest, but faced with oil, nuclear power, and North Sea gas, it is now in sharp decline, and its mechanized mines have sharply reduced the labor it needs for its lower output. Cotton textiles, wool textiles, railways, and steel will also need less labor. These and other industries have a future, but cannot hope to compete if they remain labor-intensive. On the other hand, there is a great scarcity of labor, and particularly skilled labor, in industries like engineering. We need a big shift in the next few years between these two groups of industries. But this will not be a once-for-all shift. If Britain is to keep its place in world markets, if it is to exploit the growth points in world trade, then it will need to have an economy that is more than usually flexible. This will require a labor force which can change its skills at fairly short notice. There is now and will continue to be a heavy demand for skill in training and retraining. Britain has an excellent educational system, but it has not yet been used to anything like its full potential in industrial training. Yet the adaptability of British industry in wartime has shown what can be done. In the war, schoolmasters were set to work to train their former pupils in building ships and in making guns and ammunition. Despite the long apprenticeships required by the engineering and shipbuilding industries, the ships were built and the guns and ammunition were made by people with the very minimum of training. After the war we went back to the long apprenticeship system, but there is now, I think, growing agreement that something more is needed. In the last few years we have set up industry training boards in almost every industry. These boards lay a compulsory levy on all members of the industry, and pay it out *pro rata* to the amount of training done by companies. The boards try to use their position to improve the quality and intensity of training and to shorten the time-scale. Government training centers are being set up progressively all over the country for the retraining of those cast off by old industry. This tremendous hum of activity has started in a relatively static economy. As the export-led growth following devaluation gets under-way and the rate of unemployment declines, the amount of training will have to step up even more sharply. With the scarcity of people qualified to train, it is possible that unconventional methods will come into their own; instead of a draft of schoolteachers we may rely increasingly on teaching machines and programmed instruction.

Management-union relations in Britain are, on the whole, no worse than anywhere else in the world. All statistics show that the amount of time lost by strikes in Britain is lower than in most other industrial countries, and there is only a fraction, for instance, of the time lost in the United States. Wage rates are far lower than in the United States, and the rate of annual increase is less than in most other industrial countries. There has been a strong tradition in Britain of national bargaining, and the whole of the machinery of wage-price guide-lines is geared to the idea that the major unions can govern at the national level the negotiations on the earnings of their members. But the pressure of demand for labor in the industrial Midlands and South East especially has created a high degree of wage drift arising from bargains struck at plant level. There is now some move towards pro-ductivity bargaining and an attempt to canalize through local produc-tivity committees the growth of plant bargaining. Some companies, particularly Standard Oil (N.J.) at its Fawley Refinery, have led the way, and other companies are experimenting. This kind of bargain will, of course, push a great deal more responsibility on to plant man-agement. At plant level the traditional wisdom has always dictated that consultation and negotiation should be kept separate. In practice this has meant that consultation tended to be about the state of the canteen and the washrooms, and negotiation tended to be a simple test of bargaining strength without too much regard to the produc-tivity available in the company. Plant level committees which combine consultation and negotiation and which keep the union officials and shop stewards properly informed of the company's economic state have still a long way to go. One of the most cogent arguments against them is that companies do not have the expertise to negotiate non-inflationary productivity agreements. A good many so-called non-inflationary agreements have been negotiated, but the productivity element has often been phoney and a cover-up for wage drifts. A number of companies have started experimental schemes for productivity committees, and the successful schemes may well be the proving ground for a much wider application of productivity bargaining. Since higher productivity and a much better use of labor are the key to the expansion of the British economy, tomorrow's British manager should be expert in productivity arrangements and in the operation of the machinery, such as plant production committees, through which they can be negotiated.

Although Britain has an expenditure on research and development second only to that of the United States, and it is a good deal ahead of most of its industrial competitors, Britain's record for the development of invention has not been good. Many British inventions have been developed in the United States. To some extent this is inevitable. We could not expect to sell all the jet engines in the world or all the hovercraft or all the penicillin, but, nevertheless, we could obviously use a great deal more expertise in the management of project development. Even if we do not have a continental economy and even if we do not have the resources of the United States, it ought still to be possible to tap the great sources of British inventiveness more profitably for the British economy than we now do. A higher rate of growth of the British economy following devaluation should help a good deal. In a recent report on the loss of engineers and scientists to the United States, the fact emerged that the attraction to the engineer and scientist was as much the development of new projects as money. There were more new projects in the United States with its high rate of growth than there were in Britain with its lower growth rate. As the rate of growth here goes up, there will be more projects and more scientists will stay behind to see them through and more will be attracted from the universities and from the big government research associations. We have the men; what we need is a market potential to finance project development. Because we so acutely need to solve this problem, it may be that we will bring some new insight to the building of the bridge between the laboratory and the production line. It is an area which, because it falls between research on the one hand and production and sales on the other, badly needs some new insight. Only the biggest companies can have a team continuously engaged in project development with the expertise necessary to select projects which will pay off commercially, to know when to cut losses, to know when to push the projects on, to know how to handle teething troubles, to know how to keep a tight timetable to meet market demands, to know when a scientist really has achieved a marketable breakthrough and when he is just chasing some academic hare—all of these demand a highly developed expertise which seems to me to be rare not only in Britain but probably in the world. It is vital for Britain's future that tomorrow's British manager should maximise the return from research and development.

Since Britain is so dependent on international trading and international liquidity, the fortunes of industry are very much bound up with the skill of government in managing the economy. For this reason, government's relations with industry have to be close, and that is why when a socialist government came to power in Britain in 1964, consultation and joint planning with industry were increased as socialist ministers sat down with industrialists and bankers to look at their common problems. Consultation and planning are no panaceas for solving the tough underlying problems of an economy burdened by defense and illiquidity. There have been many stresses and strains as one side or the other felt that it gave more than it got in the exchange. But even at the time of greatest strain, both government and industry were acutely aware of their interdependence and their continuing need to work together. There are many loose arrangements for consultation—each industry has its sponsoring department—e.g., the Ministry of Power for the oil industry; the Ministry of Agriculture for the farmers, food processing, fishing, and forestry; the Board of Trade for chemicals and textiles; the Ministry of Technology for engineering. But the major joint effort, the place where government and both sides of industry sit down together as equal partners is the National Economic Development Council and its twenty-two Economic Development Committees (one for each major industry) with their various subcommittees and working parties. The Prime Minister chairs the National Council, and in the industry councils six to ten management members will sit down with government representatives, top union officials, and an independent chairman and other experts to discuss the major opportunities and problems of the industry. Working parties will consider the pattern of imports, of exports, of investment, of productivity, of industry structure, of requirements for skilled labor, of use of labor, of tariffs, of taxes, and will make recommendations to the industry, to the unions, and to government. But the hard work of economic and industrial analysis cannot be carried out without a very close consultation between the committees and the industries they cover, especially with the corporate planning departments of the major corporations in each industry. This activity has stimulated the growth of corporate planning in Britain, and companies which had been content to jog along from year to year without any firm forecast of where they were going in terms of markets or resources have now been forced to do some pretty hard thinking. But corporate planners are in short supply, and there will be a shortage, for some time, of men who can distinguish between a firmly based forecast and the wildly optimistic guess of the vice-president of sales. We need men who will be able to convince their boards that not every company in the industry will be able to increase its market share, men capable of forecasting the rate of imports and the areas of the company and industry markets vulnerable to imports, men capable of seeing the growth points in world trade and persuading their boards to switch from traditional to growing markets. And it requires more than a statement of the obvious to convince many boards.

In the weeks immediately after devaluation it was clear that some British companies had already worked out a contingent corporate strategy to deal with it. Leylands, for instance, who sell trucks and Triumph sports cars, had a pricing strategy available immediately after devaluation for every major export market. Possibly the biggest gains available to any company in British industry will come from the correct use of corporate planning. Certainly those companies which have regarded the world as their market, those companies which have been aware of all the alternative corporate strategies available to them for maximization of their long-term profits, are aware too of the opportunities available in some fields and the limitations in other fields, aware of the need for reserve strategies if first choices fail— those are the companies which have gone ahead in turnover, in profitability, and in corporate high spirits. Tomorrow's British management team should, therefore, include a few of those rare corporate planners.

One final word. Professionalism has firm roots in most industrial countries, but in none does it have firmer roots than in Britain. We have a very strong professional tradition. I cannot prove that professionalism was invented in Britain, but certainly we had very early the concept of disinterested service, whether in medicine, in the law, the church, the army, the navy, the judiciary, the Indian Civil Service, the Colonial Service, the Home Civil Service, and in the newer professions such as accountancy and civil engineering, where the British professions rapidly made a worldwide reputation. Now that so many people from these older professions are coming into industrial management, they are bringing their professional traditions with them, and it is likely that management in Britain will be very firmly based on this professional tradition in the future. A profession involves a recognisable body of knowledge, an agreed code of conduct, a strong duty of care to those it serves, and an unwillingness to trade this standard of care for quick financial gain. Maybe there will be no actual profession of business management in Britain, but even so, British management will still be strongly influenced by professionalism. As the talent which was once devoted to ruling a fifth of the world is redeployed to the management of industry, it will increasingly influence the operations of British companies. It is especially important that we bring this professionalism to our overseas trade. Since we export four times as much of our gross national product as America and half as much again as the Common Market, it is by this professionalism in management that we will eventually stand or fall.

AKIO MORITA

Management in Japan

16

I

There are some fundamental differences between
Japanese and American traditions, attitudes, and
policies with respect to business organization and,
especially, with respect to the people and the way
they are being managed. These differences are so
great that they make the Japanese company behave
very differently from its western counterpart, even
though it is almost identical in its legal structure.
Having been responsible for building a major company in Japan—SONY—as well as for founding and
managing our international subsidiary in the United
States, I have been forced to think through these
differences. I have also had occasion to ask myself,
which of the basic characteristics of the Japanese
company are strengths that should be maintained and
put to work, and which, however deeply imbedded
they might be in our tradition, no longer fit the realities of Japanese economy and society, and the
demands of a competitive world economy.

Lifetime Employment

Every year in April, most Japanese companies hire
what we call freshmen—young men who have just
graduated from school or the university in March,

the end of the Japanese school year. The companies think through how many men to hire on the basis of their needs for the future rather than on the basis of current company requirements. The freshmen are first given the necessary orientation to become lifetime employees with the company. The new employee is given opportunities to develop himself by changing jobs every two or three years. As it is assumed that a man will not leave the company's employ until final retirement, it is obviously in the company's interest to have each man acquire broad experience and knowledge of all business operations. This applies, above all, to men hired for professional and management positions, that is, generally, to university graduates.

The company watches and develops a person from a long range view. It does not only evaluate him on the basis of immediate results. Through job rotation, management will gradually find the most suitable job for a person, and the person's most effective ability for the company. Every time a man changes jobs, he is being entrusted with a more demanding assignment. The more capable among the same age group are moved faster. Of course, not all personnel are promoted continually. The man who eventually becomes president of his company is the one who was advanced to more demanding assignments at the fastest rate; his colleagues have reached the age of compulsory retirement before being entrusted with top management assignments.

The promotion of capable men goes, therefore, quickly in many Japanese companies. Yet it differs radically from "promotion," as an American would use the term. The capable man in Japan gets challenging assignments fairly fast. But he gets neither more money nor, as a rule, a more impressive title. Differentiation of salary and title in Japan goes by seniority rather than by responsibility, except for the few men who get beyond the middle ranks into top management. However, that does not mean that Japanese businesses disregard the principle of authority being commensurate with responsibility. For us, however, authority is defined by the demands of the task, rather than by money or title.

Generally in a Japanese company, an employee is never fired, unless he commits a crime. As a result, his employment continues automatically up to the age of compulsory retirement (which traditionally has been fifty-five years for all except top management for whom there is, as a rule, no compulsory retirement age). This is in sharp contrast to the American system in which a company can employ personnel as needed and dismiss them or lay them off whenever they become unnecessary. It is considered quite natural in the United States for an employee to be fired whenever he does not fulfil his job, or for an employee to leave whenever he thinks he is not properly appreciated. Such mobility of employment is very rare in Japan these days.

How Lifetime Employment Came About

One hundred years have passed since Japan terminated its three hundred years of national isolation and introduced western civilization. During the first fifty years after the opening of the nation, there was mobility of employment. Changing one's place of work was the only method of obtaining higher salaries and positions at that time. Sticking to one's post in one company did not mean automatic advancement.

The depression following World War I forced modernization of Japanese industries, and the introduction of mass production and modern management systems forced companies to change the quality of employees. Companies wanted fresh, flexible, young personnel who would be more easily adaptable to modern methods. Companies rushed to hire young, educated people who had just graduated from school and gave them training to fit the new system. Through this course of training, employers gradually acquired management skills, while employees developed loyalty to the company. For the first time, a truly Japanese type of employer-employee relationship began to be formulated, based upon the traditional doctrine of mutual loyalty and mutual responsibility.

This led to a new personnel system. To keep its employees, and to discourage them from leaving and joining another company after they had been trained, an employer had to adopt a system in which wages increased and positions advanced automatically with seniority.

This seniority based on the lifetime employment system contributed greatly to the remarkable economic growth of modern Japan. Lifetime employment was a powerful factor in creating loyalty among employees, and in instilling in them the concept: this is *my* company. This concept made for high productivity and for unity among employees. From the standpoint of the employee too, this system has merit. He can plan his life in security—when to get married, when to build a house, and so forth.

Methods of Recruiting for Management

The Japanese manager is traditionally brought in as a freshman, that is, when he graduates from the university. Screening is done by way of examination, including a written test and an interview. Needless to say, this type of screening does not really tell whether a person has useful abilities for the company.

Yet the man brought in this way normally has lifetime employment, with automatic advancement in pay (doubling, on the average, every ten years) and in title and visible position. Americans may wonder why Japanese employers do not present specifications of the jobs which they want to fill, thereby screening more specifically and accurately. However, our method of hiring freshmen makes it impossible to apply such descriptions to wanted personnel. As we see it, people are there first, and then positions must be provided for them. This is just the opposite of the American viewpoint in which specific descriptions of needed personnel are drawn first—though, of course, it is not too different from the way many American companies actually recruit on college campuses. However, we in Japan do not have the rapid turnover of freshmen that many American companies have among their college recruits—ours stay once they have come aboard.

The Japanese college graduate who seeks employment generally wants to get a job in a large company. He believes a big company is unlikely to go out of business. And since an ex-employee of a company that has gone out of business is usually incapable of finding another job and may be virtually unemployable, a job at a small enterprise is a greater risk than an uninteresting or stagnant job in a large company. As long as an employer stays in business, the employee is taken care of for the rest of his business career.

On the other hand, prospective employers tend to stress the applicant's school records or, more curiously, accept a person because their sixth sense tells them there is promise in him. In short, employment is done without much relevance to the company's requirements, present or future. Once a company hires a person, it can almost never fire him—even when he is much less competent than was hoped.

Social Security Organization

An organization which hires a person with such meaningless examinations and is never able to fire him even if he does not work hard, could be called a social security organization—not a business organization.

Japanese companies have been trying to promote loyalty and the my-company concept by supplying employees with fringe benefits—

company houses, dormitories, hospitals, summer houses, recreation facilities, and so forth. Although such fringe benefits have contributed to a uniquely Japanese family-like feeling among employees, they tend to make employees forget the true purpose of business.

Personnel Evaluation

Within a family, it is not advisable to evaluate the individual member's ability. To assign rank and pay according to this evaluation is not possible. And at the same time, evaluation usually leaves behind dissatisfaction and disagreement.

In the United States, if an employee is dissatisfied with the evaluation of his performance, he may leave his employer and find another job. Evaluation of ability has value in a society where there is mobility of employment, and where both the employer and employee can choose or refuse one another.

In Japan, however, where companies mostly hire freshmen and there is little mobility of employment, dismissal by a company all but destroys the employee's life. In the same sense, an employee who leaves his employer and seeks a job in another place, risks his very livelihood. Therefore, evaluation of ability by an employer cannot have much meaning in a Japanese company.

The most acceptable compromise, if a company wants to avoid these troubles arising from individual dissatisfaction, is ranking employees by seniority—a status which no one can deny. One is less apt to be jealous of an associate who holds a higher title and receives more pay because he is older.

Emphasis on School Career

Similarly, one's school career and personal history prior to entering the company are objective, public records. The employer finds it convenient to use such information as when the applicant graduated from the university, and the prestige of the applicant's university. These are primary measures in deciding his rank and his salary. A big company usually likes to employ graduates of high-prestige universities, and these people are treated as an elite within the organization. Under these circumstances, every one wants to get a prestige school career. Often, the name of the school one graduates from is given more value than one's capability. Therefore, the purpose of education, sometimes becomes one of entering a prestige school, rather than of developing one's ability.

Communication

There is another characteristic of a Japanese company. The people in an American company represent a mixture of backgrounds—ethnic, national origin, religion, etc. In Japan, the employees have the same national and cultural background. They speak the same language and have grown up in the same environment. For Japan is a small country, a little smaller than the state of California.

Mass communication through newspapers, magazines, radio, and television is well developed. Though Japan has a population of one hundred million people, the whole country is homogeneous. In such an environment, the people's ways of thinking and feeling become similar, just as members of a family brought up in the same home tend to have a similar way of thinking and understanding.

This situation makes a difference when comparing the extent of mutual understanding among personnel in an American and in a Japanese company. In Japan, detailed instructions are not given. People believe they understand each other. In an American company, this can hardly be expected.

American management, faced with a variety of people, both new and experienced, finds it a matter of the first magnitude to establish communication among its people. Consequently, great efforts have been exerted to develop communication and understanding in the American society. The development of communications systems in the United States such as the telephone, the teletype, radio and television, and transportation systems—surface and air—represents efforts to overcome the difficulty of communication and understanding among people widely spread throughout a huge country.

Japanese management does not pay much attention to communication. People have confidence in one another and believe that they already fully understand each other. What would cause confusion in the West, is expected and shrugged off as slight and irrelevant nuances of interpretation in Japan.

Moral Attitude Toward Work

Foreigners may wonder how Japanese business is conducted if it depends only on the common ground of understanding. Japanese people have a common moral character developed over a long period of history and probably based originally upon Confucian teaching. They believe that it is a sin to be idle and that one must work hard in any situation. Therefore, a person in a company feels he must do anything which he judges to be his responsibility. Company operations are carried on by the hard work of each member, although such hard work, when it is carried on at the employee's own judgment, may not always create high efficiency for the company. For Japanese management, skill in promoting motivation and cultivating a cooperative atmosphere among the people is essential. For American management on the other hand, strong leadership is necessary in order to get across its policies to the employees.

Harmony

The effective Japanese executive tries to be like the father in a family—capable of keeping his group well motivated and in good harmony. The promotion system, based on an employee's school career and seniority, should keep every hard-working Japanese secure and motivated. From the viewpoint of Japanese management, these are about the best possible solutions to please the maximum number of members, and thus obtain the maximum efficiency from the employees whom the company in turn must support until their compulsory retirement age.

Motivating Power

By creating harmony among all the young employees and an atmosphere in which they are motivated, the management can expect the real motivating power of the company to be generated by its young employees. This gives management more time for thinking and for planning for the future of the company without being bothered too much by current routine business. In Japan, the young people are expected to do the work—top management is not expected to concern itself with what goes on day to day. Also, young employees get to know each other well through such motivating work and acquire the habit of working together cooperatively and in a group.

Under these circumstances, personal responsibility in a Japanese company is different from what it is in an American company. In the United States, the range of individual responsibility tends to be clearly defined. Everybody in America is expected to be conscious of his duty and responsibility. In a Japanese company, it is neither necessary nor wise to define individual responsibility too clearly. Everyone is expected to act like a family member and to help the next man. If something goes wrong, it would be bad taste for management to inquire who made the mistake. Rather it is advisable to inquire what caused the mistake. If the name of the person who made the mistake were disclosed, he might be kicked off the escalator of seniority promotion and lose his motivation for the rest of his business life, and yet stay on the company payroll. If, however, the cause of the mistake is clarified, the person who made the mistake will not forget it, and others will not make the same mistake.

It is very difficult to determine who has the real authority and who makes the final decisions in a Japanese company. Even a top executive must consult his colleagues before he makes a decision. He has become a top executive as much by his seniority as by his leadership ability. To keep harmony in his company, he must act as a member of a family. Decisions must be made by a group rather than by an individual. Then the responsibility will be borne by the group. In other words, a Japanese company is run by group authority and by group responsibility.

II

These traditional ways of management are now running up against two big problems, one external and the other one internal.

The external one is competition from rational profit-minded western business enterprises, as a result of the expansion of international trade. It is obvious that a company which is run like a social security organization has difficulty competing with a company which is run like a real business organization.

The internal problem is the change in the young people's way of thinking. Today's young, capable, and highly educated Japanese are no longer satisfied with the traditional escalator-like seniority system. They are demanding more opportunity and challenge. The task of Japanese management today is to reorganize to meet the new competition, and to keep the young people really motivated while maintaining the strengths of the traditional system.

The Case of SONY

We in the SONY Corporation have been trying to do just that. SONY started with twenty people in 1946, and has grown to 8,000 people in twenty years. In keeping up with such a rapid growth, we could not depend on the usual yearly hiring of freshmen. SONY gathered a wide variety of personnel by such methods as personal acquaintance, public announcement, etc. As a result, school history and seniority are never considered by SONY's management. Only the ability and qualifications of a person are considered basic factors for personnel assignments. However, as the company started to grow, SONY's management began to face pressure from the traditional Japanese social influences. To maintain its freedom to act, management thereupon decided to delete a man's school history from his personnel record. It was a bold step to take in Japan. But it resulted in greatly boosting morale among SONY employees. This decision created a sensation and was highly appreciated by the people who are trying to introduce modern management in Japan.

On the other hand, SONY management became aware that it was a mistake to disappoint the men and their families by completely abolishing the seniority promotion system. For the seniority concept is a firmly established business and social practice in Japan. Still, to keep active and adjustable to keen international competition, and to the fast-developing electronics technology, SONY must have flexibility in personnel management. A compromise has therefore been developed. SONY gives such titles as assistant manager, manager, and general manager to people on the traditional seniority basis. But the functions and the range of responsibility of a section or department are set according to the capacity of the person who assumes the management of that section or department. To carry this idea out, SONY, being flexible, changes its organization as frequently as necessary.

In the big Japanese companies, sections or departments tend to be rigid and fixed. In Japan, it is traditionally considered a vice to change the organization of the company often. This, it is thought, shows lack of confidence in management. We in SONY have shown that this tradition can be changed and that systems and organization can be adjusted quickly and often to the requirements of modern industry and to the capacities of individuals.

Knowing of capable people who are not satisfied with the old tradition and who are left unmotivated in many big companies, SONY tries to get young, aggressive professionals and technicians from the outside, in addition to hiring freshmen. Such newcomers, of a wide age range, bring with them a flexibility that overcomes the rigidities of the traditional seniority concept.

Yet, SONY believes in and practices lifetime employment. It pays according to seniority—or according to age in the case of men coming in at a later age. It uses titles by seniority to a considerable extent. However, the company makes it a point to assign work and responsibility on the basis of a man's capability and initiative, rather than according to title or pay. It tries hard to fit the employee to the position in which he can use his abilities most effectively.

What we have done in SONY will, I am convinced, have to be done by every major Japanese business, one way or another. Japanese management needs to be able to offer the educated young men the challenges and opportunities for achievement which knowledgeable workers are willing to accept. And Japanese business, in an expanding world economy, must be competitive managerially. Yet, while there is need for considerable change in practices, there is need also to preserve the fundamentally Japanese values of our social tradition. These are values of unique strength: the motivation to work and the willingness to give to a common objective, the security of membership in a family which demands dedication but which also gives unquestioning loyalty in return, the willingness of young people to compete for responsibility but to accept equality in pay and title and to help each other.

Japanese management of tomorrow needs to be as modern, as proficient, and as professional as any management found in any place in the world. But at the same time, it should—and can—be as truly Japanese, as truly representative of its own values, as our country's landscapes, culture, and art are representative of our own values.

ERNST KELLER

Management in Latin America

17 In the guiding paper prepared by the faculty of the Graduate School of Business Administration of New York University on the symposium to celebrate its fiftieth anniversary, it is said that "business and management will surely change as much in the next five decades as they have changed in the last fifty years." As far as Latin America is concerned, it can be safely said that this is a gross understatement of what business—and therefore management—will be up against in the coming decades.

Latin America Today

In order to explain the present state of business and of management in South America, and to project some of the challenges of the future, it will be necessary to describe briefly where we presently stand and what changes we will almost certainly be facing in Latin America.

Latin America, while much larger than the United States in terms of area and population, is—unlike the United States, with its wide open and vast market —split by national boundaries into economic units of varying size and potential. Area per country varies between 3.3 million square miles (for Brazil, accounting for 43 per cent of the total) and 8100 square miles (for El Salvador). Population per coun-

213

try varies between 84.7 million (for Brazil, one fourth of total) and 1.3 million (for Panama). Only three Latin American countries— Argentina, Brazil, and Mexico—have a population of over 20 million, while seventeen countries have less than 10 million inhabitants.

However, when looking at the economic potential and the size of the markets of Latin American countries, figures on area and on population are grossly misleading. With a total population of close to 235 million, Latin America has a combined Gross National Product of under 90 billion American dollars. The average per-capita income is approximately $350 per year, and it varies from a high of about $750, to a low of about $150. Over half of the population has no purchasing power and is not part of the market economy.

Except for the export to the world market of agricultural and maritime commodities, and of raw materials—primarily ores, metals, and oil—business activities in the Latin American countries are oriented almost exclusively towards supplying goods and services to domestic markets in each country. The size of these markets and the resulting scale of production and marketing of goods and services can be easily appreciated from the aforementioned figures on population and purchasing power.

Economies and domestic markets are small. With the exception of very few countries, they are vulnerable to violent fluctuations, depending upon what these countries sell to the world markets. With few exceptions, the economies are subjected to continuous or frequently recurring inflationary pressure and currency devaluation.

Trade between Latin American countries is still small, a mere 11 per cent of their total foreign trade. One reason is that many of them are exporters of the same agricultural commodities or the same raw materials. Another is that without a common trade policy and special tariff arrangements among themselves, goods manufactured in Latin America cannot compete against imports from highly industrialized nations. Industry is geared to a limited domestic market which does not permit production of scale.

Latin America's Potential

From the above, it could easily be deduced that the future for Latin America, and for business operating in Latin America, is not very bright.

I believe the contrary. Latin America has a few things which industrialized nations no longer have or will not have for very much longer. It has material resources, basic raw materials, on which a good part of the western world will become increasingly dependent. Only a small part of these resources are presently tapped, and I venture to say that less than half are presently known. It has people, an abundance of manpower to be trained and put to work. This is often quoted as a disadvantage, but most of the heavily industrialized countries will readily recognize it as an advantage. It has space to house many times its present population and it can feed it too. And the aforementioned vast resources of people represent tomorrow's potential market, the compounding effect of a rapidly growing population, an increasing number of people being incorporated in the market economy, and increasing per-capita purchasing power.

The Human Resources—Education

A country's or continent's most valuable assets for its future development are its human resources. Latin America is rich in human resources, so rich that at this time it is considered a liability rather than an asset, and this may be so for some time to come.

The peoples of Latin America are a mixture of many races, and of immigrants from many nations. To describe the characteristics and the shades in aptitude and attitude of the peoples of each nation would be the subject of a paper by itself. They vary as widely as the geographical characteristics and economic settings of their countries.

It is in the appraisal of the human resources of Latin America where the greatest errors are made and, all too frequently, where injustice is being done. More often than not, basic aptitude and attitude of the peoples are confused with their standards of education and training.

Latin American people are born with no less basic capability than Americans or Europeans. The gap opens up through the still inferior education, and—unfortunately—it seems to grow larger. By education I mean the family upbringing, elementary and secondary schooling, higher education including university, and adequate professional training. The absence of a harmonious and economically secure family upbringing as it still prevails for the majority of the younger generation, is, in my opinion, the most severe obstacle under which Latin America labors. It is the family upbringing which is all-important for shaping the attitudes of human beings towards life and work. Elementary schooling, higher education, and professional training can be entirely wasted unless a solid foundation has been laid upon which one can build.

Schooling, higher education, and professional training have a long way to go in Latin America. The means and methods are still inadequate despite the fact that in the government budgets and development plans of most countries, education occupies first place and is given highest priority. An estimated 33 per cent of Latin America's population today is illiterate. Progress towards literacy is small, and at the present pace it may take several generations before all Latin Americans can read and write. To this large percentage of the people, the road to higher education will be blocked for decades to come, and the absence of vocational training programs of massive scale makes it hard to incorporate this part of the population into the market economy, to turn them into producers and, therefore, into consumers. The peoples of Latin America are as capable as any I know. They are eager to learn and grateful for being taught and trained, but the resources—money, institutions, and teachers—are still frightfully inadequate for catching up with the existing backlog, or even for keeping pace with the growth of population.

Management's most important resource is manpower. Latin America's entrepreneurs and managers can apply the same technology and can buy the same machinery and installations and the same raw materials as are available to American or European enterprises. It is in the area of human resources where the differences in management and for management arise.

Demand and Supply of Management

Demand for management is high around the world. It has been increasing sharply with the advances in technology which in the last decades brought about a drastic change in the ratio between manual laborers and management personnel.

In the developing countries of Latin America, the demand for management—if at all measurable—may, in terms of quantity, be easily twice what it is in America or Europe. With regard to quality, I venture to say that the requirements are still greater, simply because the problems of emerging nations are so much greater and the manager's major resource, people, are presently as much of a liability as their abundance may be an asset in the future.

One of our Chilean friends said some time ago in his address to an international gathering of businessmen, that Latin American countries are not underdeveloped, but poorly managed. Though emerging nations are saddled with many problems for which there is no easy solution, the truth is that in both government and private enterprise, insufficient and inadequate management is undoubtedly the principal cause for slow progress and frequent setbacks.

Management in Latin America is in high demand and in scarce supply, with the degree of scarcity varying according to echelons and professional background. Probably the greatest demand and the greatest scarcity refer to entrepreneurs, people who can build a business from scratch and can continue to expand it on a sound basis. The supply of managers in Latin America, perhaps better described as business administrators, i.e., people who know how to operate established businesses with reasonable success but who may not develop them substantially further, has improved over the years as a result of much improved higher education and the start of schools for business administration. However, when it comes to middle management or to lowest-level management—the foremen or department head—the supply is as poor as at the top.

The supply of managerial talent at different echelons is clearly proportionate to educational facilities and training opportunities. To a recent inquiry which I received from CIOS[1] on what I thought would be the most essential future requirements in management training, I replied, "The schooling and training of entrepreneurs," as opposed to managers or business administrators. This is where I see the greatest shortage in Latin America. On our rapidly developing subcontinent, there are thousands of opportunities but few well-conceived projects, and of the existing projects, very few are translated into enterprises, into economic impact. To identify opportunities, to develop them into feasible projects, and to translate projects into profitable enterprises takes entrepreneurs, not business administrators. It would be wrong, however, to believe that by increasing the entrepreneurial potential of Latin America alone, we would emerge from the state of a developing subcontinent. It takes not only generals to make a good army, it takes cadres, officers, sergeants, corporals, and privates.

[1] *Conseil International pour l'Organisation Scientifique,* translated International Federation of Management Organization.

If asked what capability and professional skill there was currently the greatest demand for in Latin America, I would probably come up with the answer: thoroughness and depth in approach and personal work for all echelons of managements, including entrepreneurs, and knowledge of modern techniques in finance and business administration for the top echelons—entrepreneurs through middle management. Of course, in Latin America, as probably all around the world, we place integrity, honesty, and loyalty to the task and to people ahead of capability and professional knowledge in all echelons of management in private enterprise or in the public sector.

The most restrictive force imposed on achieving rapid economic and social progress in Latin America is, without doubt, the shortage of management for private enterprise and in the public sector. Development is not primarily a matter of capital, but of people and of time— the time it takes to educate, train, and incorporate people into the market economy. And this requires management on all echelons in the public sector and in private enterprise.

The One-man Show

The most salient feature of present-day management in Latin America still is the one-man show.

Only few companies in the larger countries have a corporate management with adequate depth. In the great majority of private companies, and in the public sector, the authority for making decisions is still centralized at the top. In many private enterprises, the board chairman holds practically all the authority for making decisions, though he may dedicate only a limited amount of his time to the company. In many cases, he sits on the board of numerous companies, and it is not unusual that he makes the decisions for all of them.

The one-man show is only in part a remnant of ownership management traditional in family-owned companies. To some degree, it is the result of the custom in Latin America that people will only talk to the top man, chairman or minister, no matter how unimportant the subject may be. The main reason for the still widely prevailing one-man show management is the shortage of management. Delegation of responsibility and of authority only functions where there are people willing to accept and use it. In the absence of well-trained and responsible middle management the one-man show will persist, despite the desire of most any top man I know to free himself from routine decisions and routine work.

A second reason for the still widely prevailing one-man show in Latin American business is that existing and new businesses are built by relatively few imaginative and hardworking entrepreneurs. Compared to the pressure for accelerated development present in all Latin American countries, and to the opportunities at hand, there are far too few responsible and conscientious businessmen or public officials who are prepared to face the workload and the problems connected with assisting emerging countries in their development process. The exceptional ability and the capacity of these men for doing hard and thorough work lead to a concentration of activities around them which most of them would like to avoid.

Finally, because of the shortage of management and the lack of middle management, little of the four basic management functions— plan, decide, instruct, and control—is being carried out on lower echelons. Much of the detailed planning work has to be done at the top. The function of deciding cannot be delegated many times because there are still too few people capable or willing to assume it. "Instruct" turns into "do" many times when, despite clear instructions, things are not getting done. And under the aforementioned circumstances, the function of control sometimes takes rather preposterous proportions.

One of the fairly widespread misconceptions about the Latin American entrepreneur and manager is that he is a loafer who enjoys an easy life. The past twenty years have brought about a fundamental change in the Latin American businessman's attitude. Today, the majority of present-generation businessmen clearly recognize that the responsibility for economic development and social progress is as much theirs as it is their governments'. Due to the great demand for basic planning work and for leadership, as well as for doing thorough detail work, these men work long hours. They assume responsibilities and make sacrifices which many of their colleagues in the more industrialized continents would frown at.

The one-man show is a result of the disproportion between what needs to be done in developing countries and the manpower to accomplish it. Within our own organization, we make a conscious attempt to delegate responsibility and authority to the greatest number of people, but for every task or responsibility we delegate, two or more new assignments are added to the load at the top. Most, if not all, of these new assignments are projects and undertakings which are dictated by the ever present pressure for accelerated economic development, in the relatively short time which still may be left to us to overcome the most urgent problems of developing nations. We do not take on this constantly mounting load for reasons of higher income for our companies or for ourselves, but because we cannot in good conscience reject it. Thus, despite a determined effort to decentralize functions and to delegate responsibility and authority too great a concentration at the top tends to persist, because we cannot find or train people as rapidly as we need them.

Present-day Management Techniques

With few exceptions, the activity of private enterprise and of the public sector is still oriented entirely towards domestic markets and domestic development. Except for the large producers of agricultural commodities and the extractive industries which serve the world markets, private business in Latin America is organized towards working in small, isolated, and in many cases, highly protected domestic markets. This largely determines the present state of management techniques in use.

Because of the limited size of markets and companies, in many cases managements feel no urgent need to adopt more modern management techniques or they consider them too costly. All too often, however, the lack of familiarity with modern management techniques at the top of a company leads to a summary rejection of changes which are badly needed, with the argument which was not unknown in Europe some ten to twenty years ago (and still prevails in some rather large and backward European companies) that "we have run this company since its foundation with the present methods and techniques and have been successful," or "we are a special case, where these techniques are not applicable."

The use of modern management techniques in Latin American companies is not a question of their size. Size only is involved when one talks about the means of organization, equipment, and installations which involve heavy investments. While most companies in the smaller Latin American countries could not afford or profitably use such means of organization as third generation computers, they can immensely profit from modern management techniques.

Instead the medium-size and even large company in Latin America, particularly in the smaller countries, works usually with antiquated management techniques, such as the following:

1. Absence of systematic planning and business development, and of "knowledge functions."
2. No clear concept of organizational structure, no definition of functions, responsibilities, and authority.
3. No system of communication and of information.
4. Absence of modern marketing and selling techniques ("order-taking" rather than marketing and selling).
5. Deficient, if any, planning and control of production and inventories (instead, "hand-to-mouth" practices).
6. Primitive, if any, systems of cost accounting, cost control, and pricing (due to previous or still prevailing high margins, little competition within highly protected domestic markets).
7. Antiquated accounting practices.
8. Little or no financial planning and financial management, and in many cases lack of precise and timely controls for management.

Almost any change away from antiquated practices and towards more modern techniques could be accomplished without elaborate and costly means of organization, and would result in greater effectiveness and in lower cost of marketing, lower overhead in production, and lower administration expenses.

With increasing frequency, failures of companies can be traced to the absence of modern management techniques and control instruments, particularly when a business has been rapidly growing—over the head of its management. Many times it can also be traced to the treacherous effect of using traditional methods of accounting and financial management in inflationary economies. On this count, many a large foreign company not accustomed to operating in a strongly inflationary economy, found its capital wiped out by erosion though during all the years the profit and loss statement had shown large profits in local currency. One of the most severe errors we encounter frequently with Latin American businessmen is their opinion that inflation, currency risk, and erosion of capital are an exclusive worry of the *foreign* investor, while they have themselves invested local currency, and consider profits for them in local currency a true measure of their companies' success.

There exists a large gap in management techniques which needs to be closed, but there are encouraging signs of progress. Many of the younger generation of businessmen have been sent abroad to be educated and trained. When they take over, this means in most cases a change towards modern management techniques. In other cases, companies are forced to adopt more modern management techniques by increasing competition in their markets—sometimes competition from foreign-owned companies who "import" their management techniques. And changes are imposed on many a company because it outgrows the previously employed organization and techniques. Finally, though still inadequate in dimension and quality, universities in Latin America are beginning to teach business administration and finance.

The Challenge of the Future

A change away from antiquated management techniques will come none too soon for Latin American enterprises, if one visualizes what the next decade will hold in store for them.

Within their own growing domestic markets there is now and will be more competition in the future. Virtual monopolies, as they used to exist not too far back, are rapidly disappearing.

Increasing competition in their present market is, however, a very minor threat compared to the irreversible trend towards the establishment of larger trade areas, of subregional markets, like the already functioning Central American Common Market or the Common Market now aspired to by the countries of the Andean Group and the Caribbean Islands. All of the units, by overlapping, association, or merger, may eventually lead to LAFTA—the Latin American Free Trade Area.

Economic integration will impose demands on entrepreneurs and managers against which the adoption of more modern management techniques in their existing companies and for their existing markets may look like a minor undertaking. In addition to modern management techniques, without which they will be unable to operate and survive in the new era, they will have to adopt an entirely different philosophy and approach to marketing and sales, to production of scale, and with regard to the mobilization of financial and human resources. There will be the multi-national company, established through joint ventures, through acquisition, or through merger. The greater markets and keen competition will require equally greater investments in modern production facilities, which permit manufacturing on a large scale and in turn will require vastly greater financial resources which can no longer be raised in any one country alone.

Latin American businessmen will in the years to come face the same challenge and opportunities—and also the same problems—which European businessmen faced ten years ago, when EEC and EFTA were born. At that time very few European businessmen and enterprises recognized the full dimension of the challenge and opportunities and of the changes which would be required to adapt their companies to the new era. Many of them started late, and some of them too late to survive. They were swallowed by other companies or disappeared. The changes ahead for the Latin American businessman will be at least as great and hard to face as they were for his European colleague, but most probably a good deal harder. For many European enterprises the larger trade areas only meant one jump, from the relatively well organized smaller company operating in a smaller market to a well organized company of larger dimensions facing greater competition and requiring larger resources. For many Latin American companies the coming decade means two fundamental changes: first, from antiquated to modern management techniques, and second, from small, isolated, and highly protected markets to larger trade areas, many times the size of their present domestic markets. For some companies it means a change from virtually no competition to a completely open market. In addition, Latin American businessmen will have to cope with the great differences in the economic setting, monetary systems, and social progress in the countries they may be operating in under the concept of economic integration.

The changes imposed by economic integration on the Latin American businessmen and their companies will be immensely greater and more difficult to effect, compared to what their European colleagues went through in the past ten years. Can we meet this challenge? Can the average Latin American company survive? Or will it—more so than in Europe—be swallowed by large international companies which are not presently interested in the fractured and small domestic markets but which will be attracted by larger trade areas which lead to LAFTA?

Many of the Latin American entrepreneurs and companies have what it takes to make the change, to meet the challenge, to make use of the opportunities it offers, and to survive and prosper on their own.

A large number of enterprises may become part of multi-national companies formed between Latin American businessmen through joint ventures, mergers, and acquisition. Others, the ones which are too far behind now and are unwilling to face the challenge ahead and prepare themselves for the opportunities, will either be bought up or will die.

How can we bridge the already existing gap in management techniques? How can we satisfy the demand for more and better entrepreneurs and managers and get away from the obsolete "one-man show"? How can we meet the challenge of much larger markets and of greater dimensions in production and finance?

There is no hard and fast answer to all these questions. But something which becomes evident at once is that we must multiply the number of entrepreneurs and managers of all echelons, probably by importation from the "crops" turned out by the business and management schools established in America and Europe, by forgetting nationalism and encouraging immigration, and by rapidly stepping up the "production" in Latin America. We must tap just about every possible source for additional entrepreneurs, managers, and professionals.

Of the alternatives we have, importation or local formation, the latter is, of course, preferable, though much more difficult to achieve. Latin America is and will for some decades to come be a world which is rather different from America or Europe and vastly different from Japan. A good part of the entrepreneurs' and managers' effectiveness is derived from their intimate knowledge and understanding of countries, economies, resources, development potential, and people. It takes at least a few years to acquire this, regardless of how well it may have been taught at universities in America or Europe.

Nothing short of a determined joint effort by government and private business in Latin America to establish business schools and graduate schools throughout the subcontinent can solve our present and future shortage of entrepreneurs and management.

In addition to the initial efforts of foreign and local universities to teach business administration in business schools and graduate schools in each country, we need in Latin America one or two large major universities with the character of more than a university, of what I would call an "Economic Development Institute," with a business school for young people and a graduate school for entrepreneurs, industrialists, large farmers, investment bankers, and management for the public sector. Moreover, local and continent-wide business and graduate schools in Latin America would have to teach a few things which are not being taught in the more advanced countries, for instance, the techniques of operating business enterprises in inflationary countries and of development banking. And I wonder whether we will be able to create what we need most in Latin America, *a school of entrepreneurs and developers for private enterprise and for the public sector*, instead of only managers.

Regardless of what our efforts may be to learn and to teach, in the future—more so than in the past—management knowledge is likely to be obsolete by the time we have acquired and understood it.

G. A. COSTANZO

The Multi-National
Executive

18

I

Multi-national business has become very big business. Direct United States investments abroad now total about $60 billion compared with only $8 billion at the end of World War II, and they are growing at a rate of 10 per cent per annum in spite of governmental restraints.

Another, and perhaps more significant, measure of the dimension of United States international business is a recent estimate by Dr. Judd Polk of the International Chamber of Commerce on the value of the output of American-owned production facilities abroad. His estimate is in excess of $120 billion, the third largest in the world after the United States and the Soviet Union. Obviously, an activity of this dimension can no longer merely be a peripheral concern of American businessmen; it has become a matter of central importance today. There is every indication that American businessmen will continue to increase their direct investment abroad.

Multi-national businesses based in other developed countries are growing just as fast. Sweden, for instance had about $250 million invested in manufacturing subsidiaries abroad, i.e., outside Sweden, some ten or twelve years ago. The figure is now well above one billion dollars—and growing, it appears, at a faster rate than that of the direct investments of American manufacturing industry.

But size alone does not tell us much, unless we understand the challenges it brings. One of these will be to adapt to the accelerating pace of technological change. We are on the threshold of still another era of dynamic technological progress, which is certain to alter the face of international business as we know it today. In the 1970's a network of communications satellites and coaxial cables will encircle the globe, making possible the instantaneous transmission of business data from almost any place in the world to any other. This development, plus that of the multiple-access computer, will produce an information explosion that will become a driving force in business as well as an incredible asset for management control.

Moreover, technological progress is rapidly beginning to eliminate some of the obstacles to the development of a truly international corporation as it provides more sophisticated ways to coordinate and plan operations. The development of corporate planning techniques has occurred in recent years in response to the needs of the giant domestic corporation. These techniques are already being applied by corporations with far-flung international operations to integrate the international side of their business into their over-all strategy. As a result, there will be much more freedom to allocate responsibility to those in the best position to exercise it than has been the case in the past.

The success of international businessmen in organizing their operations for maximum efficiency and flexibility will largely determine their ability to meet a second challenge in the years ahead, that of increased competition in world markets.

As more and more companies in the United States and elsewhere begin to recognize the opportunities to be found in world markets and to expand across their own national boundaries, there will be a substantial increase in competition. Indeed, trade in manufactured goods among the industrial nations in the postwar period has been growing even faster than industrial output. This development is without historical precedent.

It is clear that as American companies become more dependent on external markets, their potential vulnerability to foreign competition will increase. As a result of lower labor costs, Western European and particularly Japanese companies are posing serious price competition.

American companies are generally credited with an edge in technological development. This is a matter of particular concern to our competitors. The outcome of the struggle for markets will depend increasingly upon research and development programs, and will result in an accelerated growth of science-based products and industries.

The existence of a technological gap has already begun to arouse some anxiety among Europeans who envision themselves in a position of economic subservience if the gap continues to widen. As a result, the international businessman finds himself faced with the challenge of nationalism.

Nationalistic resentment of foreign investment is a phenomenon that poses a real threat for the future. The potential conflict between nationalism and international business arises from the fact that investment by a foreign corporation is double-edged, in that it may or may not benefit the recipient. On the plus side, foreign investment brings a capital inflow to the country together with new technology. It also means more jobs for the local labor force. In addition, it may reduce imports and/or generate exports.

But the entry of the modern international firm into a country generates revolutionary forces which permeate the whole economy. Traditional business practices suddenly become obsolete. Local, family-run industrial empires, after literally a century of profitable operations, are faced with the urgent necessity of making revolutionary changes in order to survive. Of these changes, the most difficult is the adaptation of modern business management techniques. Obviously, this may create resentment and can fan the fires of nationalism.

It is possible to envision a future in which the scale, complexity, and importance of international business spurred by technological change will increase immeasurably. Moreover, differences in economic growth, ingrained nationalistic habits, and the differing nature of competition itself all tend to change the ground rules.

The man who has been an effective executive in domestic operations is therefore not always equally effective in an international context. Experience suggests that international businessmen must possess certain qualities that are not essential for success in business at home, yet may make the difference between success and failure in overseas operations.

The question is therefore how to select and train a man who can keep pace with technology, meet competition, develop local managers, and yet avoid triggering a nationalistic backlash. What kind of man can meet the challenges of the international business world of the future? Here are some tentative suggestions.

First, and probably foremost, is the matter of a man's attitudes, and how they have been formed. He must want to live and work in any part of the world for an indefinite period of time. He must understand what this commitment entails, and he must be capable of fulfilling it.

It is not an easy matter for business recruiters to identify such a man. Certainly pre-employment tests would not be relevant here. There is probably no group of businessmen in the United States today with more diverse backgrounds than those in international business. There are English majors as well as MBA's heading up international divisions for leading American corporations. It is necessary to look at the whole man, his intelligence, background, personality, education, and skills. International business is not the place for narrow-minded individuals of limited scope.

There are, however, certain traits common to the men who succeed in international business. As a group, they tend to be flexible when confronted with new situations. They can adapt to foreign cultures and operate effectively within them. Conversely, they are not easily frustrated when they discover that the old answers no longer seem to apply to the new problems that confront them.

What is more, they have probing, analytical minds. They can reach decisions even when they must work with limited information, as is still frequently the case in international business. They possess empathy in their approach to new people and new situations. They take time to listen to an opposing point of view and proceed into new areas with an open mind. They employ a diplomatic approach in their dealings at all levels. They frequently possess a genuine interest in closer ties among nations and feel a sense of involvement in the task of economic development and in an improvement in living standards throughout the world. It is this strain of altruism that is often what attracts them into international business to begin with.

These are the personal characteristics that subtly distinguish the international businessman from his domestic counterpart. It is clear that an individual who does not possess these characteristics is ill-suited for a career in international business.

But the individual who has the right personal characteristics also needs certain knowledge and skills to do his job overseas.

The first and most obvious of these, but also the most important, is *language.* It is impossible to overemphasize the need for fluency in the language of a host country. Men who try to do business without a firm footing in the language are placing themselves at an inordinate disadvantage. It is unrealistic to rely on others knowing English. What is worse is that our foreign competitors often make a mockery of us by speaking several languages fluently. Americans have tended to delude themselves about languages, paying lip service to their importance, but rarely learning to speak them.

Second, the need for more *sophisticated business tools* is increasing as the conduct of international business itself becomes more sophisticated. In light of the developments in technology and business techniques, knowledge of the principle of corporate planning and budgeting will be helpful. So will a basic understanding of the computer.

Third, there is also a need for a broadbased familiarity with *what is going on in the world.* This goes well beyond the "literary" in history one can acquire in courses in contemporary events. It includes an attitude and a point of view.

Finally, a man must have a grounding in *international economics.* The multi-national executive needs to understand the fundamentals of the international monetary system and the interrelationships between monetary and fiscal policies, prices, the international balance of payments, and exchange rates.

To be sure, these are areas that can be filled in during the course of an individual's career. In a corporate environment which has recognized the importance of *continuing education*, the business schools have begun to work closely with corporations to provide the knowledge and skills needed to speed an individual's progress.

What I have been suggesting essentially is that the international company is looking not for readers of cook books, but for *cordon bleu* chefs; not for potential candidates who simply go by the business texts, but for those who can be creative in a foreign environment of change as well.

II

Multi-national business is becoming so important that the business school had better prepare *all* its students for it. The young man who graduates from one of our business schools without the realization of the scope and thrust of multi-national business is as unprepared for the reality of our economy as the young man who graduates without a little accounting knowledge. Surely, the speed of expansion of multi-national business makes it a primary opportunity area for the young man planning a business career.

This applies particularly to the many students from foreign countries who are attending our business schools. In many ways these young men are the ideal candidates for employment in their home countries in executive positions by a multi-national corporation. In turn, the multi-national company can often offer them opportunities to put to work what they have learned and want to apply which are superior to the opportunities other, purely domestic employers in their native countries might be willing and able to offer them.

It is then comparatively easy for the multi-national business to help this young American-educated employee to develop himself as he advances. We at First National City Bank have begun to introduce executive development programs in selected locations overseas. We have been successful enough in this experiment to amend our manpower plans for American personnel abroad. In the next five years we plan to hold recruiting of Americans for our international staff at present levels, although we anticipate a doubling of over-all manpower needs as we continue to expand rapidly abroad.

There is, in other words, a big job being done by the American business school in preparing young men for this multi-national business world. And there is an even bigger one yet to be tackled.

Still, however necessary programs in multi-national business are—a basic education for every young man and woman in our business schools today—they are only a foundation. The major need lies in the continuing education of men as they move from domestic into multi-national careers, and as they move up the ladder in the multi-national business both at headquarters and abroad. These men need to acquire specific skills—languages; knowledge of history, culture, customs; international economics and finance; often some law, and so on. They need, above all, to be helped to develop attitudes—it is not the easiest thing in the world to be a good representative of your country abroad without being a snob, or, conversely, to be appreciative of a foreign culture without becoming an expatriate.

Above all, however, the multi-national executive needs the opportunity to reflect on his experience and to think through his needs and opportunities. This is a rapidly moving, a rapidly evolving area in which everyone has to learn as he runs—but he must also teach as he himself grows and develops.

This, obviously, is not within reach of the youngster who has not yet started on a career.

Continuing, advanced education of the successful, the mature, the accomplished multi-national executive is thus our greatest need. Not all of it, obviously, can be satisfied by the schools. Indeed the major part of the task lies with the company—and, of course, with the individual himself.

But there is a great and growing opportunity for the business school to develop into the educational institution for this new, central human resource of the world economy: the multi-national executive. His vision and field of action is the world economy, and he therefore has to be a top-flight business manager; a bridge between cultures, languages, traditions; and capable of taking independent responsibility in the country in which he works and yet be a responsive and responsible member of a multi-national team.

THE MISSION OF THE BUSINESS SCHOOL

IV

EDITOR'S INTRODUCTION

Should there be one prototype, one universal model for systematic business education? Or is diversity a source of strength in business education and appropriate to its tasks? This question has been debated since business schools first emerged almost a hundred years ago. Should the business school be, first and foremost, a member of academia, or, first and foremost, a part of the business community? Should it be a tool maker—or perhaps a concept maker—for business, or should it be the conscience of the business community? Should it be altogether a business *school, or a school of* administration *embracing other organized institutions of our society in its scope? These are some of the questions considered in the fourth and last part of this book in which the challenges of environment, economy, and business are projected on the role and mission of the business school.*

HOWARD W. JOHNSON

Education for Enterprise Management

19

Change, Contrast, Interdependence

Technology and its products have revolutionized our environment—our travel, our communication, our economy. We are in the process of a social, economic, and political reformation in which only the fittest of enterprises will survive.

In this setting, the task of education for enterprise management will be to provide the climate in which men of rare imagination are nurtured and their full abilities are brought to bear creatively within the framework of their organization and within the larger environment in which it operates. The need will be for men who have entrepreneurial spirit and energy; who are innovative; who have the capacity for translating ideas and discoveries into action; who are both receptive to change and initiators of change; who have a high tolerance for ambiguity and uncertainty; who have the will to risk.

Our rapidly changing environment has encouraged a wide diversity of expectation and achievement. It has resulted also in a record of progress that is uneven. There is no harmonious advance of material and social benefits in all sectors of our society. And, again, it is technology that seems to be the common cause of the paradox—the curious coexistence of the contrasts of hope and despair, potential and reality, side by side. Technology is seen at once as our blessing and our bane, the wellspring of our aspirations and the threat to our well-being. It appears both as social benefactor and social calamity. It offers us nuclear power and holds the specter of thermonuclear destruction. It means both personal transportation and urban pollution, computation efficiency which multiplies our creative power and threatens our privacy; mass communication and mass propaganda; and an affluent but alienated youth. Technology offers the potential of the good life, but seems unable to relieve the poverty around us. There are rich nations and poor nations, and the gulf steadily widens. Huxley may well have been right to ask, "What are you going to do with all these new things?"

Clearly science, which forms the foundation for our technology, plays a critical role. But scientific knowledge alone is not enough. The effective approach lies in a partnership of technology and management —both industrial and social—which will be intensely responsive to human need, and will so order the distribution of technology's products and our national priorities as to resolve the paradox.

The holistic view of man's knowledge and problems has given rise to what some have called the "systems society," in which technological, social, political, and economic factors are seen as parts of a larger framework. Not the variables alone, but their relationship and interdependence determine the size and scope of our endeavor as well as our potential for progress.

To a large degree, the challenge for business education in a systems world is to create a wide awareness on the part of those who should understand modern culture, and, beyond that, to provide a logical approach to the manager for the solution of existing problems and for the charting of new courses for the future.

In sum, whether we will it or not, society in every country of the world is undergoing rapid transformation, and the business enterprise is at the center of this transformation. It is changing internally in products and processes, in organizational form, and in the employment of information technology to speed and refine its decisions. It is growing larger through merger and acquisition and expanding markets. Externally the firm is forced to be more responsive—to government, to society, to its customers, as well as to its employees and their unions. These changes represent both challenges and opportunities for the American business enterprise in the next decade.

It is essential, therefore, that the managerial leaders who are educated in this changing world be adaptive and innovative, themselves agents of change if they and their institutions are to survive.

Extraordinary Performance

Against a setting that is so formidable in its demands on the manager, extraordinary performance will become a standard, an expectation, and a threshold of tolerance that schools of business will have to aim for and build upon in their curricula and programs. Education for management will be the process by which creative imagination can be disciplined to produce men who will meet this specification of extraordinary performance.

Before going into a more fundamental discussion of the aims of management education in the future, it is appropriate to review some critical areas of curriculum and educational approach where revisions are necessary. Some of these revisions are underway in several institutions, and there is high hope that the quality of their results will justify the intensive effort that is expended in planning and carrying them out.

The first area of concern is *competence*, basic versus applied administrative competence. A great portion of the curriculum in business schools to date has emphasized the teaching of applied skills—accounting, production, marketing, human and labor relations, and so forth. To the extent that these skills are taught as specific techniques, they suffer the obsolescence that is so prevalent in technical products and services. But even when they are taught as principles or dynamic processes, they still fall short of achieving the wide sweep of interdependence that is required and must be established among these applied fields. And so the standard teaching of administrative competence in the applied fields will no longer provide the background for the management of large industrial enterprise and large public and service systems.

What, then, will be the new directions for the teaching of this competence? It seems clear that the emphasis in the future will be shifted more and more from techniques to basic principles of practice; and from applied business fields to basic management sciences, drawing heavily upon the physical and the social sciences.

A second area of concern is the *method of presentation* and examination of the course material in management education. It will be essential for the management student to understand, to develop, and to appreciate the skills of thorough analysis in order to understand and practice the decision-making process. A recent debate between students and faculty about the different "schools of approach" employed by well-developed schools of business illustrate this point. One of the discussants likened the teaching of management to swimming instruction without water. He described one approach as "putting the student in a room where the air was very moist and asking him to practice swimming strokes." The other approach was to "teach students hydro-dynamics and have them do push-ups." The latter approach places stress on analysis, of course. Obviously neither approach is perfect without balance, and neither is adequate without some kind of internship or real experience. But the point that should be made here is that analysis is the *sine qua non* for effective and insightful understanding of practice.

A third area for consideration is the process of finding solutions or, as it is best known, the *problem-solving* approach to management education. This is an approach and an emphasis that has been with us for a long time. It has formed the basis, one might say, for the development of American business education, certainly in the last 20 to 30 years. But so central is the problem-solving concept that, on occasion, we overemphasize one of its aspects, the seeking of definitive and final answers.

There is something very attractive indeed in the sense of accomplishment that obtaining an answer to a problem provides. The neatness of an answer has the appealing qualities of order and perfection that are hard to resist. We are especially aware of this in a university like the Massachusetts Institute of Technology where the study of elementary physics and mathematics prepares the students, by the time they enter as freshmen, to seek and expect final answers to stated problems. The dangers of applying this approach to advanced material, and especially of applying it to the social sciences and to management, cannot be overemphasized. Not only is it demoralizing to find that neat answers do not provide real solutions to complex problems, but students who wear answer-seeking blinders also tend to be carried away, and flatly refuse to face the multitude of factors and variables that make up current business problems. The result is bound to be narrow-minded and devoid of reality and depth. It often fails even to define the problem. A capital requirement of the new curricula in management should be a perspective in the identification of problems to guarantee that the whole problem will stay in focus at all times, and that partial solutions will not be elevated to the status of final answers. Perhaps the simple way to state this is that the student should be prepared for the fact that there are no final answers, and that problem-solving should be measured on progress rather than finality. To achieve this continuity of evaluation and depth of perspective, we need to provide students with a conceptual base that will allow and encourage the functions of continuing feedback between action and planning stages. This may range from a formal knowledge of communication theory and sensitivity training, to informal appreciation and sharpening of interpersonal skills.

A fourth area of concern involves the *transferability* of management skills as a critical factor to be taken into account and to be borne as an objective of a good management education.

Returning to the requirements of the environment within which management decisions will be made, it seems clear that, for managers of future organizations, the need for reshuffling of human resources, the emphasis on organic versus organizational solutions to problems, and the need to reorder priorities rapidly, midstream as it were, will require a special agility and a competence in managing ambiguity and change. These conditions will place a high premium on the manager who is able to transfer his effectiveness from one task to another.

In the past several years, we have seen an extraordinarily successful experiment with this notion of the transferability of management skills in the experiences of young master's graduates who have served for two years in positions of responsibility as M.I.T. Fellows in Africa. This program was initiated on the basis of a professor's conviction that young men with high intelligence and a problem-solving management education could be readily useful and able to carry major responsibilities and heavy workloads in the government agencies and public or private corporations of the developing nations. The Fellows had no previous familiarity with local conditions and culture; yet they were able to adapt and to produce quickly, just as managers will have to do in what Professor Warren G. Bennis has labelled the "temporary society" and the "changing organizations" of the future.

As for the specific directions in the revisions of management curricula, it might be useful to review briefly some of the changes in M.I.T.'s Sloan Fellowship Program in the past twelve years. In 1955, the whole field of organizational behavior had only a slim foothold in the curriculum. The late Douglas McGregor and his colleague Alex Bavelas were groping for ways to couple the theories of the behavioral sciences to the problems of management, and teach them effectively to the Sloan Fellows. While we are still a long way from applying in practice all that we know from behavioral science theory, the body of knowledge about the human side of enterprise has expanded enormously in the past decade.

In the field of finance, twelve years ago instruction rested largely on assessment of a firm's requirements for funds and the best means of obtaining them. The rigorous analytical approach to risk, uncertainty, and capital cost measurement in the management of corporate assets had not yet found its way into the classroom.

Application of the computer to the problems and processes of the firm was then vaguely foreshadowed. But in the intervening years, a great new field of management information systems and control has developed, which parallels the new computer and communication technology.

Marketing as a field was long on practice, short on theory and analysis. Today, increasingly, the uncertainties of the marketplace are giving way, or at any rate are being narrowed, by application of statistics and the methods of operations research.

The management of research and development as a subject of inquiry hardly existed twelve years ago. Now there is a growing body of literature and organized instruction illuminating the special problems of organization for discovery.

This is by no means a complete catalogue of changes in the body of knowledge available and appropriate to be taught to a group of young American managers. But it is an indicator of a shift in the focus and the philosophy of management education over the past decade. It is, in part, the curricular response to the requirement for extraordinary performance.

Continuous Learning

The primary point here is, of course, that the knowledge available for improving the practice of management has been growing and will grow more rapidly; that each managerial generation no longer has to learn primarily through experience, and that this changes what the manager can do and what is demanded of him. The processes of management education and management development of the future must take cognizance of the need of potential managers to acquire this body of knowledge—and skill in its application—but more than that, to recognize that the acceleration of research on management and the rising accumulation of knowledge will very quickly make obsolete the manager who switches off his formal learning apparatus the day he leaves the university.

The university's role in contributing to an individual's development by no means ends with his graduation. *Education must be continuous.* The successful companies will be in partnership with the universities in this process of human capital formation. Not all continuing education will have to take place within the university framework, but the university has a responsibility for setting standards and for innovation. In the end, of course, education is an individual rather than an institution-centered process—important as the institution must be.

Organization of Talent

It is clear that the manager must be aware of changes taking place within the organization. The American labor force is increasingly better educated, and this implies both a higher level of aspiration and a need for management to tap the creative capacities of labor, to organize talent, and to motivate it effectively. For example, by 1975 six out of every ten American workers over 25 years of age will be high school graduates, that is, with twelve years of formal schooling; one in four will have had some university education. Professional, managerial, clerical, and sales personnel will outnumber skilled craftsmen. With the vast sums being spent on research and development, men engaged in such work constitute an increasing proportion of the American work force. They are in great demand and they are highly mobile. *Management education must seek new approaches to organizing and directing their work in order to maximize the effectiveness of their efforts.*

Computation and communication technology have a profound effect on the internal structure of the firm, an effect which we are only beginning to see and cannot yet perceive in its full implications. There seems little question that the computer is becoming an indispensable and all-pervasive element in the modern corporation. By 1975 there are expected to be 85,000 computers in operation in the United States, representing an investment of more than $30 billion. The potentials of this capacity for the control of processes, for the employment of information in the firm, and for the handling of routine and increasingly sophisticated decisions is certain to have a powerful effect upon the nature of managerial work, shifting it in the direction of the unstructured, non-programmed work, and away from more routine analysis, allocation, and evaluation. Goal setting, strategy formulation, policy questions will occupy more of the manager's time and he will be aided in his thinking by the information system at his fingertips. He will be more involved in understanding the environment and in defining the system in which he makes his decisions. His education must supply him with an awareness of the potential, if not the depth, that technology makes available to him. In short, the manager need not be a technologist; but he must understand technology. He must organize human talent in ways that take full advantage of technological capability.

Focus on Entrepreneurship

The changing environment and changing role of the manager indicate the need for a shift in the focus of management education toward the basic qualities of entrepreneurship: invention, innovation, and adaptation. The universities clearly have a role in aiding the individual in the development of the knowledge, skills, motivation, and attitudes which characterize this adaptive and innovative spirit. At the undergraduate level, colleges have been examining their programs carefully with the aim of increasing the student's independence and freedom of choice, giving him an opportunity to range more broadly over the curriculum, and devising laboratory opportunities for the undergraduate to design and carry out his own projects. A particular experiment in the undergraduate program of the School of Management has attracted wide interest within M.I.T. and elsewhere by providing a selected group of students the opportunity to take essentially full responsibility for their own education in their final two years. The students define their own needs and interests, organize their programs, and involve the faculty and segments of the business community as resources in the educational pursuit. The outcome clearly has been a more confident, more venturesome spirit among the men who have taken part in that program.

Above all, the manager of enterprise must be an entrepreneur. In the graduate schools of business there is increasing concern for the development of an entrepreneurial outlook and attitude on the part of the students. This does not mean less emphasis on the development of analytical knowledge and capacity, or of organizational skills. Rather, it means a continuous search for ways to identify students with an entrepreneurial spark and to reinforce rather than inhibit these qualities throughout the educational process.

In the corporate sphere, we see that some companies have been inventive in creating opportunities for younger men to try out their entrepreneurial energies in the development of new products. These approaches have included creating product or project teams, men working together within the framework of the company, but with a sense of independence and freedom to be wholly responsible for developing and bringing a new product to the market. Their activities include design, packaging, pricing, and promotion—seeking advice within the company and use of its resources, but taking the responsibility for the outcome as individuals. This, too, is part of managerial education.

Such an approach by corporate enterprise requires the capacity and willingness of the organization to absorb risk for the sake of creativity and innovation, to push into unexplored areas where there is high potential for error. To determine whether new ideas are real contributions usually requires investigation and experiment—time and resources are required to avoid premature judgment. If an organization is too tightly run, the climate is usually unfavorable for innovation. There must also be an ethos in the organization that is conducive to change. Risk taking must be legitimate. Managers in all firms continually must ask themselves how this opportunity for risk-taking development can be improved. For in the final analysis, the most effective (though costly) management education can take place only in the world of practice where both errors and successes can have immediate and real feedback to the individual who learns by making decisions.

Commitment

American society puts an increasing demand on the manager and the firm to exercise a sense of *social and ethical responsibility*. This is another major area of challenge for management education, and it will influence the range of knowledge, values and abilities of the manager in the future. Society clearly is charging the corporate enterprise with responsibility for the safety and effectiveness of its products and for the quality of the community through an active role as a corporate citizen, and expects the corporation to apply its resources to find new solutions. It is becoming increasingly clear that the *manager must be politically and economically educated* to be sensitive to the consequences of his actions and to the consequences of environmental conditions for his enterprise. He must develop economic insight to adapt to a changing economic environment.

The evidences of the need for education to contribute more in this area are many. The public uproar over automobile safety is an illustration, and it is highly probable that the automotive industry will be increasingly challenged to take a leading role in the solution of the problems to which the automobile has contributed in our society, such as the congestion of the cities and the pollution of the air. American business is being challenged directly to take the initiative and leadership in providing job training and job opportunities for the hard-core unemployed. The opportunities are manifold for business enterprise to be innovative in solving the problems of education, housing, transportation, and of rebuilding our cities into a viable and enriching social environment.

Management education cannot afford to overlook these important new areas of learning for responsibility. A deep sense of commitment cannot be instilled, but new courses focusing on the intensity of human and social content in the decision-making process are both desirable and necessary.

CLIFFORD D. CLARK

New Directions in Professional Business Education

20

Events and Ideas

In discussing the inevitable gap between generations, Walter Lippmann recently wrote: "The movement of events is almost always a great deal faster than the movement of our own minds." He observed, further, that "as men grow older and take charge of affairs, they must battle a persistent human tendency to see the world through spectacles that fitted them twenty or thirty years earlier." (*Harper's*, October, 1967.) Few would question the truth of these comments, particularly when applied to social, economic, and political events. My purpose is to apply them to some fundamental issues of higher education for business.

Among the goals of the business schools, highest priorities must be accorded to the preparation of individuals for productive involvement in business activities today and tomorrow. The spectacles fitted to the young by an older generation of teachers must, accordingly, be designed with the utmost concern for useful service extending a period of years into the future. Transmission of accumulated knowledge is not enough. The classrooms of the business schools should provide, continually, an experimental setting for testing traditional concepts against the movement of

245

events so as to determine inadequacies and to make revisions. In these experiments, a premium is placed on empirical methods of research and on the study of business institutions and practices. As a general matter, understanding "what is" precedes the development of principles or analyses suggesting policy, or "what should be."[1] Events take place in institutional settings, and if they are to stimulate accretions to organized knowledge, they should be studied on native grounds.[2]

Business schools are aware of, and constantly resist, man's tendency to see current events in former settings and to approach current problems with obsolete methods. During the past fifteen years, they have made vast revisions in courses of study, and they now stress techniques of analysis and the understanding of relevant disciplines. Descriptive studies of fragmented business practices no longer occupy central positions in curricula.

Activities of Business and Curricula

Although no attempt is made here to classify the various approaches of business schools to academic work, there appears to be appreciation for grouping areas of business study in accord with three sets or classes of activity common to business units: (1) those involving the organization of real productive resources; (2) those involving the financial aspects of planning, control and management, and (3) those concerned with administration and environment.

Real Productive Resources

The organization or combination of real productive resources by businesses involves levels and variation in rates of production, and relates to sales, inventories, the relative scarcity of resources or constraints on their use, and technological conditions. Financial and

---

[1]There should be no misunderstanding on this point. The study of what is is not a goal in itself, but a means to the development of theoretical explanations frequently in a scientific sense.

[2]Although it is sufficient here to place emphasis on institutional research, but not to the exclusion of other methods, some would state the above proposition in stronger language by hypothesizing that institutionally-oriented research in business and economics has, historically, led to more useful theories than, say, deductive methods. (See, for example, Martin Blyn, *Essays in Innovation of American Academic Economists*, Ph.D. Dissertation, New York University, 1966. Clearly, theories do lag events in many cases, for example, in the field of social legislation.

monetary dimensions of resource use must enter into the determination of efficiency or optimal combinations, although they need not be given primary attention.

The business school curriculum approaches these problems through the study of production, marketing, accounting, operations analysis, statistics, and management science with an organizational emphasis. Not only does economics contribute directly to the study of these activities, but also indirectly by providing the other disciplines with normative propositions. Although these approaches of the business schools have not been in effect long, they are promising. Yet it is clear there are weaknesses, and these have to do primarily with the frequent, and perhaps general, teaching of the various disciplines as though they were subject to strict lines of demarcation, one from the other.

Financial Aspects

The financial aspects of management and planning include the management of the financial resources as such, financing operations and expansion, and the use of financial controls. The courses of study in business schools which deal with these matters include corporation finance, investments, accounting, financial institutions, operations analysis, statistics, and economics. All of these fields, as they apply to the financial activities of business units, have made significant progress in the past few years. Perhaps it is this rapid progress which has blinded us to the fact that few attempts have been made to apply findings from the behavioral sciences to the financial dimensions of business. Nor have economics been integrated with business decisions and financial planning. As in the previous class of business activities, the fields of study tend, too much, to be taught as separate and unrelated disciplines.

Administration and Environment

The activities of the business unit grouped under the heading of administration and environment include the methods and organizational arrangements to establish goals, the utilization and communication of information in decisions and control, the responses to and influences on markets, and circumstances and policies external to the business unit. The contributing fields of study in the business schools are management principles, marketing (both marketing management and market structure), managerial aspects of accounting and finance, behavioral approaches to organization theory, statistics, operations analysis, and studies of the environment either with legal or economic emphasis. Frequently attempts are made to relate the divisions of business study through courses in policy, simulation exercises, or cases. Although these approaches to the understanding of business administration and environment are of great value, improvements must be made in the formal study of environment, in fusing the various fields of business inquiry, and, perhaps most important, in developing and applying concepts derived from the behavioral sciences.

Although the discussion above contains some suggested changes in business education, particularly as they apply at the graduate level, there is need to review these tentative conclusions in juxtaposition with some identifiable forces affecting the future conditions of business.

Evolving Patterns and Business Education

The previous discussion focused attention on the business unit and on the nature of educational efforts to prepare individuals for careers in business. Attention is given below to forces of economic and social change and to some of their implications for business and for business education. It is useful in this regard to organize thoughts in accord with the major determinants of economic growth. Although they may be grouped in different ways, five factors influencing growth have been selected. They are:

1. Increases in population, the labor force, and productive hours of labor.
2. Growth of the capital stock, with primary emphasis on physical plant and equipment.
3. Increases in the rate of productivity which are related, in turn, to the development of knowledge regarding methods of employing productive resources, to the enhancement of managerial skills, and to the dissemination of innovations.
4. Expansion of the market place with the implied scale effects of mass production and mass marketing techniques.
5. Changes in the institutional environment including monetary and fiscal measures, and, in general, the relationship of government to business.

Population and Labor Force

If quantitative projections were derived from this classification, it would be necessary to note, for example, that the population of the United States in 1980 might reach about 250 million people. It would also be necessary to take into account the age composition of the population, the probable size of the work force, which may grow at an annual rate which is from 20 per cent to 50 per cent faster than in the postwar years, the shortening of the work week, and finally, the rate of unemployment. By making these adjustments, a figure for hours worked by the total labor force would be determined. Primary concern here, however, is with qualitative, not quantitative, factors, and the importance of growth in the labor force is to be measured in terms of skills, not numbers. In the mid-fifties, for example, the number of white collar workers began to exceed, for the first time, the number of blue collar members of the labor force, and by 1975 the white collar workers will outnumber blue collar workers by 50 per cent or more. Concurrently, the number of unskilled workers will increase very little, if at all.[3]

There are various reasons for changes in the composition of the labor force. They are related to the fact that an increasing proportion of our national economic effort is devoted to the production of services, rather than of goods. The growth of federal, state, and local governmental activities also contributes. Changes in the mix of required labor and productive skills are influenced in large part by increased sophistication of business processes, including automated production and control methods.[4] Businesses today draw on research and advisory services to an unprecedented degree.

[3]Projections to 1975 have been made by the National Industrial Conference Board, *Economic Potentials of the United States in the Next Decade* (1965).

[4]Some quantitative projections are based on the expectation that a significant portion of the future labor force will be technologically unemployed. Despite its initial strength, the structural hypothesis, as set forth, for example, by Professor Charles Killingsworth, has been largely discredited by recent events. Had the hypothesis been stated with a greater degree of flexibility, it would have withstood much of the criticism, for surely, the need for training, retraining, and general improvement of labor skills will remain in the future. It is unlikely, however, that a large fraction of the labor force will consist of the structurally unemployed.

Capital Stock

A quantitative projection would also estimate growth of the capital stock or of investment expenditures and utilize the results in a model designed to estimate gross national product.[5] In considering capital expenditures, the projection would depend largely on the future course of governmental policy. Is it expected, for example, that policy will be designed to encourage investment as in recent years, or will policy give greater emphasis to the production of consumer goods, or will the policy vary over the cycle? Recent experience with the investment credit suggests it may be used as a counter-cyclical weapon rather than as a long-term instrument.[6] It is sufficient to note that the qualitative issue here is one of governmental policy.

Productivity and Management

A quantitative projection would also take into account trends in output per man hour, and project rates of from 3 to 4 per cent per year. Productivity rates have been much higher in the past thirty years than in preceding periods of our history, and they may account for as much as two-thirds of our growth in recent years. Further, they are undoubtedly related to educational and research accomplishments. It is not by chance, for example, that one of the largest productivity increases has been registered for some time by the agricultural sector. Significant research efforts, jointly sponsored by universities and government, were made in agriculture many years ago. The growth of research and development expenditures in the private sector and the relations of these efforts to the research activities of government is one of the fascinating issues which has emerged in the postwar years.

Improved productive processes and managerial skills have contributed and will continue to assist productivity. Herman Kahn and Anthony Wiener in the recent book, *The Year 2000*, suggest that "modern management and production techniques" can be considered the instruments of contemporary expansion.[7] Their view is related to

[5]The Industrial Conference Board projects an increase in capital stock of 3.6 per cent per year to 1975.

[6]Despite this recent experience with the investment credit, it seems likely that long term policy will be favorable to investment as an avenue to growth.

[7]Herman Kahn and Anthony J. Wiener, *The Year 2000* (New York: The Macmillan Company, 1967), p. 45.

the assumption provided by Daniel Bell that "the United States is becoming a post-industrial society ... defined as one in which the organization of theoretical knowledge becomes paramount for innovation in the society."[8]

The combined result of the growth of the labor force, of capital stock, and of productivity may serve to increase national product from 4 per cent to 4.5 per cent per year, and yield a GNP in 1980 two-thirds larger than at present. Of course, a number of assumptions are necessary to support any such projection. For example, it is reasonable to anticipate the continuation of a relatively peaceful world and of an adequate supply of natural and energy resources. With respect to the international climate, the economist can only state his assumptions underlying the projections. It is reasonable to assume that the pressures on our energy resources will be overcome through imaginative use of materials available to us and through international trade.[9]

The composition of the projected national product will be significantly influenced by the extent to which national income is derived from private market activities and by the extent to which it is derived from public activities. Particularly important in this respect is the expected rapid increase in state and local expenditures.

Markets

There is every reason to suspect that markets will continue to expand both internally and internationally. Associated with this expansion will be larger scale production and larger management units. In general, increases in scale of production lead to increased efficiency, although this may not be true in particular cases.[10] Expected growth

---

[8]*Ibid.*, p. xxvii.

[9]See, for example, Harrison Brown, James Bonner, and John Weir, *The Next Hundred Years.* The authors of the book are less optimistic about the development of required scientific and engineering manpower than they are about energy resources. However, the economic forces of the market are more effective in directing human resources than is frequently believed. Professor George Stigler's analysis of the supply of engineers is persuasive. There are, however, other aspects in which the market may not bring about a socially optimum allocation of scientific resources, and this applies to those pursuing or potentially capable of engaging in basic research. The external or "spillover" consequences of such research are not fully taken into account by market forces.

Alternative projections of G.N.P. and population to 1985 and to 2000 are given in: Herman Kahn and Anthony J. Wiener, *The Year 2000*, Table XII, p. 159.

[10]The growth of large corporations in the sense recently suggested by John Kenneth Galbraith is not at issue. His concern was with the growth of relative economic power. It is suggested here only that absolute size will increase, and emphasis is given to production, not marketing.

in the size of the typical business unit and its increasing involvement in other cultures and countries seems well supported by historical trends and economic reasons.

Government and Business

The unprecedented economic expansion enjoyed by the American economy during the past few years must be attributed, in part, to the recognition that government has responsibilities to influence general economic activity. Surely, governmental responsibilities will continue to extend to other areas as increasing affluence permits certain problems formerly accorded low priorities to receive attention. It is not only a matter of priorities, but also a matter of new technology, such as that associated with space research and exploration, which virtually require joint efforts. These developments need not be such as to reduce the private sector. They may be structured, with imaginative planning, so as to permit expansion of the private sector into areas formerly reserved for governmental activity—for example, in urban development.

Some Questions

The various developments or evolving forces sketched out above raise a number of questions, some of considerable significance for educational institutions. A few examples are:

What will be the result of involving a larger and larger proportion of our human resources in service activities, in highly skilled occupations, and in professional pursuits?

What are the implications of the fact that high rates of productivity increase can be associated with educational and research efforts supported by business, by public bodies, and universities?

What implications flow from the fact that managerial skills contribute powerfully to economic development?

What are the challenges presented by the exceptionally rapid growth of state and local expenditures, and the related concentration of our population in urban centers?

What are the ramifications of public acceptance of responsibility for rates of unemployment, income distribution and maintenance, changes in price levels and the extent of economic growth?[11]

What are some of the implications of growth in size of the market place, including continual extension beyond national boundaries, and of technical achievements implied by larger productive units?

Although it is not possible to foresee the implications of all these questions, some suggestions are possible.

Some Implications

Upgrading of the labor force necessarily involves greater educational activity and raises such questions as the relative emphasis given to technical courses of study as compared to those based on the liberal arts.[12] Whatever the proper balance between the liberal and technical courses may be, the trend to greater skills—skills which are viable in the presence of vast change—will place a premium on those aspects of education which give guidance and permit adaptation in the face

---

[11]A related concern of public policy is the structure of our international balance of payments. Emphasis is given to employment, prices, and growth, to suggest these as goals. The state of the balance of payments becomes, in consequence, a constraint on achievement of the national goals, but is not, *per se*, a goal.

[12]There are two facets, at least, to this question. In secondary education the issue is that of vocational versus college preparatory courses. Growing concern for the circumstances of the low skilled, frequently in the youngest age group of the labor force, has given strength to the arguments for vocational training. Whether responsibility for such training rests with the schools or with programs designed to promote economic development or to combat poverty is the current issue. In the universities the question is that of professional versus liberal education. This question is properly cast in the form of a conflict, provided that the curricula of the two forms of education are fixed and relatively rigid. The question, however, is not properly stated as a conflict if the curricula, particularly of the professional schools, are responsive to relevant social changes. In *Educating Tomorrow's Managers*, the Committee for Economic Development (October, 1964) has stated it this way: "Although a liberal education has its traditional and timeless aspects, it is not a static concept. As the social, economic, and technological conditions of a free society change, so must the content of a liberal education. One cannot be considered a liberally educated person in our society without a knowledge of the nature and role of business institutions. Nor is there any necessary conflict between a liberal and a professional education; on the contrary, each should be shaped to enrich and strengthen the other." (p. 27)

of uncertainty. Concurrently, the upgrading of skills is a significant challenge to professionally oriented study programs. These programs must try to visualize, however hazily, the nature of the relevant sector of the world in the years ahead in order to provide professional training which gives rise to new procedures. It will no longer be possible to provide training only in procedures now in existence and adaptable primarily to present circumstances.

The apparent causal relationships between high productivity increases today and research and educational efforts of earlier years suggest the necessity for the development of guidelines regarding the sharing of activities by business and public bodies. New relationships are emerging, or at least we are becoming aware of them. It is quite clear that the public and private sectors will become affiliated under a myriad of contractual arrangements in the future, which will affect the nature of property rights. Since these relationships involve the institutional structure of our socio-economic system, and though they may be necessary to accomplish desirable social goals, their development must be guided by carefully formulated principles if we are to retain our liberal society.

To name a few areas involving this affiliation:

1. There is the relationship of government research activities and the related innovations in the private sector involving "spillover" effects. Already the magnitude of this activity is great, and we need only mention the concern of some universities to conduct government-sponsored research, to illustrate the need for new guidelines. An important question in this respect is: what group will sponsor basic research, and how can the drain on such research talents to employment in highly structured pursuits be avoided?[13]

2. Increases in federal aid to higher education when there is a growing disparity between the cost of education at private and public institutions, when social demands for higher education are increasing, and when many capable students are unable to pursue university training for financial reasons, deserve attention. The question of whether higher education is a social good with benefits accruing to the whole society and not only to the person educated must

[13]Economic reward for research conducted either by government or business is tied closely to identifiable applications flowing from the research. Research of a basic nature, thus, frequently lags due to inadequate support. Effective business and education, or government and education partnerships, with few limitations attached, would do much to correct this imbalance.

be answered without equivocation, at least for policy purposes, in the next few years.

3. The business and government partnership in assuming responsibility for training unskilled members of the labor force and persons with obsolete skills requires further understanding. Although it may not be a partnership in a formal sense, there is a change in the degree of responsibility accepted by the private sector and by the public sector during cyclical fluctuations in economic activity. During recessions, for example, government accepts relatively more responsibility.

4. The development of communications satellites and public and private sponsorship of new high-speed railroad equipment and passenger aircraft involves new relationships. These relationships also affect the use of our air and water resources and most of our energy sources.

5. The changing relationship of government and business in assuring competitive markets, in involving the public interest in labor negotiations, in providing tax incentives, and in social and medical services requires careful study.

These are but examples of the emerging institutional and real relationships which demand the greatest attention from schools of higher education. Students in the modern university must be given the opportunity to explore such issues. Only then can the new generation develop the guidelines which are so necessary if the society is to retain its effective respect for individual choice.

The educational implications of the importance of managerial talents, coupled with the fact that many aspects of human performance are better understood today than yesterday, suggest that educational institutions should give greater attention to the training of managers not only for business units but for government, non-profit, and other organizations. In this respect, too, the public and business sectors can learn from each other. For example, one of the new tools of analysis referred to as the systems approach, is being as avidly applied in the private sector as it is in the public sector.

Acceleration of state and local expenditures may be expected, since it is related to the increase in urbanization, the low level of local government services compared to total government services, and to changes in representation in legislative bodies. It is not unreasonable to expect that the services provided by state and local governments in the future will be such as to modify the boundary lines of political subdivisions and bring into being quasi-governmental units designed to provide special services, such as the Port of New York Authority. Will the individual find his governmental unit more or less responsive to his needs under these new arrangements? The answer depends on whether he wants it to. In all of this, business education has a crucial and guiding role.

Public responsibility for high employment, stable prices, and rapid rates of economic growth may be translated into action in many different ways. It is up to the educational world, in large part, to assist in the selection of intelligent policies consistent with traditional values. This must be done by increasing our understanding of the effects of various policies. If, for example, we are to choose between price stability and low rates of unemployment, on what basis do we make the choice? Is it not necessary for us to know more about the nature of the losses incurred by those who are hurt by inflation and more about the nature of the gains of those who receive employment because of the policy? This choice, so similar in nature to many others, cannot be made on the basis of prejudice or on the basis of past history.

The growth of the market place and of related technical innovations in production will—if the past gives a clue to the future—be associated with the growth of large scale organizations, but not necessarily at the expense of the small productive units.

Whatever the balance of organizations may be, there is no denying that we shall need to understand a great deal about the behavior of organizations and of individuals functioning within these organizations.

New Directions in Business Education

Emerging social and economic patterns also lead to the suggestions for changes in curriculum. Development of the various disciplines relating to business must be accompanied by movements to relate or integrate the branches of business study. The movement to greater fusion is taking place, and will continue, in the functional fields of accounting, finance, marketing, and production. In a sense, the business unit is viewed increasingly as economists view an economic system in full equilibrium with simultaneously determined solutions. There are, however, limitations to the development of a fully integrated study of business, and these have to do with methods of analysis and with the ways disciplines develop. Methodologically, when the scope of study widens and more variables are taken into account, there is a loss in operational value. The primary purpose of the business schools, however, is to assist individuals to make operational decisions. Hence, the schools cannot be expected to stress formal methods too far.

Related to methods of inquiry, but with substance beyond, is the fact that disciplines tend to develop through concentrated efforts on problems of limited scope and through the development of a literature and of an esprit by practicing scholars. Hence, members of business school faculties must give attention to two sets of pursuits—those which contribute to their chosen field of inquiry and those which contribute to the understanding of business activity in a broad sense. These pursuits will be given different priorities depending on individual and group attitudes. If an estimate of outcomes is to be made, it would seem likely that the most frequent choice will be in favor of the disciplines. Hence, although greater formal interrelation among fields of business study will take place, primary emphasis on the disciplines will remain.

The student, however, must be provided with the opportunity to relate the various branches of business study since sometime in his career he will be called upon to do so. The solution to this dilemma will be provided, not so much by formal developments within disciplines, as through techniques and experiments in instruction and teaching. Use of management simulation exercises, in which a large number of business factors are retained in the memory of a computer, would seem promising. More promising, perhaps, is the establishment of common elements of purpose by the business school faculties. Symposia, such as the one reflected in this book, which call the attention of students, alumni, and faculties to the nature of business and its environment and to the range of choices available to business and society, should serve to emphasize the importance of business school missions. If the community of scholars who make up the business school teaching staffs are persuaded that their activities count, and count significantly, a more even balance between the discipline and broad business perspective is likely to occur.

Behavioral Sciences

Curriculum review suggested the need to give greater attention to propositions derived from behavioral studies. A glimpse at probable future conditions underscores this conclusion. Improvement in managerial skills has contributed importantly to economic growth. If they are to continue to do so, they must adapt to and exercise control over sophisticated methods for solving business problems. Increased understanding of individuals in their productive pursuits must accompany improved understanding of business technology and growth in the proportion of economic activity which takes place within formal national and multi-national organizations.

How the behavioral sciences are to be included in full measure in curricula is one of the most difficult problems facing business schools. Certain branches or facets of the behavioral sciences have been applied to courses of study in marketing, accounting, and organizational behavior. There is widespread expectation, however, that behavioral propositions may serve eventually as those most basic to effective business studies. Consequently, experimentation will abound with different courses of action to develop the field and to incorporate it into the curriculum. Some schools will single out a particular discipline, such as social psychology, and expect developments to branch out from there. Others will appoint individual faculty members with skills and understanding derived from several disciplines, but who give emphasis to applications in business. Indeed, these latter efforts may very well succeed as new branches of knowledge, just as those who have applied quantitative procedures of investigation to business have developed the new fields of operations analysis, management science, and systems analysis. Seldom will a school be sufficiently affluent to pursue both courses with equal vigor. Generally, a higher priority must be given to one of the two approaches. If one were to make estimates of the magnitudes of risk and return attached to each course of development, it is likely that the discipline-based approach would have a lower risk attached and probably a smaller immediate return than the eclectic approach. Over a longer period, the discipline-based approach may prove superior.

Environment

A glimpse at emerging social and economic patterns suggested that the environment of business will undergo substantial change within the next two or three decades. Thus, added support is given the conclusion derived from review of current curricula which suggested that greater attention be given to circumstances beyond the control of the firm. There are conflicting approaches to formal study of the environment. Some would suggest the proper stance is that of an observer who seeks to discern trends so that he may react in accord and take advantage of them. Others would suggest that the study include normative or social values in large measure, and the stance taken would frequently be that of a person or leader who provides guidance for change. As suggested in the discussion of future problems, there are many reasons why the businessman of the present must be concerned with the nature of the social and economic system of tomorrow; he cannot escape acceptance of responsibility for providing guidance to the forces of change. Although some sectors of business may escape this responsibility, at least for a short period of time, the business school cannot. It is clear, therefore, the environment of business must be studied in the broader context of responsible citizenship. Hopefully, the business community will provide leadership in the process of social change to come.[14]

Business and Business Schools

The business schools, by emphasizing basic and analytical disciplines, have become academically accepted and educationally exacting institutions. They have added to the understanding of business and have vastly improved the quality of instruction offered. By virtue of these efforts, and because of their success, the distance between business and the business schools has tended to widen. There is, in consequence, a significant and expanded role for institutions which act as intermediaries between the worlds of business and education. Indeed, properly conceived, there are important functions to be served by satellite institutions attached to business schools and designed as platforms for effective communication between business and education. Satellite units could serve to transmit ideas derived from academia to business for application and experimentation. The nature of the response of the business world would provide direction to inquiries and, when reinforcing, may be the source of changes in curriculum.

[14]Some argue that there is no role for "responsible" action by business managers in a framework of a highly competitive economy. The pursuit of profits is a sufficient norm. This conclusion would follow provided that the forces which establish the *conditions* of business enterprise change quickly and properly. These conditions, however, are frequently man-made institutions, many of them operated or greatly assisted by businessmen and their design is affected by the personal or social values of the designers.

Satellite units could try out new approaches to business study, particularly involving new ways of integrating branches of knowledge through management training programs, with results to be introduced into curricula. Development of new approaches to management training would in many instances involve the use of faculty "task forces" which, once formed, may be applied in providing courses in the regular student programs. Indeed, satellite units that are in close communication with business school faculties would serve as common ground for faculty members. I have deliberately taken an evolutionary, indeed, a gradualist approach in this paper. What the business school needs to do today to serve tomorrow is to organize what we have learned and to exploit what we have achieved.

MICHAEL SCHIFF

Ends and Means in
Business Education

21 One basic difference between general and professional education is the different relationship between ends and means. In general education, e.g. the traditional "liberal arts" program, the ends are forever in flux and change with every major change in the values and the structure of society. But the means are amazingly stable. Subjects, courses, and curricula in general education change their labels, but rarely their contents.

In professional education, by contrast, the means are always in lively ferment, with subjects, departments, courses, and methods changing continually. But the ends tend to remain the same for very long periods. However great the changes in medical knowledge and methods, Hippocrates' ideal of the physician still gives direction and goal to medical education. Justinian's code-trained *jurisconsult* was taught quite differently from the case-trained modern American lawyer. But Justinian's idea of the lawyer's role and conduct still informs the American law school of today.

Business education shares with these schools of the tradition-hallowed professions the relationship between ends and means. Since business was first seen as a field for professional university-level education when the Wharton School was founded in 1881 at the University of Pennsylvania, we have been debating its means, subjects, curricula, methods, courses, prerequisites, and so on. But there rarely has been much quarrel about the ends of professional education in business. It aims first at the formation of accomplished, responsible business executives who know their job, do it successfully, and set an example both in the business community and in society. It aims second at finding new knowledge, developing it, and disseminating it. Third, professional business education is the conscience of the profession. It defines the standards of craftsmanship, as well as the standards of conduct for the practitioner.

Finally, all business education aims, as a central purpose, at making business and businessmen capable of managing change in a complex, dynamic, and rapidly shifting economy and technology.

But while business education is similar to all other professional education in its relationship between ends and means, it differs drastically from the old professions and their schools in the relationship between specialist and generalist.

In all the older professions the beginner is the generalist. As the practitioner and the scholar in law and medicine advance in the profession, they become increasingly specialized. In business, however, the beginner works, of necessity, as a specialist, in one "function," or in one skill area. As he advances in business and becomes a "manager," he is concerned increasingly with wholes, with the interrelationships between specialties, disciplines, and techniques, and with building and maintaining an "organization" that is a complex human community in which individual specialists work together for joint performance and results. Increasingly in business, advancement means moving from "specialist" to "generalist."

The reason for this is, of course, that the older professions have traditionally been practiced alone or in small partnerships. Business is practiced in and through an institution. It is the purpose of this institution to make specialists productive—and this is its strength. But this means that the progress of the business executive is almost exactly the opposite of the progress any professional education of the past assumed for its practitioners.

This has, of course, been known all along. But it has not been taken into account in the business school. This explains, in large measure, the confusion that has been so prevalent in American business education and the dissatisfaction of business educators with their own work, despite their impressive success, both within academia and in the business community. For the distinct and different relationship between specialist and generalist in business has profound implications for business education—its publics, its structure, and its subject matter.

I

The first implication, and the one which we are beginning to understand, is that professional business education has, in effect, four student bodies. There are four distinct groups, each with specific needs which require professional education in business. The first of these groups is not the traditional "student," that is, the young man or woman who has not yet entered upon his life's work. The first category is clearly the one "generalist" in business, that is, the people who actually manage businesses. On their performance depends ultimately the performance of all other people in business enterprise. Their standards, their competence, their knowledge, and their seriousness determine how the entire business profession performs, if not indeed whether one can even speak of a "business profession."

In every discipline the general knowledge is and has to be the starting point for the definition and development of specializations. But where in the other professions this comes at the beginning of a career, in the profession of business—and in all other professional work within institutions—this is in effect the climax. It is the end point towards which all business knowledge trends.

Senior managers are, therefore, the first "student body." But they are also the first public of the business school for its other ends. They are the first public for the development of standards of craftsmanship and standards of conduct.

They are also—or should be—the first publics for "research," that is, for the development of new knowledge. We have, during the last twenty years, developed the beginnings of an educational effort for and with senior managers. We are today very much concerned with standards—though most of the work still remains to be done. But there are few systematic efforts to create the knowledge that is appropriate to the senior manager and pertains to his work. This is one of the weaknesses of our current system. By contrast, the physical sciences have at least the framework for communication. Basic research in the sciences is carried on by government, by universities, and by industry.

The fact that all three are involved permits the interchange of ideas and provides a vital communication link. Applied scientific research is also carried on by each of these units and here again communication is encouraged. Within the firm we move from applied scientific research to engineering to product or service to market.

There is no equivalent research structure in business and, hence, only limited communication. Very few businesses engage in business research. They do marketing research, but most of this research aims at solving immediate problems. The universities have extended their research efforts in the field of business. Yet even here, research has been in large measure compartmentalized into specialties, and communication with business is almost non-existent. The luxury of research in business being limited to scholars writing for other scholars is something we cannot afford. This is not meant to constrain research. But a continuing dialogue with business managers receiving the fruits of research and pressing for new research would fill a large gap in management development and business scholarship. For this, however, senior management must be brought close to the business school, must become one of the school's "publics."

The second student body of the business school is younger people who are about to become managers or have recently been moved from being individual contributors in a specialty into a management position. These people who are in a mid-career need to understand the entire business. They need the "generalist's" vision and knowledge. They also have enough experience to understand it and enough scope in their work to apply it. Yet they still need to become more proficient in specialties. Indeed, at this stage one of the great needs is to acquire an understanding of specialties that were not hitherto important in one's work. This group is today offered business instruction by a few large business schools, such as the Graduate School of Business Administration at New York University, which are willing to accept well qualified men in mid-career, holding full-time jobs, as part-time students for advanced degrees. They are, perhaps, the students who most closely correspond in their capacity as well as in their needs to the traditional student in the traditional schools of the older professions dominated by the individual practitioner.

There is a third group, namely, specialists, who have the need to perfect themselves in their specialty. They are the group in the business school that requires what is now coming to be known as "continuing" education. They are the people who need "refresher" courses because their knowledge, after ten years out of school, is becoming obsolescent. They are the people who need "updating" and acquaintanceship with new ideas, new knowledge, new concepts, and new techniques. In many ways the professional societies are geared to furnish this "continuing" education. But some of the larger metropolitan business schools—again GBA is an example—also have developed the necessary programs for these men.

Finally, there is the young man, the young graduate with a liberal arts or science degree, who still has to be trained for his first job as an adult. But unlike the man of the same age in the older professional schools, this man, to be trained for entry into business, should be trained as a *specialist*.

The position taken here is that at the point of entry into business, the graduate needs to know a field well—in short, he should be a specialist. This specialized knowledge prepares him earlier for productive work. But more importantly, the initial work assignment will undoubtedly be in the field of specialization giving immediate opportunity to apply knowledge.

At this level it is not meaningful to define the end of the educational experience as preparation for general management. There is little chance that the student will be able to put to work such knowledge. And all our work in learning theory amply proves that knowledge that cannot be applied very soon to achievement rapidly evaporates, and indeed, becomes an obstacle to understanding and to performance.

It is not, I believe, necessary for each professional business school to address itself to all four publics of professional business education. But it is necessary for effectiveness, I would maintain, for each professional business school to distinguish between these four different groups and to treat each differently.

II

At the same time, the specific structure of professional work in business also raises serious questions regarding the traditional "disciplines" and "subjects."

In the other professions, in which the starting point is the "generalist," the student first receives a foundation in the basic disciplines. He then, as he advances, learns increasingly specialized subjects and becomes acquainted with increasingly narrower areas.

In business we have tried to follow the same approach. But the "foundations" in business are the disciplines that belong at the end, the disciplines that integrate for general management. These, however, have not proven to be meaningful for the young, inexperienced student who, so far, has been the majority of our student population throughout the nation. As a result, business schools have addressed themselves primarily to what they call "specialties," but which, in reality, are immediately salable skills and rather narrow techniques. The result has been uncontrolled proliferation and a great deal of duplication. Above all, what is taught as "new knowledge" often tends to be only refinement of technique, if not the newest fad. At the same time, significant new developments, which, as a rule, cut across traditional skill demarcations, cannot be accommodated. They are left out, or they become "departments" or "disciplines" of their own. One example is the way in which we have recently multiplied the departments dealing with quantitative methods, each advertising its own wares as "the answer"—whether accounting or econometrics, statistics, operations research, or decision theory.

I submit that any area of knowledge has to define its subject matter in terms of the foundations. This means, applied to business education, three rather fundamental changes.

1. It means first that the entire business school curriculum be developed from and organized within what I would consider the six permanent concerns of business management, that is, of the entire business. I would define them as:

1. Planning
2. Management information, analysis, and control
3. Marketing
4. Innovation—the management of change
5. Managing people
6. The social, political, and cultural environment.

These are the areas which the general managers need and in which they should engage in a continuing dialogue with the scholars. These are also the areas to which the scholar needs to orient his vision and his work, if he wants to be a scholar of business.

2. What are traditionally considered the "foundation disciplines," that is, the essentials of economics, quantitative methods, accounting, finance, and human behavior, are in fact "information" rather than

"knowledge" for business. Everybody in business, from the youngest specialist on, should know the essentials here, and these can best be learned by the student in the systematic, self-administered form of a computerized self-study program. There needs to be no instructor with his own special training or interest. The result would be a group of courses geared to students' own speed, broadly concerned, and quite economical to administer.

Insofar as manufacturing—production planning and control—and business logistics belong in a business school, they could be learned the same way. I strongly suspect, however, that these subjects are better taught within schools of industrial engineering. The performance and achievement of business schools in these areas have not been too impressive, and the skills developed are essentially those of the engineer, that is, skills of efficiency.

3. The traditional student, that is, the young man who has not yet entered upon his business career, and who requires training as a specialist, should be offered work focused on specific performance as a beginner. But this work should be integrated into the fundamental business disciplines, that is, into planning; management information, analysis, and control; marketing; innovation; managing people; and the environment of business. This will require new "specialties." They will, of course, utilize in large measure the traditional skills. But they will present these skills not as ends in themselves, but as means towards business performance. They will present these skills not as entities in themselves, but as tools from the tool kit of the well-trained business craftsman. They will, therefore, prepare the young man both for work as a specialist when he enters business, and for growth towards becoming a manager as he matures and advances.

I realize that these may sound like very radical ideas, but the distinct "publics" for business education have already emerged. What still remains to be done is to develop the proper means for the ends of business education on which all of us seem to be in agreement.

Actually the task may go well beyond designing new *business* school curricula. We may have the opportunity of designing the prototype of tomorrow's new professional school. Business enterprise was only the first of the new institutions to emerge. Increasingly all major tasks of our society are being performed in and through large organizations. In every one the structure of the work is similar to work in business: the beginner starts as a specialist but advances towards the generalist. Where the older professions have "foundations" at the beginning of a career, the new professions of the professional executive—whether in business, in the hospital, in the government agency, in the armed services or in research—derive their cohesion from the capstone. The older professions were, so to speak, designed like a Greek temple in which each column carries the load of the entire building. The new professions resemble the Gothic cathedral in which the whole weight is suspended from the top of the arch.

In designing professional business education to attain its ends, we might, therefore, well design the education for effectiveness in today's society altogether.

REINALDO SCARPETTA

Management Education as a Key to Social Development

22 In developing countries, the business school has special competence to bring together the business community and the university. It also can, and must, bring together those two with government as well. The distance that traditionally exists between these key sectors of society has seriously damaged educational efforts in many developing countries, especially by the misrepresentation to students or managers or public officials of the nature and intentions of the other sectors. This tragic breakdown in communications is gradually disappearing, thanks to the efforts of business schools to present management and management education as a universal institution and necessity.

Two movements in the field of management and management education in Latin America may serve as examples of the changes that can be brought about by management education.

The first of these is the graduate program in management at the Universidad del Valle in Cali, Colombia, commonly called the del Valle experiment. The second is an organization now called CLADEA (Committee of Deans of Latin American Graduate Schools of Management), informally known as the "healthy baby group."

269

I

Dr. Marshall Robinson of the Ford Foundation described the del Valle experiment in his paper, *A Worldwide Campus of Management.* "One of the youngest of the Latin American business administration programs is at the Universidad del Valle in Cali, Colombia. An economically thriving region, a brilliant university rector, an aggressive young dean, and an energetic and knowledge-thirsty group of young business leaders have combined to design a graduate program with unique qualities. For the moment, its principal students are the businessmen. They work on cases, are exposed to a variety of visiting professors, use the school as a consulting organization, and are attempting to adapt what is known in the field to their own setting. Business educators from more settled institutions might not recognize all that goes on in the program, but they would envy the enthusiasm and intensity with which it is produced and consumed."

The total story of the del Valle experiment will perhaps never be known, for in it are now involved hundreds of people. However, the initial concept is still very clear to many of us who took part in its initial formulation. It has not changed much in application.

The needs of the Cauca Valley gave birth to the concept that a beleaguered society could generate from itself the elements which would allow it to overcome its limitations and face the challenges before it. The fundamental element in effecting such a change was considered to be the managerial capital of the region.

After carefully studying the problems facing the different sectors of the region, a group of people came to the conclusion that a small, though in many cases exceptionally able, group of executives were holding together a turbulent and rapidly expanding power structure. It was felt that these people and the institutions they represented needed an immediate transfusion of managerial help if development was going to be creatively managed and forces of change channeled constructively.

Since a transfusion of managerial blood was impossible in management-short Colombia, the group decided to establish a management-talent generator, composed of several institutions and powered by the existing managers.

In essence, the top managers of the Cauca Valley were invited to take part in an adventure of self-development in the philosophies and tools of modern management. In this way, they would involve themselves, the local University (Universidad del Valle), the local Productivity Center (Incolda-Cali), and other institutions in a joint process of study of their society's problems and its opportunities for the businessman.

The University assumed the role of catalyst and chief research agent in this process, and the Productivity Center took on an aggressive extension role. University-based professors of management joined senior businessmen in a joint learning process: studying the Colombian managerial situation, using the executives' own companies and institutions as laboratories, and applying new concepts of management which focused on development on a short and long-term basis without forgetting sound corporate management and bottom-line performance.

Throughout the eighteen months (six hours of class and six hours of group study per week), senior executives and del Valle staff worked together in generating the course content, trying out new concepts, and focusing the student-executives' term projects on long and short term opportunities facing their specific companies. This process gave the whole exercise tangible relevance and applicability.

As the senior men came to del Valle, Incolda—the Colombian management association—using del Valle staff, developed in depth year-long courses for functional managers (such as production, marketing, finance, etc.), whereas the more junior executives were given the same concepts as their chiefs, but with greater detail and depth as far as application was concerned.

At the same time—and also jointly—Incolda and del Valle overhauled a night school program through which middle management could be massively, though rigorously, trained. Finally, Incolda stepped up short-term programs of general interest for a region in a process of full development, attracting to them not only private-sector managers, but also executives of all other sectors of society, such as education, government and health care.

During the first couple of years, the concept of creation of incremental intellectual capital took deep roots within the society. The University was crowded with young executives from business and government anxious to get on to the right thing which self-improvement had become. Company attitudes toward helping personnel better themselves were changed radically. All of a sudden, a considerable amount of money and time was being poured into training the region's management force. The concept had partially succeeded.

But it was only in the third year that the original total concept began to take full effect. The original idea was to create managerial capital and have part of the new capital flow towards such management-poor sectors as the public sector.

It is impossible to say whether this would have happened had not Dr. Carlos Lleras assumed the Presidency of our country. Able and respected, President Lleras called the best men he could find to his side in guiding Colombia. These last few years, the del Valle experiment has supplied a governor for the state and four of his key secretaries, a mayor for Cali and five of his key staff, three senior men for the National Planning Office, and the Minister of Public Works. These men had all participated in del Valle's executive management program. In this way, leaders of the private sector have found themselves immersed in public affairs. It is interesting to note that a great amount of teamwork between former participants in the project was achieved in expediting communication and getting things done.

These community activities had a profound impact on the management work at the University as well. Gradual changes in course content reflected the new areas of interest in the community. Such courses as Colombian economic topics and Colombian government-industry relations were overhauled. New areas, such as information sciences, applied behavioral sciences, and multi-national business issues were introduced into the curriculum.

The University has incorporated its business and economics schools into a Division of Social and Economic Sciences which includes departments of political sciences and sociology. The over-all research effort of the Division became oriented towards understanding and solving the region's most pressing problems. Graduate-level programs were established in agricultural economics and management, bringing full-time students from other regions of Colombia and from other countries to the campus.

In its first four years of operation, the Graduate School of Management trained over two hundred managers at the MBA level. The night school, together with the extension courses given with Incolda and the undergraduate activities of the Division, contributed several hundred more men, ready to enter different levels of managerial activity in the private and public sector.

The School of Agricultural Economics placed several of its brightest graduates in the National Planning Office. Very soon, these young men were taking an active part in determining the country's agricultural development policies.

Society's problems themselves began to help redefine the future areas of interest of the business school. Having involved leaders of most sectors of society in the graduate-level executive course, the school became responsible for helping them create the wherewithal to improve their managerial performance. To do this, the school started developing a full-time, highly trained Colombian staff which could help managers, in addition to training future managers.

For instance, a group of businessmen proposed and incorporated a time-sharing computer company. The computer will link the University, the main hospital, the main government agencies of state and city, and the region's leading business companies, in one information utility. To respond to this innovation, the University is developing a strong program in information sciences.

Through an aggressive program in applied behavioural sciences including labs, T. groups and other forms of sensitivity training, the business school is helping managers create a greater receptivity to managerial tools within growing enterprises. This experiment is of tremendous importance, for it seeks to leap-frog a cultural lag inherent in rapid organizational and technological change.

Having involved more than a dozen leaders of the health sector in its top management programs, the business school is helping the University's Health Sciences Division set up a comprehensive plan to upgrade and enhance health care and medical facilities for the people of the region. The experience with this effort promises to lead to a joint program to educate managers for health enterprises.

Another area in which the del Valle experiment has become deeply involved is education. Based at the School of Education, but with help from the business school, an education-management program, as well as experimentation with new systems and techniques for education, was started at the graduate level. Through these efforts, the region is laying foundations for entry into the knowledge industry.

Finally, as explained above, the public sector began requiring better trained people for top jobs and some rapid method of retraining middle-level executives. In answer to this need, a number of government employees have been admitted to all programs conducted by Incolda and the University—in the majority of cases, on a direct scholarship basis. This interaction not only strengthened the public sector, but brought together public and private executives in the same classroom.

The program at del Valle is now entering its fifth year of operation. It is still too soon to determine whether the impact on directing social change it has had in the past will be intensified as the social and political science efforts of del Valle are strengthened, or whether the school will fall back into a more passive role in the design and creation of the future.

The symptoms, however, are indicative of the former. It seems likely that as forces of technological, economic, political, and social change emerge, the braintrust at del Valle will be tremendously important in channeling them constructively towards the sound social and economic development of the region.

II

A second example of business schools taking active part in bringing about necessary economic and managerial change is the creation and operations of CLADEA, the Committee of Deans of Latin American Graduate Schools of Management.

The Committee is formed and is financed by twelve schools of management operating in Latin America. From North to South, they are: Escuela de Graduados en Administracion del Instituto Tecnologico y de Estudios Superiores de Monterrey, Mexico; the Instituto Centroamericano de Administracion de Empresas (INCAE), Managua, Nicaragua; the Division de Ciencias Sociales y Economicas de la Universidad del Valle, Cali, Colombia, and the Facultad de Economia de la Universidad de Los Andes, Bogota, Colombia; the Escuela de Administracion de Negocios para Graduados (ESAN), Lima, Peru; the Escola de Administracao de Empresas de Sao Paulo of Getulio Vargas Institute, Sao Paulo, Brazil; the Facultad de Ciencias Economicas de la Universidad de Chile; and the Facultad de Ciencias Economicas y Sociales de la Universidad Catolica de Chile, both in Santiago, Chile.

In addition, it has as observers three institutions that are developing graduate programs in management: the Facultad de Comercio y Administracion de la Universidad Nacional Autonoma de Mexico, in Mexico City; the Instituto de Estudios Superiores de Administracion (IESA), Caracas, Venezuela; and the Instituto para el Desarrollo de Ejecutivos en la Argentina (IDEA), Buenos Aires, Argentina.

PACCIOS, the Pan American division of the *Conseil International pour l'Organization Scientifique* (C.I.O.S.) is also an observer.

These institutions all have a full-time faculty with Ph.D. or, at least, Master's degrees, offer programs at the graduate level, and grant academic degrees.

The purposes of the Committee are to promote the international dimension of the curriculum in business education in Latin America (which is especially important in the light of Latin American integration, and the movement towards a Common Market), and to achieve efficient operations by pooling and sharing academic resources among the schools.

To accomplish these general purposes the Committee designed a program composed of eight projects. The first and most important project is to have work groups formed of Latin American professors. Since a different work group is created for each field of study (production, finance, marketing, etc.), these groups create effective international academic collaboration in specific academic areas. The work groups meet at least once a year in a Latin American city and are sponsored by a member institution.

During one week, professors discuss academic matters, exchange academic experiences, analyze the similarities and differences of working with undergraduates, graduates, and executives in their respective fields in the various Latin American countries, recommend major research projects to be executed by the schools, and finally, analyze the future trends in the development of their fields in Latin America.

In many cases, visiting professors conduct seminars for a group of local executives. Such a work group provides an exchange of information among the professors, as well as on the spot trials for teaching methods. These seminars broaden the views of both lecturers and businessmen. In addition, fees from the local executives' courses help finance the work group gathering.

The second project is an exchange of professors among the member institutions, oriented towards internationalizing faculty, and, therefore, internationalizing the students and their horizons. It also maximizes the use of the human resources and, in the long run, should stimulate specific schools to concentrate on specific areas of strength.

The remaining projects deal with:

3. The design of a special program for faculty development that contemplates the specific needs of Latin America.

4. The establishment of an academic clearing-house to which all the institutions send cases, articles, translations of books, etc.

5. The exchange of students (Colombians to Chile, Chileans to Mexico, Mexicans to Brazil, etc.). Again, the main purpose is to internationalize students and, in the long run, stimulate a certain specialization of the schools. Hopefully, the students will decide in which field and at which graduate school of management they would prefer to study.

Finally, the schools work together on (6.) the standardization of admission tests (7.), the selection of applicants with the highest professional and academic potential, and (8.) the selection of students for study in other parts of the world.

The member schools meet in a yearly Deans' Conference. The first conference was held at Universidad del Valle in February, 1966, and the second in March, 1967, in Lima. The third conference was held at the Escuela para Graduados en Administracion in Monterrey in May, 1968. The Deans also hold frequent round-table discussions with representatives from business and from Latin American governments. Conferences are also held with top international executives whose companies operate in Latin America.

At these conferences, participants try to anticipate how political, sociological, economic, and technological changes will affect future business, and how these changes should affect business education in Latin America.

Finally, six seminars in the field of international marketing are held every year. These are four-week, full-time seminars given by faculty members of Universidad del Valle and other schools.

The committee's formation has obvious implications for business education. But, perhaps equally important are the implications for the region's managers. It provides a way for executives in various Latin American countries to meet with their counterparts and to think through their common needs for people, for knowledge, and for standards. It makes it possible for people in several countries to ask, why don't we get together and do X or Y? Managers are doers, and management educators should train doers. The linking of these major Latin American business schools thus encourages the linking of managers who are doing things.

Then again, the linking of management education necessarily links together the study of the relationship between government and business in one country and between various businesses and governments in various countries.

The strongest integration force in Latin America will be the manager—public or private. Therefore, to understand integration, managers and management must be understood. Finally, the committee provides a means for association between people whose interests exceed business and encompass wider aspects of social and economic development.

III

Business schools train the men in charge—the managers—whose role is to manage and create change. Business schools, therefore, should play a particularly important role in a society undergoing rapid growth and development. In such a society the business school is the fuel cell.

But, perhaps the role business education is increasingly playing in the rapidly changing societies of Latin America is only an early example of the role it should—and can—play everywhere. For, all our societies are in rapid change. All need men who have been responsibly trained to take charge.

The business school of the future may well have to be a place where the best professional competence of many disciplines mixes in such a way as to prepare the people who will perform the tasks necessary to keep a society developing.

In the past, we have thought of business education as something oriented almost exclusively towards the management of an enterprise. Today, we are confronted with the fact—evident in developing countries as well as in others—that management comprises much more than the management of a business enterprise.

We are, therefore, becoming aware of how essential it is for these schools to turn to the management problems of other affairs of society, especially those related to the management of knowledge and education, health, social security, and public affairs.

We have seen public affairs management extend beyond the creation of organization patterns necessary to provide basic services for citizens, to the interpretation, quantification, and energization of public opinion and politics. On a wider basis, social scientists are adding the *why* to the managers' grasp of *how* to deal with social groups, and thereby improving it.

In the field of international relations and politics, a new force—the multi-national corporation—is changing the rules by which international lawyers and politicians manage world affairs. Due to the impact this essentially managerial force has on a country's economy, economists are reorganizing their thoughts on the factors affecting economic development.

More and more, we see the people of the world—whatever their particular situation—looking to managers to shape their future. At the same time, we see those managers—many of whom were trained in financial methods of internal control alone—wrestling with a widening variety of social and political variables in their efforts to steer new courses within a changing society, and to maintain, at the same time, creative order in those affairs entrusted to them to manage.

Management is no longer a procedure-oriented discipline. It must act as a profession with philosophical content and with growing analytical tools with which to accomplish its mission of maintaining creative order within a changing or developing society.

These new tools make it possible for management to have an accurate, over-all view in its association with all its publics, from the immediate enterprise, to the community, to government.

The time horizon of management and management education has also changed because of the advent of these tools and of the widening social scope of managerial responsibility. It has become essential to continually retrain management and continually upgrade its tools, constantly checking them for relevance and applicability.

Modern management must think far ahead in order to orient policies that guide a giant enterprise in which communications and acceptance of change require a long time. It must also be able properly to interpret trends of the past and present them as elements of future planning. New information processes work at spellbinding speed to give the modern manager the timely data which he may use to calmly and thoughtfully make the right decisions.

Social and economic development needs an institution which provides efficient coordination of developmental efforts, understands variables involved in such development, and provides the leadership to bring about organized creative change. This, in my opinion, is the role of management as an institution. The business school is the place where the people who manage today, and who will manage tomorrow, can become acquainted with management's tasks, philosophies and tools.

The business school must, then, be able to create and interpret change as a challenge to entrepreneurial and managerial spirit. To help produce, at the university or within the enterprises themselves, managers capable of managing creative change in society's institutions is, in my opinion, the role of the business school in social and economic development. In any case, the business school will have a growing role in society's education and may well become the center where thought and action, analysis and decision, objectives and human energies, meet and are welded into one achieving society.

PETER F. DRUCKER

Summing Up: Preparing
Tomorrow's Business Leaders Today

23

We hear and read a good many speculations today about "the year 2000." Judging by past experience, few of these speculations will come to pass.

But one thing is already certain today about "the year 2000." The men who will make the decisions in the year 2000, the men, above all, who will be in charge of our businesses and of our economies, are among the young men who will graduate in the next few years from the business schools of the free world. They are among the young men business now hires as young professionals and management trainees. The decision makers for the year 2000 are now learning what they will put to work in "the year 2000."

Opinions differ widely, of course, as to what they will need the most to do their job. But a few threads run through all the discussions in this book in respect to the needs of the business leader of tomorrow. A few major areas of decision, of knowledge, of competence, can already be seen as needed. Even a cursory glance at the chapters of this volume on tomorrow's business and tomorrow's business leader brings out again and again the same areas of emphasis.

1. Tomorrow's business leader, it is clear, will need to be able to organize for entrepreneurship. He will have to build and lead organizations, including very large ones, that will be capable of effective economic decisions regarding the future. He will have to make

whole organizations capable of doing what in the past only the individual by himself could do, that is, systematically make a new and different future.

2. Closely connected to this is the capacity for systematic innovation. The business leader of tomorrow will have to know how to anticipate innovation and how to make innovation economically effective—rapidly and profitably. He will have to see innovation as part of the economic system rather than as a force working on the economic system from the outside. And he will have to know the dynamics of technology and its relationship to economic resources and economic results.

3. The organization he will build and lead will primarily be an organization of knowledge workers, that is, of highly educated people who put to work knowledge and concepts, and who work with their minds rather than with their hands. The business leader of tomorrow will have to know how to organize knowledge workers for performance, how to motivate them, how to reward them, and, above all, how to make them productive. They will be the main resource of tomorrow's business—but also its main cost.

4. The business leader of tomorrow will have to be able to run businesses that operate across national boundaries and are truly "multi-national." He himself will have to be able to operate in diverse cultures and under a diversity of laws and sovereignties. He will have to be at home in a number of languages and in the cultural traditions they symbolize. And he will have to be able to work together for joint performance with men from a diversity of cultural, linguistic, and ethnic backgrounds.

5. Finally, the business leader of tomorrow will have to know as much about other institutions of our society, and especially about government, as he knows about business. He will live in a society in which every major task of society is being performed in and through a large institution organized for perpetuity. He will, so to speak, live in symbiosis with government and government agencies, but also with educational institutions, with the large hospital, with the armed services, and so on. And he will need to understand how each of these—and especially, of course, the government agency—works, what its rationale and its procedures are, and what it can do, as well as what it cannot do.

It may well be said that none of these is "new." All of these have been with us before. But the importance of these areas of knowledge, competence, and performance is likely to increase very fast as is also their complexity. While not "new" in the sense that they have not been known before, they are truly new dimensions of the businessman's job, new major challenges to him.

There are also new tools becoming available—tools of great power but also of high demands on the business that uses them. One area is that of quantification and data processing, of course. Altogether information—which is energy for mind work—is becoming available for the first time in human history. To use this new capacity, however, requires new skills, new knowledge, and new attitudes.

And simultaneously the behavioral sciences are making available increasing information about the behavior of people and of organizations—with resulting major effects on the structure of business, but also on the demands which employees on all levels will make on business and on business managements.

Economics, too, increasingly provides new tools, especially new tools of analysis, to the businessmen. It is likely to provide a great deal more as the concepts of macro-economics are being translated into analysis and understanding of markets, of industries, and of business.

One conclusion we can draw from this is surely that business schools will become more important to business, as well as to education. They will become more important as centers of instruction. For more and more, the new knowledge and competence the business leader of tomorrow will need, require systematic foundation and systematic preparation. They will also become more important as centers of study, thinking, and new knowledge. The new challenges the business leader faces all require new concepts as well as new data.

I

How business and business schools will respond to these new challenges, I do not presume to know. I have, of course, my own opinions. But opinions are all anyone can have today. There are a great many questions. But there are, so far, no "right answers." Indeed, if there is one thing clear today, it is that there is going to be no *one* "right answer." We need a diversity of approaches. We need a great deal of experimentation. We need, in other words, a period of high innovative activity in both business and the business schools to make ourselves capable of dealing with tomorrow.

But there are some clear *implications* for the direction both business and business schools will have to go. These implications can be indicated as follows:

1. Preparing and developing tomorrow's business leaders is not a job that either business or the business school can do alone. It must be done by the two working together. It requires both systematic learning and developmental work experiences.

The tasks ahead also require much more active participation of our businessmen in the work of the business school than we have seen so far. In particular, top management needs to be much closer to the schools than it has usually been—both in its own interest and that of the schools. Top management needs to know what the young think and what the young need—and the school is the place where the young can make their needs and desires known. Top management needs to know what goes on in research and teaching in the school in order to be ready for the new knowledge and the new tools that it will need to do its new jobs.

The school, too, needs top management and needs close rapport with it. The business school needs to see business whole. All the new tasks are tasks that embrace the entire business rather than this or that function or technique. Yet, in a faculty the great majority are, of necessity, specialists concerned with this or that function or technique. Unless these specialists can relate their own narrow field to the totality of a business, they are unlikely to be productive, both in terms of new knowledge and in terms of their contribution to business. Such vision, however, requires close relationship between the scholar and the practitioner. It requires the kind of relationship that prevails between the two in our other "clinical discipline," medicine.

2. It will also be necessary for business to learn how to maintain relationships with the other institutions of society, and especially with the government agency. Above all, it will be necessary for business to learn how to bring about a "circulation of the elites" in which accomplished men from other institutions, e.g. from the government agency, the university, or the hospital, move into executive positions in business, while accomplished men in business move into executive positions in these other institutions—and back again.

This is the only effective way in which we can create the general understanding of institutions—their points of view, their methods, and their behavior patterns—which is needed above all by business.

Today, such "circulation of the elites" takes place, if at all, only at the very top. There is a great deal of evidence to suggest that this is not enough. The right time is the early, formative years of a man's career, when he has already proven his capacity for executive work, but before he is ready to assume a senior position in an organization.

3. There are implications also for the business school. The most important perhaps is that the business school can no longer define its audience as one group. To make its contribution to business and to our society, it must organize itself for effective work with four distinct audiences.

First, there are the *young*, who need to be prepared so that they can start working effectively, successfully, and with high dedication. They need tools and techniques which they can put to work fast. They also need values. And they do need an overview, a vision of the whole, that gives sense and meaning to their work. Maybe they also need something akin to the physician's internship. They may need such a period of actual business experience under the guidance of an accomplished practitioner while still students. "Case study," or "business games" cannot be an adequate substitute for realistic exposure in work to the major new challenges tomorrow's business leader will have to tackle.

A second, and equally important audience—perhaps a more important one—are *men in mid-career*. The young executive or professional who has proven his competence and his capacity to perform is not only the student who profits the most from what a professional school has to offer; he is also the student who needs the most what a professional school can teach. Though still working in one area, he is, as a rule, no longer merely a technician. He needs to relate his own work to the universes of management, business, economy, and society. He has experience. But he has, as a rule, not learned how to organize it, how to reflect on it, and how to generalize from it.

Indeed the challenges which tomorrow's business leaders will have to tackle make it, I submit, reasonably clear that "continuing education" is the central core of educational preparation for business leadership.

Third, an important audience for the business school should be the *specialist* who needs upgrading and updating in his specialty.

And finally, to say it again, *top management* is an audience for the business school, both as an important student category and as a source of stimulation, knowledge, and understanding. Top management is also a source of critical appraisal for business schools, their faculties, and their other and younger student groups.

The strength of a profession lies very largely in its professional schools and in the relationship between the practitioner, the teacher, and the scholar. The strong and effective profession does not consider its professional school to be "outside." It is an integral part of the profession and of its practice. Conversely, a strong professional school does not see the practitioner as being "outside." It sees itself as an integral part of the practice.

In the educated society of today, there is no terminal point for going to school. The educated professional man never "finishes" his education. And the schools do not see in any one degree the "terminal" degree or in any one age the age at which one "graduates." Education has to be continuing education in its approach, in its curriculum, and in its structure.

How to build the two concepts—the integration of practice and scholarship, and continuing education—into business and the business school will be a major preoccupation, especially for the business educator. That it will have to be done, in the interests of both business and the business school—let alone in the interest of the greater society —can hardly be doubted.

II

The challenges and tasks which preparing tomorrow's business leader will pose for both today's business leader and today's business school, also raise a good many *issues* to which we do not as yet have the answers.

Again, they raise, above all, issues for business. Several of these may be summarized as follows:

1. The first question raised is whether entrepreneurship can be organized within the existing managerial structure of a business. Perhaps it requires separate structures, outside the existing ongoing businesses. Can one and the same division or component both manage today and make a very different tomorrow? And if not—and the pre- ponderance of evidence today is that these two tasks are not truly compatible—how does one organize a business so that two different structures can yet live together in effective and productive unity?

2. And what must the top-management relationships look like in a business that is organized for systematic entrepreneurship and for the systematic anticipation of technology and innovation? Can we even recruit tomorrow's top management the same way we have been

recruiting top management historically? Or do we need to build different experiences and different tests into the preparation of top managers? Maybe we will even have to think in terms of top managements rather than "top management."

3. Altogether the whole career concept in business will have to be thought through again. We now know that we need career ladders for individual professional contributors that parallel the career ladders of men in managerial positions. But do we also need career ladders that are entrepreneurial and innovative? Do we have to think through career ladders that take a man through different institutions, business and non-business, on his way to greater responsibilities? Altogether the problem of enabling people who, of necessity, must start out today in specialized work to become capable of taking an entire business into the future, will force us to think through very carefully what "performance" in a man's career means and what it should mean.

But these are only aspects of the whole area of manager development which is likely to become highly controversial ground. Other important issues can be added to our list:

4. Today our manager development approaches are primarily focused on remedying the deficiencies of a man. Tomorrow we may be much more concerned with manager development that tries to remedy the deficiencies of the organization as a developmental experience. Tomorrow we may be much more concerned with providing a man with the experiences and the knowledges which his work and his organization cannot provide, and which he still needs to be an executive in tomorrow's business, let alone a leader in it.

But we may also have to change our approach to organization and structure. Traditionally organization has been seen as focused on the logic of the work. And work, in turn, has been seen as essentially unchanging if not eternal. Typical of our approaches has been the concept that there are four or five "typical functions" in the "typical manufacturing business." Tomorrow we may have to start out with the question: what is the best organization to develop the kind of *people* we need? Tomorrow we may see the main purpose—but also the main test of organization—in the development of people for the tasks ahead. This is bound to lead to very different organizational structures from any we have seen yet.

5. We will have to think through how to use the international opportunities and needs of our world for the development of managers.

It would seem to me, for instance, that we may come to look upon service in the developing countries as one of the best ways (and certainly one of the cheapest) to develop young executives. Today few businesses are willing to let their young and promising executives work for a few years as, say, consultants to a business, a government agency, or a business school in Colombia or Nigeria. The International Executive Service Corps, for instance, is using primarily retired men for such work. But we may have to learn that this is, above all, work that develops the rising young executive and prepares him for the challenges and opportunities of a multi-national corporation and of a world economy.

6. Similarly we may, as has been said already, look upon service and experience in other institutions as a highly desirable preparation for the executive job. We may have to organize systematically the "circulation of the elites." Above all, we may have to look upon an experience as a teacher in a business school for a few years as an ideal testing and proving ground for the rising executive.

The issues which tomorrow's challenges pose for the business school are no less great and no less difficult. These also need to be added to our list and carefully examined:

7. Above all, the challenges ahead raise serious doubt about the direction the American business school is traveling today. It is trying today to be "academically respectable," that is, to put its emphasis on "scholarly disciplines," and especially, of course, on areas that can be considered "scientific" and capable of quantification. This is undoubtedly desirable and indeed necessary. *But is it enough?* Or is it equally important to develop the business school as a "clinical" and as a "professional" institution, concerned with the practice of business and with the areas of uncertainty and ignorance, as well as with the areas of certainty and quantification?

Is this also the time to lock up the curriculum? During the last ten years great efforts have been made, especially by the Association of Collegiate Schools of Business, to lay down "requirements." But one can only codify what one already knows—and one can only know the past. One can never know the future. Is this the time, however, to allow the past, that is, the areas which traditionally have been considered major disciplines, to control the instruction, the organization, and very largely thereby, also, the thinking and research of the business school? Or is this the time to be flexible, to be imaginative, to experiment, and to develop new and quite different areas of specialization, of instruction, and of research?

8. Altogether the new challenges raise the question what the role and mission of the business school should be.

During the last fifty years, the business school has emerged as the largest single school within the American academic community. It has, at the same time, moved into a central position in respect to business. But it has not tackled the question of what it is really trying to do and what it should be trying to be. Can it still continue in this undefined role? Or does it have to think through the alternatives and make decisions?

Specifically, is it the function of the business schools to prepare employees or to prepare leaders? Historically, it has always done the former. Is this still enough?

Is the business school a tool maker or a policy maker, let alone a vision maker? Historically it has been, above all, a tool maker. Is this still enough?

Is the business school a "vocational school" or a "professional" school? Does it concern itself with the skills needed to be effective in business? Or is it also the conscience of a profession? Historically, the business school has, by and large, been a supplier of skills. Does it have to become a leader as well?

9. Finally, should the business school be a "business school" or should it be a "school of administration"?

In the title of many schools, including that of the Graduate Business School of New York University, this question is neatly straddled. We are *schools of business administration.* Actually we have been primarily "schools of business techniques." We will, of course, have to continue to teach techniques—one has to know what the tools are and how they are to be used. But to live up to the challenges ahead, we may have to become increasingly "schools of business." There is truth to the old gibe that our business schools teach everything except business. Tomorrow we will no longer be able to afford this.

But at the same time, will we also have to become "schools of administration"? Will we, in other words, also become schools for the preparation and development of the leaders in other major institutions in our society? To a large extent, these institutions require exactly the same knowledge and the same concepts as the business enterprise does. Is it not rational, therefore, to extend the scope of the business school to these other institutions as well? After all, business was only the first of the major organizations of our society to emerge. It first had to face such problems as those of large-scale management, of the utilization of human resources, and of the allocation and analysis of costs. But these are problems and challenges wherever men band together in organization for joint performance.

Yet, wherever we have attempted to extend the scope of the business school to other organizations, we have, in essence, failed. There are schools that call themselves "schools of business and public administration"—but they really concern themselves with business only. Is this necessary? Is this right? Is it going to continue?

Perhaps the line is not between "business" and "other institutions." It may lie between policy-making institutions—such as the major policy-making agencies of a government—and organizations where the emphasis is on execution and action—such as business. In other words, it may make sense for the business school to extend its scope to the hospital, the administration and management of educational institutions, the armed services, perhaps, and those agencies of government that are actually operating agencies (as are most agencies of local government, for instance). It may, however, make little sense to try to embrace the policy-making and decision-making functions we usually mean when we say "government." These are different.

This clearly is an issue of major importance, of major impact, and of great complexity.

In conclusion, let me say that I have not even started to summarize the questions raised in this book. I have only picked out a few that struck me as particularly important and as particularly difficult.

I have not attempted to give answers to the questions that were raised, nor to the questions any similar group of business and academic leaders would ask today about the direction of economy and business and the preparation of tomorrow's business leaders. Yet I think I have said enough to bring out clearly one fundamental conclusion to which everything that the contributors to this book have been saying leads inescapably: in the last fifty years, since the graduate Business School of New York University first offered advanced and graduate work to young executives in mid-career, American business—and business throughout the free world altogether—has changed very greatly. The business school has probably changed a good deal less—perhaps not enough. Yet it certainly occupies today a very different place in education, as well as in business, economy, and society, than the place it occupied fifty years ago. The American business school is also increasingly a major "export" product. Indeed it has proven itself to be one of the most effective tools of economic and social development.

Yet *the major period of change in business education is still ahead.* The major tasks of preparing tomorrow's business leaders—whether in business or in systematic instruction—are yet to be tackled.

But they are not tasks for tomorrow. For the forecasters who are so busy today, the "year 2000" is still more than thirty years away. For us, whether in business or in the business school, who are concerned with preparing tomorrow's business leader, "the year 2000" is today. What we do now and in the next few years, in our businesses as well as in our classrooms, will very largely decide what American business and American society altogether will be able to do in "the year 2000." What we do now will very largely determine the one crucial quality of "the year 2000": the vision, self-respect, and performance capacities of the leaders of tomorrow's America.

This fiftieth anniversary volume of New York University's Graduate Business School discusses our vision of the future. But tomorrow's vision is today's work assignment.

DATE DUE

DATE DUE